DOVER · THRIFT · EDITIONS

Gorgias and Timaeus

PLATO

Translated by

B. Jowett

DOVER PUBLICATIONS, INC.
Mineola, New York

DOVER THRIFT EDITIONS

GENERAL EDITOR: PAUL NEGRI

EDITOR OF THIS VOLUME: TOM CRAWFORD

Bibliographical Note

This Dover edition, first published in 2003, is an unabridged reprint of the dialogues *Gorgias* and *Timaeus* from the third edition of *The Dialogues of Plato*, published by The Macmillan Company, 1892. Translated by B. Jowett. The Jowett introduction to *Gorgias* has been reprinted from the fourth edition, published by Oxford University Press. The Note has been specially prepared for this edition.

Library of Congress Cataloging-in-Publication Data

Plato.
    [Gorgias. English]
    Gorgias ; and, Timaeus / Plato ; translated by B. Jowett.
        p. cm. — (Dover thrift editions)
    ISBN 0-486-42759-5 (pbk.)
    1. Ethics—Early works to 1800. 2. Political science—Early works to 1800.
3. Cosmology—Early works to 1800. I. Jowett, Benjamin, 1817–1893. II. Plato.
Timaeus. English. III. Title. IV. Title: Timaeus. V. Series.

B371.A5J69 2003
170—dc21
                                                                    2002041786

Manufactured in the United States of America
Dover Publications, Inc., 31 East 2nd Street, Mineola, N.Y. 11501

Note

One of the founders of Western philosophy and, in the range and depth of his thought, one of the greatest of all thinkers, Plato (c. 428 B.C.– c. 347 B.C.) was born into an aristocratic Athenian family, some of whose members were deeply involved in the extremist politics of the day. He originally entertained political ambitions himself, but after witnessing the violent abuses of the democracy restored after the oligarchic terror of 404, and the execution of his master Socrates, Plato left Athens and traveled for some years in Greece, Italy, and Egypt.

Upon his return, about 387 B.C., he founded the Academy, intended as a center of philosophical and scientific inquiry. Located about a mile outside the walls of Athens, the Academy comprised pleasant groves, gardens, a gymnasium, and other facilities where students were encouraged to study mathematics, solid geometry, astronomy, natural science, and, of course, philosophy. Here Plato spent much of the rest of his life, teaching and writing. Considered by many the first "university," the Academy lasted for more than 900 years until it was closed in A.D. 529 by the emperor Justinian, who considered it a "pagan establishment."

Written for educated laymen, the Dialogues represent a rich repository of Platonic thought, although since many points of view are expressed, even within the same dialogue, it is not always clear which point of view is Plato's own. Certain ideas, however, such as the doctrine of eternal "forms"; the idea that knowledge is recollection, and the theory of the tripartite soul were probably espoused by Plato himself. Scholars generally divide the Dialogues into three periods: early, middle, and late. *Gorgias* belongs to the early period, while *Timaeus* falls among Plato's mature works, offering an interesting vantage point for analyzing the evolution of his thought.

Devoted to political and ethical themes, *Gorgias* begins ostensibly as an investigation of the importance and role of rhetoric, but over the course of the dialogue evolves into an eloquent and powerful plea for a life lived according to high moral principles. No act which is immoral (unjust) ever brings happiness; moreover, true happiness only comes as a result of the control of desire by the individual's commitment to justice, virtue, and self-knowledge.

In *Timaeus*, Plato offers an extensive, detailed exposition of cosmology, physics, and biology. Some scholars regard the work as an attempt to combine the astronomy and mathematics of the Pythagoreans with the biology of Empedocles, who originated the concept of the four elements: earth, air, water, and fire. Ranging widely over many subjects, this dialogue discusses such topics as the creation of the universal soul, the nature of space, the state of the world prior to creation, being and becoming, truth and belief, opinion versus knowledge, health and disease, the classes of animals, and much else. *Timaeus* is also the source of the great myth of the vanished island kingdom of Atlantis.

Fascinating and thought-provoking, these two great dialogues offer rich insight into the thought and influential methodology of one of the supreme minds of the ancient world, whose philosophy is "perhaps the most notable effort in the history of Western thought to construct a doctrine of absolute and objective values."[1]

---

1. Raphael Demos, Introduction, *The Dialogues of Plato*, Random House, 1937.

Contents

GORGIAS

INTRODUCTION

IN SEVERAL of the dialogues of Plato, doubts have arisen among his interpreters as to which of the various subjects discussed in them is the main thesis. The speakers have the freedom of conversation; no severe rules of art restrict them, and sometimes we are inclined to think, with one of the dramatis personae in the *Theaetetus*, that the digressions have the greater interest. Yet in the most irregular of the dialogues there is also a certain natural growth or unity; the beginning is not forgotten at the end, and numerous allusions and references are interspersed, which form the loose connecting links of the whole. We must not neglect this unity, but neither must we attempt to confine the Platonic dialogue on the Procrustean bed of a single idea. (Compare Introduction to the *Phaedrus*.)

Two tendencies seem to have beset the interpreters of Plato in this matter. First, they have endeavoured to hang the dialogues upon one another by the slightest threads; and have thus been led to opposite and contradictory assertions respecting their order and sequence. The mantle of Schleiermacher has descended upon his successors, who have applied his method with the most various results. The value and use of the method has been hardly, if at all, examined either by him or them. Secondly, they have extended almost indefinitely the scope of each separate dialogue; in this way they think that they have escaped all difficulties, not seeing that what they have gained in generality they have lost in truth and distinctness. Metaphysical conceptions easily pass into one another; and the simpler notions of antiquity, which we can only realize by an effort, imperceptibly blend with the more familiar theories of modern philosophers. An eye for proportion is needed (his own art of measuring) in the study of Plato, as well as of other great artists. We may readily admit that the moral antithesis of good and pleasure, or the intellectual antithesis of knowledge and opinion, being and appearance, are never far off in a Platonic discussion. But because they are in the background, we should not bring them into the foreground, or expect to discern them equally in all the dialogues.

1

There may be some advantage in drawing out a little the main out-lines of the building; but the use of this is limited, and may be easily exaggerated. We may give Plato too much system, and alter the natural form and connexion of his thoughts. Under the idea that his dialogues are finished works of art, we may find a reason for everything, and lose the highest characteristic of art, which is simplicity. Most great works receive a new light from a new and original mind. But whether these new lights are true or only suggestive, will depend on their agreement with the spirit of Plato, and the amount of direct evidence which can be urged in support of them. When a theory is running away with us, criticism does a friendly office in counselling moderation, and recall-ing us to the indications of the text.

Like the *Phaedrus*, the *Gorgias* has puzzled students of Plato by the appearance of two or more subjects. Under the cover of rhetoric higher themes are introduced; the argument expands into a general view of the good and evil of man. After making an ineffectual attempt to obtain a sound definition of his art from Gorgias, Socrates assumes the exis-tence of a universal art of flattery or simulation having several branches;—this is the genus of which rhetoric is only one, and not the highest species. To flattery is opposed the true and noble art of life which he who possesses seeks always to impart to others, and which at last triumphs, if not here, at any rate in another world. These two as-pects of life and knowledge appear to be the two leading ideas of the di-alogue. The true and the false in individuals and states, in the treat-ment of the soul as well as of the body, are conceived under the forms of true and false art. In the development of this opposition there arise various other questions, such as the two famous paradoxes of Socrates (paradoxes as they are to the world in general, ideals as they may be more worthily called): (1) that to do is worse than to suffer evil; and (2) that when a man has done evil he had better be punished than un-punished; to which may be added (3) a third Socratic paradox or ideal, that bad men do what they think best, but not what they desire, for the desire of all is towards the good. That pleasure is to be distinguished from good is proved by the simultaneousness of pleasure and pain, and by the possibility of the bad having in certain cases pleasures as great as those of the good, or even greater. Not merely rhetoricians, but poets, musicians, and other artists, the whole tribe of statesmen, past as well as present, are included in the class of flatterers. The true and false fi-nally appear before the judgment-seat of the gods below.

The dialogue naturally falls into three divisions, to which the three characters of Gorgias, Polus, and Callicles respectively correspond; and the form and manner change with the stages of the argument. Socrates is deferential towards Gorgias, playful and yet cutting in dealing with the youthful Polus, ironical and sarcastic in his encounter with Callicles. In the first division the question is asked—What is rhetoric? To this there is no answer given, for Gorgias is soon made to contradict himself by Socrates, and the argument is transferred to the hands of his disciple Polus, who rushes to the defence of his master. The answer has at last to be given by Socrates himself, but before he can even explain his meaning to Polus, he must enlighten him upon the great subject of shams or flatteries. When Polus finds his favourite art reduced to the level of cookery, he replies that at any rate rhetoricians, like despots, have great power. Socrates denies that they have any real power, and hence arise the three paradoxes already mentioned. Although they are strange to him, Polus is at last convinced of their truth; at least, they seem to him to follow legitimately from the premises. Thus the second act of the dialogue closes. Then Callicles appears on the scene, at first maintaining that pleasure is good, and that might is right, and that law is nothing but the combination of the many weak against the few strong. When he is confuted he withdraws from the argument, and leaves Socrates to arrive at the conclusion by himself. The conclusion is that there are two kinds of statesmanship, a higher and a lower—that which makes the people better, and that which only flatters them, and he exhorts Callicles to choose the higher. The dialogue terminates with a mythus of a final judgment, in which there will be no more flattery or disguise, and no further use for the teaching of rhetoric.

The characters of the three interlocutors also correspond to the parts which are assigned to them. Gorgias is the great rhetorician, now advanced in years, who goes from city to city displaying his talents, and is celebrated throughout Greece. Like all the sophists in the dialogues of Plato, he is vain and boastful, yet he has also a certain dignity, and is treated by Socrates with considerable respect. But he is no match for him in dialectics. Although he has been teaching rhetoric all his life, he is still incapable of defining his own art. When his ideas begin to clear up, he is unwilling to admit that rhetoric can be wholly separated from justice and injustice, and this lingering sentiment of morality, or regard for public opinion, enables Socrates to detect him in a contradiction. Like Protagoras, he is described as of a generous nature; he expresses his approbation of Socrates' manner of approaching a question; he is quite 'one of Socrates' sort, ready to be refuted as well as to refute,' and very eager that Callicles and Socrates should have the game out. He knows by experience that rhetoric exercises great influence over other men, but he is unable to explain the puzzle how rhetoric can teach everything and know nothing.

Polus is an impetuous youth, a runaway 'colt,' as Socrates describes him, who wanted originally to have taken the place of Gorgias under the pretext that the old man was tired, and now avails himself of the earliest opportunity to enter the lists. He is said to be the author of a work on rhetoric, and is again mentioned in the *Phaedrus,* as the inventor of balanced or double forms of speech (cf. *Gorg.* 448c, 467c; *Symp.* 185c). At first he is violent and ill mannered, and is angry at seeing his master overthrown. But in the judicious hands of Socrates he is soon restored to good-humour, and compelled to assent to the required conclusion. Like Gorgias, he is overthrown because he compromises; he is unwilling to say that to do is fairer or more honourable than to suffer injustice. Though he is fascinated by the power of rhetoric, and dazzled by the splendour of success, he is not insensible to higher arguments. Plato may have felt that there would be an incongruity in a youth maintaining the cause of injustice against the world. He has never heard the other side of the question, and he listens to the paradoxes, as they appear to him, of Socrates with evident astonishment. He can hardly understand the meaning of Archelaus being miserable, or of rhetoric being only useful in self-accusation. When the argument with him has fairly run out,

Callicles, in whose house they are assembled, is introduced on the stage: he is with difficulty convinced that Socrates is in earnest; for if these things are true, then, as he says with real emotion, the foundations of society are upside down. In him another type of character is represented; he is neither sophist nor philosopher, but man of the world, and an accomplished Athenian gentleman. He might be described in modern language as a cynic or materialist, a lover of power and also of pleasure, and unscrupulous in his means of attaining both. There is no desire on his part to offer any compromise in the interests of morality; nor is any concession made by him. Like Thrasymachus in the *Republic,* though he is not of the same weak and vulgar class, he consistently maintains that might is right. His great motive of action is political ambition; in this he is characteristically Greek. Like Anytus in the *Meno,* he is the enemy of the sophists; but favours the new art of rhetoric, which he regards as an excellent weapon of attack and defence. He is a despiser of mankind as he is of philosophy, and sees in the laws of the state only a violation of the order of nature, which intended that the stronger should govern the weaker (cf. *Republic* ii. 358–60). Like other men of the world who are of a speculative turn of mind, he generalizes the bad side of human nature, and has easily brought down his principles to his practice. Philosophy and poetry alike supply him with distinctions suited to his view of human life. He has a good will to Socrates, whose talents he evidently admires, while he censures the puerile use which he makes of them. He expresses a keen intellectual interest in the argument. Like Anytus, again, he has a sympathy with other men of the world; the Athenian statesmen of a former generation, who showed no weakness and made no mistakes, such as Miltiades, Themistocles, Pericles, are his favourites. His ideal of human character is a man of great passions and great powers, which he has developed to the utmost, and which he uses in his own enjoyment and in the government of others. Had Critias been the name instead of Callicles, about whom we know nothing from other sources, the opinions of the man would have seemed to reflect the history of his life.

And now the combat deepens. In Callicles, far more than in any sophist or rhetorician, is concentrated the spirit of evil against which Socrates is contending, the spirit of the world, the spirit of the many contending against the one wise man, of which the sophists, as he describes them in the *Republic*, are the imitators rather than the authors, being themselves carried away by the great tide of public opinion. Socrates approaches his antagonist warily from a distance, with a sort of irony which touches with a light hand both his personal vices (probably in allusion to some scandal of the day) and his servility to the populace. At the same time, he is in most profound earnest, as Chaerephon remarks. Callicles soon loses his temper, but the more he is irritated, the more provoking and matter-of-fact does Socrates become. A repartee of his which appears to have been really made to the 'omniscient' Hippias, according to the testimony of Xenophon (*Mem.* iv. 4, 6, 10), is introduced (490e). He is called by Callicles a popular declaimer, and certainly shows that he has the power, in the words of Gorgias, of being 'as long as he pleases,' or 'as short as he pleases' (cf. *Protag.* 336d). Callicles exhibits great ability in defending himself and attacking Socrates, whom he accuses of trifling and word-splitting; he is scandalized that the legitimate consequences of his own argument should be stated in plain terms; after the manner of men of the world, he wishes to preserve the decencies of life. But he cannot consistently maintain the bad sense of words; and getting confused between the abstract notions of better, superior, stronger, he is easily turned round by Socrates, and only induced to continue the argument by the authority of Gorgias. Once, when Socrates is describing the manner in which the ambitious citizen has to identify himself with the people, he partially recognizes the truth of his words.

The Socrates of the *Gorgias* may be compared with the Socrates of the *Protagoras* and *Meno*. As in other dialogues, he is the enemy of the sophists and rhetoricians; and also of the statesmen, whom he regards as another variety of the same species. His behaviour is governed by that of his opponents; the least forwardness or egotism on their part is met by a corresponding irony on the part of Socrates. He must speak, for philosophy will not allow him to be silent. He is indeed more ironical and provoking than in any other of Plato's writings: for he is 'fooled to the top of his bent' by the worldliness of Callicles. But he is also more deeply in earnest. He rises higher than even in the *Phaedo* and *Crito*: at first enveloping his moral convictions in a cloud of dust and dialectics, he ends by losing his method, his life, himself, in them. As in the *Protagoras* and *Phaedrus*, throwing aside the veil of irony, he makes a speech, but, true to his character, not until his adversary has refused to answer any more questions. The presentiment of his own fate is hanging over him. He is aware that Socrates, the single real teacher of politics, as he ventures to call himself, cannot safely go to war with the whole world, and that in the courts of earth he will be condemned. But he will be justified in the world below. Then the position of Socrates and Callicles will be reversed; all those things 'unfit for ears polite' which Callicles has prophesied as likely to happen to him in this life, the insulting language, the box on the ears, will recoil upon his assailant. (Compare *Republic*, and the similar reversal of the position of the lawyer and the philosopher in the *Theaetetus*, 173–6).

There is an interesting allusion to his own behaviour at the trial of the generals after the battle of Arginusae, which he ironically attributes to his ignorance of the manner in which a vote of the assembly should be taken (473e). This is said to have happened 'last year' (406 B.C.), and therefore the assumed date of the dialogue has been fixed at 405 B.C., when Socrates would already have been an old man. The date is clearly marked, but is scarcely reconcilable with another indication of time, viz. the 'recent' usurpation of Archelaus, which occurred in the year 413 (470d); and still less with the 'recent' death of Pericles, who really died twenty-four years previously (429 B.C.) and is afterwards reckoned among the statesmen of a past age (cf. 517a); or with the mention of Nicias, who died in 413, and is nevertheless spoken of as a living witness (472 a,b). But we shall hereafter have reason to observe, that although there is a general consistency of times and persons in the dialogues of Plato, a precise dramatic date is an invention of his commentators (Introduction to *Republic*, p. 6).

The conclusion of the dialogue is remarkable, (1) for the truly characteristic declaration of Socrates (509a) that he is ignorant of the true nature and bearing of these things, while he affirms at the same time that no one can maintain any other view without being ridiculous. The profession of ignorance reminds us of the earlier and more exclusively Socratic dialogues. But neither in them, nor in the *Apology*, nor in the *Memorabilia* of Xenophon, does Socrates express any doubt of the fundamental truths of morality. He evidently regards this 'among the multitude of questions' which agitate human life 'as the principle which alone remains unshaken.' (527b) He does not insist here, any more

than in the *Phaedo*, on the literal truth of the myth, but only on the
soundness of the doctrine which is contained in it, that doing wrong is
worse than suffering, and that a man should be rather than seem; for
the next best thing to a man's being just is that he should be corrected
and become just; also that he should avoid all flattery, whether of himself or of others; and that rhetoric should be employed for the mainte-
nance of the right only. The revelation of another life is a recapitula-
tion of the argument in a figure.

(2) Socrates makes the singular remark, that he is himself the only
true politician of his age. In other passages, especially in the *Apology*,
he disclaims being a politician at all. There he is convinced that he or
any other good man who attempted to resist the popular will would be
put to death before he had done any good to himself or others. Here he
anticipates such a fate for himself, from the fact that he is 'the only man
of the present day who performs his public duties at all.' The two points
of view are not really inconsistent, but the difference between them is
worth noticing: Socrates is and is not a public man. Not in the ordinary
sense, like Alcibiades or Pericles, but in a higher one; and this will
sooner or later entail the same consequences on him. He cannot be a
private man if he would; neither can he separate morals from politics.
Nor is he unwilling to be a politician, although he foresees the dangers
which await him; but he must first become a better and wiser man, for
he as well as Callicles is in a state of perplexity and uncertainty (527d,
e). And yet there is an inconsistency: for should not Socrates too have
taught the citizens better than to put him to death (519)?

And now, as he himself says (506c), we will 'resume the argument
from the beginning.'

Analysis

Socrates, who is attended by his inseparable disciple, Chaerephon,
meets Callicles in the streets of Athens. He is informed that he has just
missed an exhibition of Gorgias, which he regrets, because he was desirous, not of hearing Gorgias display his rhetoric, but of interrogating
him concerning the nature of his art. Callicles proposes that they shall
go with him to his own house, where Gorgias is staying. There they
find the great rhetorician and his younger friend and disciple Polus.

Soc: Put the question to him, Chaerephon. *Ch*: What question? *Soc*:
Who is he?—such a question as would elicit from a man the answer, 'I
am a cobbler.' Polus suggests that Gorgias may be tired, and desires to
answer for him. 'Who is Gorgias?' asks Chaerephon, imitating the
manner of his master Socrates. 'One of the best of men, and a profi-

cient in the best and noblest of experimental arts,' &c., replies Polus, in rhetorical and balanced phrases. Socrates is dissatisfied at the length and unmeaningness of the answer; he tells the disconcerted volunteer that he has mistaken the quality for the nature of the art, and remarks to Gorgias, that Polus has learnt how to make a speech, but not how to answer a question. He wishes that Gorgias would answer him. Gorgias is willing enough, and replies to the question asked by Chaerephon,— that he is a rhetorician, and in Homeric language, 'boasts himself to be a good one.' At the request of Socrates he promises to be brief; for 'he can be as long as he pleases, and as short as he pleases.' Socrates would have him bestow his length on others, and proceeds to ask him a number of questions, which are answered by him to his own great satisfaction, and with a brevity which excites the admiration of Socrates. The result of the discussion may be summed up as follows:—

Rhetoric treats of discourse; but music and medicine, and other particular arts, are also concerned with discourse; in what way then does rhetoric differ from them? Gorgias draws a distinction between the arts which deal with words, and the arts which have to do with external actions. Socrates extends this distinction further, and divides all productive arts into two classes: (1) arts which may be carried on in silence; and (2) arts which have to do with words, or in which words are coextensive with action, such as arithmetic, geometry, rhetoric. But still Gorgias could hardly have meant to say that arithmetic was the same as rhetoric. Even in the arts which are concerned with words there are differences. What then distinguishes rhetoric from the other arts which have to do with words? 'The words which rhetoric uses relate to the best and greatest of human things.' But tell me, Gorgias, what are the best? 'Health first, beauty next, wealth third,' in the words of the old song, or how would you rank them? The arts will come to you in a body, each claiming precedence and saying that her own good is superior to that of the rest—How will you choose between them? 'I should say, Socrates, that the art of persuasion, which gives freedom to all men, and to individuals power in the state, is the greatest good.' But what is the exact nature of this persuasion?—is the persevering retort: You could not describe Zeuxis as a painter, or even as a painter of figures, if there were other painters of figures; neither can you define rhetoric simply as an art of persuasion, because there are other arts which persuade, such as arithmetic, which is an art of persuasion about odd and even numbers. Gorgias is made to see the necessity of a further limitation, and he now defines rhetoric as the art of persuading in the law courts, and in the assembly, about the just and unjust. But still there are two sorts of persuasion: one which gives knowledge, and another which gives belief without knowledge; and knowledge is always true, but belief may be either true or false, — there is therefore a further question: which of the two sorts of persuasion does rhetoric effect in courts of law and assemblies? Plainly that which gives belief and not that which gives knowledge; for no one can impart a real knowledge of such matters to a crowd of persons in a few minutes. And there is another point to be considered: — when the assembly meets to advise about walls or docks or military expeditions, the rhetorician is not taken into counsel, but the architect, or the general. How would Gorgias explain this phenomenon? All who intend to become disciples, of whom there are several in the company, and not Socrates only, are eagerly asking: — About what then will rhetoric teach us to persuade or advise the state?

Gorgias illustrates the nature of rhetoric by adducing the example of Themistocles, who persuaded the Athenians to build their docks and walls, and of Pericles, whom Socrates himself has heard speaking about the middle wall of the Piraeus. He adds that he has exercised a similar power over the patients of his brother Herodicus. He could be chosen a physician by the assembly if he pleased, for no physician could compete with a rhetorician in popularity and influence. He could persuade the multitude of anything by the power of his rhetoric; not that the rhetorician ought to abuse this power any more than a boxer should abuse the art of self-defence. Rhetoric is a good thing, but, like all good things, may be unlawfully used. Neither is the teacher of the art to be deemed unjust because his pupils are unjust and make a bad use of the lessons which they have learned from him.

Socrates would like to know before he replies, whether Gorgias will quarrel with him if he points out a slight inconsistency into which he has fallen, or whether he, like himself, is one who loves to be refuted. Gorgias declares that he is quite one of his sort, but fears that the argument may be tedious to the company. The company cheer, and Chaerephon and Callicles exhort them to proceed. Socrates gently points out the supposed inconsistency into which Gorgias appears to have fallen, and which he is inclined to think may arise out of a misapprehension of his own. The rhetorician has been declared by Gorgias to be more persuasive to the ignorant than the physician, or any other expert. And he is said to be ignorant, and this ignorance of his is regarded by Gorgias as a happy condition, for he has escaped the trouble of learning. But is he as ignorant of just and unjust as he is of medicine or building? Gorgias is compelled to admit that if he did not know them previously he must learn them from his teacher as a part of the art of rhetoric. But he who has learned carpentry is a carpenter, and he who has learned music is a musician, and he who has learned justice is just. The rhetorician then must be a just man, and rhetoric is a just thing. But Gorgias has already admitted the opposite of this, viz.

that rhetoric may be abused, and that the rhetorician may act unjustly. How is the inconsistency to be explained?

The fallacy of this argument is twofold; for in the first place, a man may know justice and not be just—here is the old confusion of the arts and the virtues;—nor can any teacher be expected to counteract wholly the bent of natural character; and secondly, a man may have a degree of justice, but not sufficient to prevent him from ever doing wrong. Polus is naturally exasperated at the sophism, which he is unable to detect; of course, he says, the rhetorician, like everyone else, will admit that he knows justice (how can he do otherwise when pressed by the interrogations of Socrates?), but he thinks that great want of manners is shown in bringing the argument to such a pass. Socrates ironically replies, that when old men trip, the young set them on their legs again; and he is quite willing to retract, if he can be shown to be in error, but upon one condition, which is that Polus studies brevity. Polus is in great indignation at not being allowed to use as many words as he pleases in the free state of Athens. Socrates retorts, that yet harder will be his own case, if he is compelled to stay and listen to them. After some altercation they agree (cf. *Protag.* 338), that Polus shall ask and Socrates answer.

'What is the art of Rhetoric?' says Polus. Not an art at all, replies Socrates, but a thing which in your book you affirm to have created art. Polus asks, 'What thing?' and Socrates answers, A sort of practical skill in making a sort of delight or gratification. 'But is not rhetoric a fine thing?' I have not yet told you what rhetoric is. Will you ask me another question—What is cookery? 'What is cookery?' A sort of practical skill in making a sort of delight or gratification. Then they are the same, or rather fall under the same class, and rhetoric has still to be distinguished from cookery. 'What is rhetoric?' asks Polus once more. A part of a not very creditable whole, which may be termed flattery, is the reply. 'But what part?' A shadow of a part of politics. This, as might be expected, is wholly unintelligible, both to Gorgias and Polus; and, in order to explain his meaning to them, Socrates draws a distinction between shadows or appearances and realities; e.g. there is real health of body or soul, and the appearance of them; real arts and sciences, and the simulations of them. Now the soul and body have two arts waiting upon them, first the art of politics, which attends on the soul, having a legislative part and a judicial part; and another art attending on the body, which has no generic name, but may also be described as having two divisions, one of which is medicine and the other gymnastic. Corresponding with these four arts or sciences there are four shams or simulations of them, mere experiences, as they may be termed, because they give no reason of their own existence. The art of dressing up is the sham or simulation of gymnastic, the art of cookery, of medicine; rhetoric is the simulation of justice, and sophistic of legislation. They may be summed up in an arithmetical formula:—

> Tiring:gymnastic::cookery:medicine::sophistic:legislation.

And,

> Cookery:medicine::rhetoric:the art of justice.

And this is the true scheme of them, but when measured only by the gratification which they procure, they become jumbled together and return to their aboriginal chaos. Socrates apologizes for the length of his speech, which was necessary to the explanation of the subject, and begs Polus not unnecessarily to retaliate on him.

'Do you mean to say that the rhetoricians are esteemed flatterers?' They are not esteemed at all. 'Why, have they not great power, and can they not do whatever they desire?' They have no power, and they only do what they think best, and never what they desire; for they never attain the true object of desire, which is the good. 'As if you, Socrates, would not envy the possessor of despotic power, who can imprison, exile, kill anyone whom he pleases.' But Socrates replies that he has no wish to put anyone to death; he who kills another, even justly, is not to be envied, and he who kills him unjustly is to be pitied; it is better to suffer than to do injustice. He does not consider that going about with a dagger and putting men out of the way, or setting a house on fire, is real power. To this Polus assents, on the ground that such acts would be punished, but he is still of opinion that evildoers, if they are unpunished, may be happy enough. He instances Archelaus, son of Perdiccas, the usurper of Macedonia. Does not Socrates think him happy?—Socrates would like to know more about him; he cannot pronounce even the great king to be happy, unless he knows his mental and moral condition. Polus explains that Archelaus was a slave, being the son of a woman who was the slave of Alcetas, brother of Perdiccas king of Macedon—and he, by every species of crime, first murdering his uncle and then his cousin and half-brother, obtained the kingdom. This was very wicked, and yet all the world, including Socrates, would like to have his place. Socrates dismisses the appeal to numbers; Polus, if he will, may summon all the rich men of Athens, Nicias and his brothers, Aristocrates, the house of Pericles, or any other great family—this is the kind of evidence which is adduced in courts of justice, where truth depends upon numbers. But Socrates employs proof of another sort; his appeal is to one witness only,—that is to say, the person with whom he is speaking; him he will convict out of his own mouth. And he is prepared to show, after his manner, that Archelaus cannot be a wicked man and yet happy.

The evil-doer is deemed happy if he escapes, and miserable if he suffers punishment; but Socrates thinks him less miserable if he suffers than if he escapes. Polus is of opinion that such a paradox as this hardly deserves refutation, and is at any rate sufficiently refuted by the fact. Socrates has only to compare the lot of the successful tyrant who is the envy of the world, and of the wretch who, having been detected in a criminal attempt against the state, is crucified or burnt to death. Socrates replies, that if they are both criminal they are both miserable, but that the unpunished is the more miserable of the two. At this Polus laughs outright, which leads Socrates to remark that laughter is a new species of refutation. Polus replies, that he is already refuted; for if he will take the votes of the company, he will find that no one agrees with him. To this Socrates rejoins, that he is not a public man, and (referring to his own conduct at the trial of the generals after the battle of Arginusae) is unable to take the suffrages of any company, as he had shown on a recent occasion; he can only deal with one witness at a time, and that is the person with whom he is arguing. But he is certain that in the opinion of any man to do is worse than to suffer evil.

Polus, though he will not admit this, is ready to acknowledge that to do evil is considered the more foul or dishonourable of the two. But what is fair and what is foul; whether the terms are applied to bodies, colours, figures, laws, habits, studies, must they not be defined with reference to pleasure and utility? Polus assents to this latter doctrine, and is easily persuaded that the fouler of two things must exceed either in pain or in hurt. But the doing cannot exceed the suffering of evil in pain, and therefore must exceed in hurt. Thus doing is proved by the testimony of Polus himself to be worse or more hurtful than suffering.

There remains the other question: Is a guilty man better off when he is punished or when he is unpunished? Socrates replies, that what is done justly is suffered justly: if the act is just, the effect is just; if to punish is just, to be punished is just, and therefore fair, and therefore beneficent; and the benefit is that the soul is improved. There are three evils from which a man may suffer, and which affect him in estate, body, and soul;—these are poverty, disease, injustice; and the foulest of these is injustice, the evil of the soul, because that brings the greatest hurt. And there are three arts which heal these evils—trading, medicine, justice—and the fairest of these is justice. Happy is he who has never committed injustice, and happy in the second degree he who has been healed by punishment. And therefore the criminal should himself go to the judge as he would to the physician, and purge away his crime. Rhetoric will enable him to display his guilt in proper colours, and to sustain himself and others in enduring the necessary penalty. And similarly if a man has an enemy, he will desire not to punish him, but that he shall go unpunished and become worse and worse, taking care only that he does no injury to himself. These are at least conceivable uses of the art, and no others have been discovered by us.

Here Callicles, who has been listening in silent amazement, asks Chaerephon whether Socrates is in earnest, and on receiving the assurance that he is, proceeds to ask the same question of Socrates himself. For if such doctrines are true, life must have been turned upside down, and all of us are doing the opposite of what we ought to be doing.

Socrates replies in a style of playful irony, that before men can understand one another they must have some common feeling. And such a community of feeling exists between himself and Callicles, for both of them are lovers, and they have both a pair of loves; the beloved of Callicles are the Athenian Demos and Demos the son of Pyrilampes; the beloved of Socrates are Alcibiades and philosophy. The peculiarity of Callicles is that he can never contradict his loves; he changes as his Demos changes in all his opinions; he watches the countenance of both his loves, and repeats their sentiments, and if anyone is surprised at his sayings and doings, the explanation of them is that he is not a free agent, but must always be imitating his two loves. And this is the explanation of Socrates' peculiarities also. He is always repeating what his mistress, Philosophy, is saying to him, who, unlike his other love, Alcibiades, is ever the same, ever true. Callicles must refute her, or he will never be at unity with himself; and discord in life is far worse than the discord of musical sounds.

Callicles answers that Gorgias was overthrown because, as Polus said, in compliance with popular prejudice he had admitted that if his pupil did not know justice the rhetorician must teach him; and Polus has been similarly entangled, because his modesty led him to admit that to suffer is more honourable than to do injustice. By custom 'yes,' but not by nature, says Callicles. And Socrates is always playing between the two points of view, and putting one in the place of the other. In this very argument, what Polus only meant in a conventional sense has been affirmed by him to be a law of nature. For convention says that 'injustice is dishonourable,' but nature says that 'might is right.' And we are always taming down the nobler spirits among us to the conventional level. But sometimes a great man will rise up and reassert his original rights, trampling under foot all our formularies, and then the light of natural justice shines forth. Pindar says, 'Law, the king of all, does violence with high hand'; as is indeed proved by the example of Heracles, who drove off the oxen of Geryon and never paid for them.

This is the truth, Socrates, as you will be convinced, if you leave philosophy and pass on to the real business of life. A little philosophy is an excellent thing; too much is the ruin of a man. He who has not 'passed his metaphysics' before he has grown up to manhood will never know the world. Philosophers are ridiculous when they take to politics, and I dare say that politicians are equally ridiculous when they take to philosophy: 'Every man,' as Euripides says, 'is fondest of that in which he is best.' Philosophy is graceful in youth, like the lisp of infancy, and should be cultivated as a part of education; but when a grown-up man lisps or studies philosophy, I should like to beat him. None of those over-refined natures ever come to any good; they avoid the busy haunts of men, and skulk in corners, whispering to a few admiring youths, and never giving utterance to any noble sentiments.

For you, Socrates, I have a regard, and therefore I say to you, as Zethus says to Amphion in the play, that you have 'a noble soul disguised in a puerile exterior.' And I would have you consider the danger which you and other philosophers incur. For you would not know how to defend yourself if anyone accused you in a law-court,—there you would stand, with gaping mouth and dizzy brain, and might be murdered, robbed, boxed on the ears with impunity. Take my advice, then, and get a little common sense; leave to others these frivolities; walk in the ways of the wealthy and be wise.

Socrates professes to have found in Callicles the philosopher's touchstone; and he is certain that any opinion in which they both agree must be the very truth. Callicles has all the three qualities which are needed in a critic—knowledge, goodwill, frankness; Gorgias and Polus, although learned men, were too modest, and their modesty made them contradict themselves. But Callicles is well-educated; and he is not too modest to speak out (of this he has already given proof), and his goodwill is shown both by his own profession and by his giving the same caution against philosophy to Socrates, which Socrates remembers hearing him give long ago to his own clique of friends. He will pledge himself to retract any error into which he may have fallen, and which Callicles may point out. But he would like to know first of all what he and Pindar mean by natural justice. Do they suppose that the rule of justice is the rule of the stronger or of the better? 'There is no difference.' Then are not the many superior to the one, and the opinions of the many better? And their opinion is that justice is equality, and that to do is more dishonourable than to suffer wrong. And as they are the superior or stronger, this opinion of theirs must be in accordance with natural as well as conventional justice. 'Why will you continue splitting words? Have I not told you that the superior is the better?' But what do you mean by the better? Tell me that, and please to be a little milder in your language, if you do not wish to drive me away. 'I mean the worthier, the wiser.' You mean to say that one man of sense ought to rule over ten thousand fools? 'Yes, that is my meaning.' Ought the physician then to have a larger share of meats and drinks? or the weaver to have more coats, or the cobbler larger shoes, or the farmer more seed? 'You are always saying the same things, Socrates.' Yes, and on the same subjects too; but you are never saying the same things. For, first, you defined the superior to be the stronger and then the wiser, and now something else;—what *do* you mean? 'I mean men of political ability, who ought to govern and to have more than the governed.' What about themselves? 'What do you mean?' I mean that every man is his own governor. 'So you really identify temperance with folly! But my doctrine is, that a man should let his desires grow, and take the means of satisfying them. To the many this is impossible, and therefore they combine to prevent him. But if he is a king, and has power, how base would he be in submitting to them! To invite the common herd to be lord over him, when he might have the enjoyment of all things! For the truth is, Socrates, that luxury and self-indulgence are virtue and happiness; all the rest is mere talk.'

Socrates compliments Callicles on his frankness in saying what other men only think. According to his view, those who want nothing are not happy. 'Why,' says Callicles, 'if they were, stones and the dead would be happy.' Socrates in reply is led into a half-serious, half-comic vein of reflection. 'Who knows,' as Euripides says, 'whether life may not be death, and death life?' Nay, there are philosophers who maintain that even in life we are dead, and that the body (σῶμα) is the tomb (σῆμα) of the soul. And some ingenious Sicilian has made an allegory, in which he represents fools as the uninitiated, who are supposed to be carrying water to a vessel, which is full of holes, in a similarly holey sieve, and this sieve is their own soul. The idea is fanciful, but nevertheless is a figure of a truth which I want to make you acknowledge, viz. that the life of contentment is better than the life of indulgence. Are you disposed to admit that? 'Far otherwise.' Then hear another parable. The life of self-contentment and self-indulgence may be represented respectively by two men, who are filling jars with streams of wine, honey, milk,—the jars of the one are sound, and the jars of the other leaky; the first fills his jars, and has no more trouble with them; the second is always filling them, and would suffer extreme misery if he desisted. Are you of the same opinion still? 'Yes, Socrates, and the figure expresses what I mean. For true pleasure is a perpetual stream, flowing in and flowing out. To be hungry and always eating, to be thirsty and always drinking, and to have all the other desires and to satisfy them, that, as I admit, is my idea of happiness.' And to be itching and always scratching? 'I do not deny that there may be happiness even in that.'

And to indulge unnatural desires, if they are abundantly satisfied? Callicles is indignant at the introduction of such topics. But he is reminded by Socrates that they are introduced, not by him, but by the maintainer of the identity of pleasure and good. Will Callicles still maintain this? 'Yes, for the sake of consistency, he will.' The answer does not satisfy Socrates, who fears that he is losing his touchstone. A profession of seriousness on the part of Callicles reassures him, and they proceed with the argument. Pleasure and good are the same, but knowledge and courage are not the same either with pleasure or good, or with one another. Socrates disproves the first of these statements by showing that two opposites cannot coexist, but must alternate with one another—to be well and ill together is impossible. But pleasure and pain are simultaneous, and the cessation of them is simultaneous; e.g. in the case of drinking and thirsting, whereas good and evil are not simultaneous, and do not cease simultaneously, and therefore pleasure cannot be the same as good.

Callicles has already lost his temper, and can only be persuaded to go on by the interposition of Gorgias. Socrates, having already guarded against objections by distinguishing courage and knowledge from pleasure and good, proceeds:—The good are good by the presence of good, and the bad are bad by the presence of evil. And the brave and wise are good, and the cowardly and foolish are bad. And he who feels pleasure is good, and he who feels pain is bad, and both feel pleasure and pain in nearly the same degree, and sometimes the bad man or coward in a greater degree. Therefore the bad man or coward is as good as the brave or may be even better.

Callicles endeavours now to avert the inevitable absurdity by affirming that he and all mankind admitted some pleasures to be good and others bad. The good are the beneficial, and the bad are the hurtful, and we should choose the one and avoid the other. But this, as Socrates observes, is a return to the old doctrine of himself and Polus, that all things should be done for the sake of the good.

Callicles assents to this, and Socrates, finding that they are agreed in distinguishing pleasure from good, returns to his old division of empirical habits, or shams, or flatteries, which study pleasure only, and the arts which are concerned with the higher interests of soul and body. Does Callicles agree to this division? Callicles will agree to anything, in order that he may get through the argument. Which of the arts then are flatteries? Flute-playing, harp-playing, choral exhibitions, the dithyrambics of Cinesias are all equally condemned on the ground that they give pleasure only; and Meles the harp-player, who was the father of Cinesias, failed even in that. The stately muse of Tragedy is bent upon pleasure, and not upon improvement. Poetry in general is only a rhetorical address to a mixed audience of men, women, and children. And the orators are very far from speaking with a view to what is best; their way is to humour the assembly as if they were children.

Callicles replies, that this is only true of some of them; others have a real regard for their fellow citizens. Granted; then there are two species of oratory; the one a flattery, another which has a real regard for the citizens. But where are the orators among whom you find the latter? Callicles admits that there are none remaining, but there were such in the days when Themistocles, Cimon, Miltiades, and the great Pericles were still alive. Socrates replies that none of these were true artists, setting before themselves the duty of bringing order out of disorder. The good man and true orator has a settled design, running through his life, to which he conforms all his words and actions, he desires to implant justice and eradicate injustice, to implant all virtue and eradicate all vice in the minds of his citizens. He is the physician who will not allow the sick man to indulge his appetites with a variety of meats and drinks, but insists on his exercising self-restraint. And this is good for the soul, and better than the unrestrained indulgence which Callicles was recently approving.

Here Callicles, who had been with difficulty brought to this point, turns restive, and suggests that Socrates shall answer his own questions. 'Then,' says Socrates, 'one man must do for two'; and though he had hoped to have given Callicles an 'Amphion' in return for his 'Zethus,' he is willing to proceed; at the same time, he hopes that Callicles will correct him, if he falls into error. He recapitulates the advantages which he has already won: —

The pleasant is not the same as the good — Callicles and I are agreed about that, — but pleasure is to be pursued for the sake of the good, and the good is that of which the presence makes us good; we and all things good have acquired some virtue or other. And virtue, whether of body or soul, of things or persons, is not attained by accident, but is due to order and harmonious arrangement. And the soul which has order is better than the soul which is without order, and is therefore temperate and is therefore good, and the intemperate is bad. And he who is temperate is also just and brave and pious, and has attained the perfection of goodness and therefore of happiness, and the intemperate whom you approve is the opposite of all this and is wretched. He therefore who would be happy must pursue temperance and avoid intemperance, and if possible escape the necessity of punishment, but if he have done wrong he must endure punishment. In this way states and individuals should seek to attain harmony, which, as the wise tell us, is the bond of heaven and earth, of gods and men. Callicles has never discovered the power of geometrical proportion in both worlds; he would have men aim at disproportion and excess. But if he be wrong in this, and if self-control is the true secret of happiness, then the paradox is true that the only use of rhetoric is in self-accusation, and Polus was right in saying that to do wrong is worse than to suffer wrong, and Gorgias was right in saying that the rhetorician must be a just man. And you were wrong in taunting me with my defence-less condition, and in saying that I might be accused or put to death or boxed on the ears with impunity. For I may repeat once more, that to strike is worse than to be stricken—to do than to suffer. What I said then is now made fast in adamantine bonds. I myself know not the true nature of these things, but I know that no one can deny my words and not be ridiculous. To do wrong is the greatest of evils, and to suffer wrong is the next greatest evil. He who would avoid the last must be a ruler, or the friend of a ruler; and to be the friend he must be the equal of the ruler, and must also resemble him. Under his protection he will suffer no evil, but will he also do no evil? Nay, will he not rather do all the evil which he can and escape? And in this way the greatest of all evils will befall him. 'But this imitator of the tyrant,' rejoins Callicles, 'will kill anyone who does not similarly imitate him.' Socrates replies that he is not deaf, and that he has heard that repeated many times, and can only reply that a bad man will kill a good one. 'Yes, and that is the provoking thing.' Not provoking to a man of sense who is not studying the arts which will preserve him from danger; and this, as you say, is the use of rhetoric in courts of justice. But how many other arts are there which also save men from death, and are yet quite humble in their pretensions—such as the art of swimming, or the art of the pilot? Does not the pilot do men at least as much service as the rhetorician, and yet for the voyage from Aegina to Athens he does not charge more than two obols, and when he disembarks is quite unassuming in his demeanour? The reason is that he is not certain whether he has done his passengers any good in saving them from death, if one of them is diseased in body, and still more if he is diseased in mind—who can say? The engineer too will often save whole cities, and yet you despise him, and would not allow your son to marry his daughter, or his son to marry yours. But what reason is there in this? For if virtue only means the saving of life, whether your own or another's, you have no right to despise him or any practiser of saving arts. But is not virtue something different from saving and being saved? I would have you rather consider whether you ought not to disregard length of life, and think only how you can live best, leaving all besides to the will of Heaven. For you must not expect to have influence either with the Athenian Demos or with Demos the son of Pyrilampes, unless you become like them. What do you say to this?

'There is some truth in what you are saying, but I do not entirely believe you.'

That is because you are in love with Demos. But let us have a little more conversation. You remember the two processes—one which was directed to pleasure, the other which was directed to making men as good as possible. And those who have the care of the city should make the citizens as good as possible. But who would undertake a public building, if he had never had a teacher of the art of building, and had never constructed a building before? or who would undertake the duty of state physician, if he had never cured either himself or anyone else? Should we not examine him before we entrusted him with the office? And as Callicles is about to enter public life, should we not examine him? Whom has he made better? For we have already admitted that this is the statesman's proper business. And we must ask the same question about Pericles, and Cimon, and Miltiades, and Themistocles. Whom did they make better? Nay, did not Pericles make the citizens worse? For he gave them pay, and at first he was very popular with them, but at last they almost put him to death. Yet surely he would be a bad tamer of animals who, having received them gentle, taught them to kick and butt, and man is an animal; and Pericles who had the charge of man only made him wilder, and more savage and unjust, and therefore he could not have been a good statesman. The same tale might be repeated about Cimon, Themistocles, Miltiades. But the charioteer who keeps his seat at first is not thrown out when he gains greater experience and skill. The inference is, that the statesman of a past age were no better than those of our own. They may have been cleverer constructors of docks and harbours, but they did not improve the character of the citizens. I have told you again and again (and I purposely use the same images) that the soul, like the body, may be treated in two ways—there is the meaner and the higher art. You seemed to understand what I said at the time, but when I ask you who were the really good statesmen, you answer—as if I asked you who were the good trainers, and you answered, Thearion, the baker, Mithaecus, the author of the Sicilian cookery-book, Sarambus, the vintner. And you would be affronted if I told you that these are a parcel of cooks who make men fat only to make them thin. And those whom they have fattened applaud them, instead of finding fault with them, and lay the blame of their subsequent disorders on their physicians. In this respect, Callicles, you are like them; you applaud the statesmen of old, who pandered to the vices of the citizens, and filled the city with docks and harbours, but neglected virtue and justice. And when the fit of illness comes, the citizens who in like manner applauded Themistocles, Pericles, and others, will lay hold of you and my friend Alcibiades, and you will suffer

for the misdeeds of your predecessors. The old story is always being repeated—'after all his services, the ungrateful city banished him, or condemned him to death.' As if the statesman should not have taught the
city better! He surely cannot blame the state for having unjustly used
him, any more than the sophist or teacher can find fault with his pupils
if they cheat him. And the sophist and orator are in the same case; although you admire rhetoric and despise sophistic, whereas sophistic is
really the higher of the two. The teacher of the arts takes money, but
the teacher of virtue or politics takes no money, because this is the only
kind of service which makes the disciple desirous of requiting his
teacher.

Socrates concludes by finally asking to which of the two modes of
serving the state Callicles invites him:—'to the inferior and ministerial one,' is the ingenuous reply. That is the only way of avoiding
death, replies Socrates; and he has heard often enough, and would
rather not hear again, that the bad man will kill the good. But he
thinks that such a fate is very likely reserved for him, because he sees
that he is the only Athenian practising the true art of politics. And
very probably, as in the case which he described to Polus, he may be
the physician who is tried by a jury of children. He cannot say that he
has procured the citizens any pleasure, and if anyone charges him
with perplexing them, or with reviling their elders, he will not be able
to make them understand that he has only been actuated by a desire
for their good. And therefore there is no saying what his fate may be.
'And do you think that a man who is unable to help himself is in a
good condition?' Yes, Callicles, if he have the true self-help, which is
never to have said or done any wrong to himself or others. If I had not
this kind of self-help, I should be ashamed; but if I die for want of
your flattering rhetoric, I shall die in peace. For death is no evil, but
to go to the world below laden with offences is the worst of evils. In
proof of which I will tell you a tale:—

Under the rule of Cronus, men were judged on the day of their
death, and when judgement had been given upon them they de-
parted—the good to the islands of the blest, the bad to the house of
vengeance. But as they were still living and had their clothes on at the
time when they were being judged, there was favouritism, and Zeus,
when he came to the throne, was obliged to alter the mode of proce-
dure, and try them after death, having first sent down Prometheus to
take away from them the foreknowledge of death. Minos,
Rhadamanthus, and Aeacus were appointed to be the judges;
Rhadamanthus for Asia, Aeacus for Europe, and Minos was to hold the
court of appeal. Now death is the separation of soul and body, but after

death soul and body alike retain their characteristics; the fat man, the dandy, the branded slave, are all distinguishable. Some prince or potentate, perhaps even the great king himself, appears before Rhadamanthus, and he instantly detects him, though he knows not who he is; he sees the scars of perjury and iniquity, and sends him away to the house of torment.

For there are two classes of souls who undergo punishment—the curable and the incurable. The curable are those who are benefited by their punishment; the incurable are such as Archelaus, who benefit others by becoming a warning to them. The latter class are generally kings and potentates; meaner persons, happily for themselves, have not the same power of doing injustice. Sisyphus and Tityus, not Thersites, are supposed by Homer to be undergoing everlasting punishment. Not that there is anything to prevent a great man from being a good one, as is shown by the famous example of Aristeides, the son of Lysimachus. But to Rhadamanthus the souls are only known as good or bad; they are stripped of their dignities and preferments; he despatches the bad to Tartarus, labelled either as curable or incurable, and looks with love and admiration on the soul of some just one, whom he sends to the islands of the blest. Similar is the practice of Aeacus; and Minos overlooks them, holding a golden sceptre, as Odysseus in Homer saw him

'Wielding a sceptre of gold, and giving laws to the dead.'

My wish for myself and my fellow men is, that we may present our souls undefiled to the judge in that day; my desire in life is to be able to meet death. And I exhort you, and retort upon you the reproach which you cast upon me,—that you will stand before the judge, gaping, and with dizzy brain, and anyone may box you on the ear, and do you all manner of evil.

Perhaps you think that this is an old wives' fable. But you, who are the three wisest men in Hellas, have nothing better to say, and no one will ever show that to do is better than to suffer evil. A man should study to be, and not merely to seem. If he is bad, he should become good, and avoid all flattery, whether of the many or of the few.

Follow me, then; and if you are looked down upon, that will do you no harm. And when we have practised virtue, we will betake ourselves to politics, but not until we are delivered from the shameful state of ignorance and uncertainty in which we are at present. Let us follow in the way of virtue and justice, and not in the way to which you, Callicles, invite us; for that way is nothing worth.

Introduction

We will now consider in order some of the principal points of the dialogue.

(1) In the *Gorgias*, as in nearly all the other dialogues of Plato, we are made aware that formal logic has as yet no existence. The old difficulty of framing a definition recurs. The illusive analogy of the arts and the virtues also continues. The ambiguity of several words, such as nature, custom, the honourable, the good, is not cleared up. The sophists are still floundering about the distinction of the real and seeming. Figures of speech are made the basis of arguments. The possibility of conceiving a universal art or science, which admits of application to a particular subject-matter, is a difficulty which remains unsolved, and has not altogether ceased to haunt the world at the present day (cf. *Charmides* 166 foll.). The defect of clearness is also apparent in Socrates himself, unless we suppose him to be practising on the simplicity of his opponent, or rather perhaps trying an experiment in dialectics. Nothing can be more fallacious than the contradiction which he pretends to have discovered in the answers of Gorgias (see Analysis). The advantages which he gains over Polus are also due to a false antithesis of pleasure and good, and to an erroneous assertion that an agent and a patient may be described by similar predicates; — a mistake which Aristotle partly shares and partly corrects in the *Nicomachean Ethics*, v.i.4; xi.2. Traces of a 'robust sophistry' are likewise discernible in his argument with Callicles (490, 496, 516).

(2) Although Socrates professes to be convinced by reason only, yet the argument is often a sort of dialectical fiction, by which he conducts himself and others to his own ideal of life and action. And we may sometimes wish that we could have suggested answers to his antagonists, or pointed out to them the rocks which lay concealed under the ambiguous terms good, pleasure, and the like. But it would be as useless to examine his arguments by the requirements of modern logic, as to criticise this ideal from a merely utilitarian point of view. If we say that the ideal is generally regarded as unattainable, and that mankind will by no means agree in thinking that the criminal is happier when punished than when unpunished, any more than they would agree to the stoical paradox that a man may be happy on the rack, Plato has already admitted that the world is against him. Neither does he mean to say that Archelaus is tormented by the stings of conscience; or that the sensations of the impaled criminal are more agreeable than those of the tyrant drowned in luxurious enjoyment. Neither is he speaking, as in the *Protagoras*, of virtue as a calculation of pleasure, an opinion which he afterwards repudiates in the *Phaedo*. What then is his meaning? His meaning we shall be able to illustrate best by parallel notions, which, whether justifiable by logic or not, have always existed among mankind. We must remind the reader that Socrates himself implies that he will be understood or appreciated by very few.

He is speaking not of the consciousness of happiness, but of the idea of happiness. When a martyr dies in a good cause, when a soldier falls in battle, we do not suppose that death or wounds are without pain, or that their physical suffering is always compensated by a mental satisfaction. Still we regard them as happy, and we would a thousand times rather have their death than a shameful life. Nor is this only because we believe that they will obtain an immortality of fame, or that they will have crowns of glory in another world, when their enemies and persecutors will be proportionably tormented. Men are found in a few instances to do what is right, without reference to public opinion or to consequences. And we regard them as happy on this ground only, much as Socrates' friends in the opening of the *Phaedo* are described as regarding him; or as was said of another, 'they looked upon his face as upon the face of an angel.' We are not concerned to justify this idealism by the standard of utility or public opinion, but merely to point out the existence of such a sentiment in the better part of human nature.

The idealism of Plato is founded upon this sentiment. He would maintain that in some sense or other truth and right are alone to be sought, and that all other goods are only desirable as means towards these. He is thought to have erred in 'considering the agent only, and making no reference to the happiness of others as affected by him.' But the happiness of others or of mankind, if regarded as an end, is really quite as ideal and almost as paradoxical to the common understanding as Plato's conception of happiness. For the greatest happiness of the greatest number may mean also the greatest pain of the individual which will procure the greatest pleasure of the greatest number. Ideas of utility, like those of duty and right, may be pushed to unpleasant consequences. Nor can Plato in the *Gorgias* be deemed purely self-regarding, considering that Socrates expressly mentions the duty of imparting the truth when discovered to others. Nor must we forget that the side of ethics which regards others is by the ancients merged in politics. Both in Plato and Aristotle, as well as in the Stoics, the social principle, though taking another form, is really far more prominent than in most modern treatises on ethics.

The idealizing of suffering is one of the conceptions which have exercised the greatest influence on mankind. Into the theological import of this, or into the consideration of the errors to which the idea may have given rise, we need not now enter. All will agree that the ideal of the Divine Sufferer, whose words the world would not receive, the man of sorrows of whom the Hebrew prophets spoke, has sunk deep into the heart of the human race. It is a similar picture of suffering goodness which Plato desires to portray, not without an allusion to the fate of his master Socrates. He is convinced that, somehow or other, such a one must be happy in life or after death. In the *Republic*, he endeavours to show that his happiness would be assured here in a well-ordered state. But in the actual condition of human things the wise and good are weak and miserable; such a one is like a man fallen among wild beasts, exposed to every sort of wrong and obloquy.

Plato, like other philosophers, is thus led on to the conclusion, that if 'the ways of God' to man are to be 'justified,' the hopes of another life must be included. If the question could have been put to him, whether a man dying in torments was happy still, even if, as he suggests in the *Apology*, 'death be only a long sleep,' we can hardly tell what would have been his answer. There have been a few, who, quite independently of rewards and punishments or of posthumous reputation, or any other influence of public opinion, have been willing to sacrifice their lives for the good of others. It is difficult to say how far in such cases an unconscious hope of a future life, or a general faith in the victory of good in the world, may have supported the sufferers. But this extreme idealism is not in accordance with the spirit of Plato. He supposes a day of retribution, in which the good are to be rewarded and the wicked punished. Though, as he says in the *Phaedo*, no man of sense will maintain that the details of the stories about another world are true, he will insist that something of the kind is true, and will frame his life with a view to this unknown future. Even in the *Republic* he introduces a future life as an afterthought, when the superior happiness of the just has been established on what is thought to be an immutable foundation. At the same time he makes a point of determining his main thesis independently of remoter consequences.

(3) Plato's theory of punishment is partly vindictive, partly corrective. In the *Gorgias*, as well as in the *Phaedo* and *Republic*, a few great criminals, chiefly tyrants, are reserved as examples. But most men have never had the opportunity of attaining this pre-eminence of evil. They are not incurable, and their punishment is intended for their improvement. They are to suffer because they have sinned; like sick men, they must go to the physician and be healed. On this representation of Plato's the criticism has been made, that the analogy of disease and injustice is partial only, and that suffering, instead of improving men, may have just the opposite effect.

Like the general analogy of the arts and the virtues, the analogy of disease and injustice, or of medicine and justice, is certainly imperfect. But ideas must be given through something; the nature of the mind which is unseen can only be represented under figures derived from visible objects. If these figures are suggestive of some new aspect under which the mind may be considered, we cannot find fault with them for not exactly coinciding with the ideas represented. They partake of the imperfect nature of language, and must not be construed in too strict a manner. That Plato sometimes reasons from them as if they were not figures but realities, is due to the defective logical analysis of his age.

Nor does he distinguish between the suffering which improves and the suffering which only punishes and deters. He applies to the sphere of ethics a conception of punishment which is really derived from criminal law. He does not see that such punishment is only negative, and supplies no principle of moral growth or development. He is not far off the higher notion of an education of man to be begun in this world, and to be continued in other stages of existence, which is further developed in the *Republic*. And Christian thinkers, who have ventured out of the beaten track in their meditations on the 'last things,' have found a ray of light in his writings. But he has not explained how or in what way punishment is to contribute to the improvement of mankind. He has not followed out the principle which he affirms in the *Republic*, that 'God is the author of evil only with a view to good,' and that 'they were the better for being punished.' Still his doctrine of a future state of rewards and punishments may be compared favourably with that perversion of Christian doctrine which makes the everlasting punishment of human beings depend on a brief moment

of time, or even on the accident of an accident. And he has escaped the difficulty which has often beset divines, respecting the future destiny of the meaner
sort of men (Thersites and the like) who are neither very good nor very bad, by
not counting them worthy of eternal damnation.

We do Plato violence in pressing his figures of speech or chains of argument; and not less so in asking questions which were beyond the horizon of his
vision, or did not come within the scope of his design. The main purpose of
the *Gorgias* is not to answer questions about a future world, but to place in antagonism the true and false life, and to contrast the judgements and opinions
of men with judgement according to the truth. Plato may be accused of representing a superhuman or transcendental virtue in the description of the just
man in the *Gorgias*, or in the companion portrait of the philosopher in the
Theaetetus; and at the same time may be thought to be condemning a state of
the world which always has existed and always will exist among men. But such
ideals act powerfully on the imagination of mankind. And such condemna-
tions are not mere paradoxes of philosophers, but the natural rebellion of the
higher sense of right in man against the ordinary conditions of human life. The
greatest statesmen have fallen very far short of the political ideal, and are therefore justly involved in the general condemnation.

Subordinate to the main purpose of the dialogue are some other questions,
which may be briefly considered:—

(a) The antithesis of good and pleasure, which as in other dialogues is supposed to consist in the permanent nature of the one compared with the transient and relative nature of the other. Good and pleasure, knowledge and
sense, truth and opinion, essence and generation, virtue and pleasure, the real
and the apparent, the infinite and finite, harmony or beauty and discord, dialectic and rhetoric or poetry, are so many pairs of opposites, which in Plato
easily pass into one another, and are seldom kept perfectly distinct. And we
must not forget that Plato's conception of pleasure is the Heracleitean flux
transferred to the sphere of human conduct. There is some degree of unfair-
ness in opposing the principle of good, which is objective, to the principle of
pleasure, which is subjective. For the assertion of the permanence of good is
only based on the assumption of its objective character. Had Plato fixed his
mind, not on the ideal nature of good, but on the subjective consciousness of
happiness, that would have been found to be as transient and precarious as
pleasure.

(b) The arts or sciences, when pursued without any view to truth or the improvement of human life, are called flatteries. They are all alike dependent
upon the opinion of mankind, from which they are derived. To Plato the
whole world appears to be sunk in error, based on self-interest. To this is opposed the one wise man hardly professing to have found truth, yet strong in the
conviction that a virtuous life is the only good, whether regarded with reference to this world or to another. Statesmen, sophists, rhetoricians, poets, are
alike brought up for judgement. They are the parodies of wise men, and their
arts are the parodies of true arts and sciences. All that they call science is
merely the result of that study of the tempers of the Great Beast, which he describes in the *Republic*.

(c) Various other points of contact naturally suggest themselves between the *Gorgias* and other dialogues, especially the *Republic*, the *Philebus*, and the *Protagoras*. There are closer resemblances both of spirit and language in the *Republic* than in any other dialogue, the verbal similarity tending to show that they were written at the same period of Plato's life. For the *Republic* supplies that education and training of which the *Gorgias* suggests the necessity. The theory of the many weak combining against the few strong in the formation of society (which is indeed a partial truth), is similar in both of them, and is expressed in nearly the same language. The sufferings and fate of the just man, the powerlessness of evil, and the reversal of the situation in another life, are also points of similarity. The poets, like the rhetoricians, are condemned because they aim at pleasure only; as in the *Republic* they are expelled the state, because they are imitators, and minister to the weaker side of human nature. That poetry is akin to rhetoric may be compared with the analogous notion, which occurs in the *Protagoras*, that the ancient poets were the sophists of their day. In some other respects the *Protagoras* rather offers a contrast than a parallel. The character of Protagoras may be compared with that of Gorgias, but the conception of happiness is different in the two dialogues; being described in the former, according to the old Socratic notion, as deferred or accumulated pleasure, while in the *Gorgias*, and in the *Phaedo*, pleasure and good are distinctly opposed.

This opposition is carried out from a speculative point of view in the *Philebus*. There neither pleasure nor wisdom are allowed to be the chief good, but pleasure and good are not so completely opposed as in the *Gorgias*. For innocent pleasures, and such as have no antecedent pains, are allowed to rank in the class of goods. The allusion to Gorgias' definition of rhetoric (*Philebus* 58a, b; cf. *Gorg.* 452d, e), as the art of persuasion, of all arts the best, for to it all things submit, not by compulsion but of their own free will—marks a close and perhaps designed connexion between the two dialogues. In both the ideas of measure, order, harmony, are the connecting links between the beautiful and the good.

In general spirit and character, that is, in irony and antagonism to public opinion, the *Gorgias* most nearly resembles the *Apology*, *Crito*, and portions of the *Republic*, and like the *Philebus*, though from another point of view, may be thought to stand in the same relation to Plato's theory of morals which the *Theaetetus* bears to his theory of knowledge.

(d) A few minor points still remain to be summed up: (1) The extravagant irony in the reason which is assigned for the pilot's modest charge (511e); and in the proposed use of rhetoric as an instrument of self-condemnation (480c–e); and in the mighty power of geometrical equality in both worlds (508a). (2) The reference of the mythus to the previous discussion should not be overlooked: the fate reserved for incurable criminals such as Archelaus (525c, d); the retaliation of the box on the ears (527a); the nakedness of the souls and of the judges who are stript of the clothes or disguises which rhetoric and public opinion have hitherto provided for them (523e; cf. Swift's notion that the universe is a suit of clothes, *Tale of a Tub*). The fiction seems to have involved Plato in the necessity of supposing that the soul retained a sort of corporeal likeness after death (524b–d). (3) The appeal to the authority of Homer, who says that Odysseus saw Minos in his court 'holding a golden sceptre,' which gives verisimilitude to the tale (526c, d).

It is scarcely necessary to repeat that Plato is playing 'both sides of the game,' and that in criticizing the characters of Gorgias and Polus, we are not passing any judgement on historical individuals, but only attempting to analyse the dramatis personae as they were conceived by him. Neither is it necessary to enlarge upon the obvious fact that Plato is a dramatic writer, whose real opinions cannot always be assumed to be those which he puts into the mouth of Socrates, or any other speaker who appears to have the best of the argument; or to repeat the observation that he is a poet as well as a philosopher; or to remark that he is not to be tried by a modern standard, but interpreted with reference to his place in the history of thought and the opinion of his time.

It has been said that the most characteristic feature of the *Gorgias* is the assertion of the right of dissent, or private judgement. But this mode of stating the question is really opposed both to the spirit of Plato and of ancient philosophy generally. For Plato is not asserting any abstract right or duty of toleration, or advantage to be derived from freedom of thought; indeed, in some other parts of his writings (e.g. *Laws*), he has fairly laid himself open to the charge of intolerance. No speculations had as yet arisen respecting the 'liberty of prophesying'; and Plato is not affirming any abstract right of this nature: but he is asserting the duty and right of the one wise and true man to dissent from the folly and falsehood of the many. At the same time he acknowledges the natural result, which he hardly seeks to avert, that he who speaks the truth to a multitude, regardless of consequences, will probably share the fate of Socrates.

GORGIAS

Persons of the Dialogue:
CALLICLES, SOCRATES, CHAEREPHON, GORGIAS, POLUS.

SCENE: The house of CALLICLES.

CALLICLES: The wise man, as the proverb says, is late for a fray, but not for a feast.

SOCRATES: And are we late for a feast?

CALLICLES: Yes, and a delightful feast; for Gorgias has just been exhibiting to us many fine things.

SOCRATES: It is not my fault, Callicles; our friend Chaerephon is to blame; for he would keep us loitering in the Agora.

CHAEREPHON: Never mind, Socrates; the misfortune of which I have been the cause I will also repair; for Gorgias is a friend of mine, and I will make him give the exhibition again either now, or, if you prefer, at some other time.

CALLICLES: What is the matter, Chaerephon—does Socrates want to hear Gorgias?

CHAEREPHON: Yes, that was our intention in coming.

CALLICLES: Come into my house, then; for Gorgias is staying with me, and he shall exhibit to you.

SOCRATES: Very good, Callicles; but will he answer our questions? for I want to hear from him what is the nature of his art, and what it is which he professes and teaches; he may, as you [Chaerephon] suggest, defer the exhibition to some other time.

CALLICLES: There is nothing like asking him, Socrates; and indeed to answer questions is a part of his exhibition, for he was saying only just now, that any one in my house might put any question to him, and that he would answer.

SOCRATES: How fortunate! will you ask him, Chaerephon—?

CHAEREPHON: What shall I ask him?

SOCRATES: Ask him who he is.

CHAEREPHON: What do you mean?

SOCRATES: I mean such a question as would elicit from him, if he had been a maker of shoes, the answer that he is a cobbler. Do you understand?

CHAEREPHON: I understand, and will ask him: Tell me, Gorgias, is our friend Callicles right in saying that you undertake to answer any questions which you are asked?

GORGIAS: Quite right, Chaerephon: I was saying as much only just now; and I may add, that many years have elapsed since any one has asked me a new one.

CHAEREPHON: Then you must be very ready, Gorgias.

GORGIAS: Of that, Chaerephon, you can make trial.

POLUS: Yes, indeed, and if you like, Chaerephon, you may make trial of me too, for I think that Gorgias, who has been talking a long time, is tired.

CHAEREPHON: And do you, Polus, think that you can answer better than Gorgias?

POLUS: What does that matter if I answer well enough for you?

CHAEREPHON: Not at all:—and you shall answer if you like.

POLUS: Ask:—

CHAEREPHON: My question is this: If Gorgias had the skill of his brother Herodicus, what ought we to call him? Ought he not to have the name which is given to his brother?

POLUS: Certainly.

CHAEREPHON: Then we should be right in calling him a physician?

POLUS: Yes.

CHAEREPHON: And if he had the skill of Aristophon the son of Aglaophon, or of his brother Polygnotus, what ought we to call him?

POLUS: Clearly, a painter.

CHAEREPHON: But now what shall we call him—what is the art in which he is skilled?

POLUS: O Chaerephon, there are many arts among mankind which are experimental, and have their origin in experience, for experience makes the days of men to proceed according to art, and inexperience according to chance, and different persons in different ways are proficient in different arts, and the best persons in the best arts. And our friend Gorgias is one of the best, and the art in which he is a proficient is the noblest.

SOCRATES: Polus has been taught how to make a capital speech, Gorgias; but he is not fulfilling the promise which he made to Chaerephon.

GORGIAS: What do you mean, Socrates?

SOCRATES: I mean that he has not exactly answered the question which he was asked.

GORGIAS: Then why not ask him yourself?

SOCRATES: But I would much rather ask you, if you are disposed to answer: for I see, from the few words which Polus has uttered, that he has attended more to the art which is called rhetoric than to dialectic.

POLUS: What makes you say so, Socrates?

SOCRATES: Because, Polus, when Chaerephon asked you what was the art which Gorgias knows, you praised it as if you were answering some one who found fault with it, but you never said what the art was.

POLUS: Why, did I not say that it was the noblest of arts?

SOCRATES: Yes, indeed, but that was no answer to the question: nobody asked what was the quality, but what was the nature, of the art, and by what name we were to describe Gorgias. And I would still beg you briefly and clearly, as you answered Chaerephon when he asked you at first, to say what this art is, and what we ought to call Gorgias: Or rather, Gorgias, let me turn to you, and ask the same question,— what are we to call you, and what is the art which you profess?

GORGIAS: Rhetoric, Socrates, is my art.

SOCRATES: Then I am to call you a rhetorician?

GORGIAS: Yes, Socrates, and a good one too, if you would call me that which, in Homeric language, 'I boast myself to be.'

SOCRATES: I should wish to do so.

GORGIAS: Then pray do.

SOCRATES: And are we to say that you are able to make other men rhetoricians?

GORGIAS: Yes, that is exactly what I profess to make them, not only at Athens, but in all places.

SOCRATES: And will you continue to ask and answer questions, Gorgias, as we are at present doing, and reserve for another occasion the longer mode of speech which Polus was attempting? Will you keep your promise, and answer shortly the questions which are asked of you?

GORGIAS: Some answers, Socrates, are of necessity longer; but I will do my best to make them as short as possible; for a part of my profession is that I can be as short as any one.

SOCRATES: That is what is wanted, Gorgias; exhibit the shorter method now, and the longer one at some other time.

GORGIAS: Well, I will; and you will certainly say, that you never heard a man use fewer words.

SOCRATES: Very good then; as you profess to be a rhetorician, and a maker of rhetoricians, let me ask you, with what is rhetoric concerned: I might ask with what is weaving concerned, and you would reply (would you not?), with the making of garments?

GORGIAS: Yes.

SOCRATES: And music is concerned with the composition of melodies?

GORGIAS: It is.

SOCRATES: By Herè, Gorgias, I admire the surpassing brevity of your answers.

GORGIAS: Yes, Socrates, I do think myself good at that.

SOCRATES: I am glad to hear it; answer me in like manner about rhetoric: with what is rhetoric concerned?

GORGIAS: With discourse.

SOCRATES: What sort of discourse, Gorgias?—such discourse as would teach the sick under what treatment they might get well?

GORGIAS: No.

SOCRATES: Then rhetoric does not treat of all kinds of discourse?

GORGIAS: Certainly not.

SOCRATES. And yet rhetoric makes men able to speak?

GORGIAS: Yes.

SOCRATES: And to understand that about which they speak?

GORGIAS: Of course.

SOCRATES: But does not the art of medicine, which we were just now mentioning, also make men able to understand and speak about the sick?

GORGIAS: Certainly.

SOCRATES: Then medicine also treats of discourse?

GORGIAS: Yes.

SOCRATES: Of discourse concerning diseases?

GORGIAS: Just so.

SOCRATES: And does not gymnastic also treat of discourse concerning the good or evil condition of the body?

GORGIAS: Very true.

SOCRATES: And the same, Gorgias, is true of the other arts:—all of them treat of discourse concerning the subjects with which they severally have to do.

GORGIAS: Clearly.

SOCRATES: Then why, if you call rhetoric the art which treats of discourse, and all the other arts treat of discourse, do you not call them arts of rhetoric?

GORGIAS: Because, Socrates, the knowledge of the other arts has only to do with some sort of external action, as of the hand; but there is no such action of the hand in rhetoric which works and takes effect only through the medium of discourse. And therefore I am justified in saying that rhetoric treats of discourse.

SOCRATES: I am not sure whether I entirely understand you, but I dare say I shall soon know better; please to answer me a question:—you would allow that there are arts?

GORGIAS: Yes.

SOCRATES: As to the arts generally, they are for the most part concerned with doing, and require little or no speaking; in painting, and statuary, and many other arts, the work may proceed in silence; and of such arts I suppose you would say that they do not come within the province of rhetoric.

GORGIAS: You perfectly conceive my meaning, Socrates.

SOCRATES: But there are other arts which work wholly through the medium of language, and require either no action or very little, as, for example, the arts of arithmetic, of calculation, of geometry, and of playing draughts; in some of these speech is pretty nearly co-extensive with action, but in most of them the verbal element is greater—they depend wholly on words for their efficacy and power: and I take your meaning to be that rhetoric is an art of this latter sort?

GORGIAS: Exactly.

SOCRATES: And yet I do not believe that you really mean to call any of these arts rhetoric; although the precise expression which you used was, that rhetoric is an art which works and takes effect only through the medium of discourse; and an adversary who wished to be captious might say, 'And so, Gorgias, you call arithmetic rhetoric.' But I do not think that you really call arithmetic rhetoric any more than geometry would be so called by you.

GORGIAS: You are quite right, Socrates, in your apprehension of my meaning.

SOCRATES: Well, then, let me now have the rest of my answer:—seeing that rhetoric is one of those arts which works mainly by the use of words, and there are other arts which also use words, tell me what is that quality in words with which rhetoric is concerned:—Suppose that a person asks me about some of the arts which I was mentioning just now; he might say, 'Socrates, what is arithmetic?' and I should reply to him, as you replied to me, that arithmetic is one of those arts which take effect through words. And then he would proceed to ask: 'Words about what?' and I should reply, Words about odd and even numbers, and how many there are of each. And if he asked again: 'What is the art of calculation?' I should say, That also is one of the arts which is concerned wholly with words. And if he further said, 'Concerned with what?' I should say, like the clerks in the assembly, 'as aforesaid' of arithmetic, but with a difference, the difference being that the art of calculation considers not only the quantities of odd and even numbers, but also their numerical relations to themselves and to one another. And suppose, again, I were to say that astronomy is only words—he would ask, 'Words about what, Socrates?' and I should answer, that astronomy tells us about the motions of the stars and sun and moon, and their relative swiftness.

GORGIAS: You would be quite right, Socrates.

SOCRATES: And now let us have from you, Gorgias, the truth about rhetoric: which you would admit (would you not?) to be one of those arts which act always and fulfil all their ends through the medium of words?

GORGIAS: True.

SOCRATES: Words which do what? I should ask. To what class of things do the words which rhetoric uses relate?

GORGIAS: To the greatest, Socrates, and the best of human things.

SOCRATES: That again, Gorgias, is ambiguous; I am still in the dark: for which are the greatest and best of human things? I dare say that you have heard men singing at feasts the old drinking song, in which the singers enumerate the goods of life, first health, beauty next, thirdly, as the writer of the song says, wealth honestly obtained.

GORGIAS: Yes, I know the song; but what is your drift?

SOCRATES: I mean to say, that the producers of those things which the author of the song praises, that is to say, the physician, the trainer, the money-maker, will at once come to you, and first the physician will say: 'O Socrates, Gorgias is deceiving you, for my art is concerned with the greatest good of men and not his.' And when I ask, Who are you? he will reply, 'I am a physician.' What do you mean? I shall say. Do you mean that your art produces the greatest good? 'Certainly,' he will answer, 'for is not health the greatest good? What greater good can men have, Socrates?' And after him the trainer will come and say, 'I too, Socrates, shall be greatly surprised if Gorgias can show more good of his art than I can show of mine.' To him again I shall say, Who are you, honest friend, and what is your business? 'I am a trainer,' he will reply, 'and my business is to make men beautiful and strong in body.' When I have done with the trainer, there arrives the money-maker, and he, as I expect, will utterly despise them all. 'Consider, Socrates,' he will say, 'whether Gorgias or any one else can produce any greater good than wealth.' Well, you and I say to him, and are you a creator of wealth? 'Yes,' he replies. And who are you? 'A money-maker.' And do you consider wealth to be the greatest good of man? 'Of course,' will be his reply. And we shall rejoin: Yes; but our friend Gorgias contends that his art produces a greater good than yours. And then he will be sure to go on and ask, 'What good? Let Gorgias answer.' Now I want you, Gorgias, to imagine that this question is asked of you by them and by me; What is that which, as you say, is the greatest good of man, and of which you are the creator? Answer us.

GORGIAS: That good, Socrates, which is truly the greatest, being that which gives to men freedom in their own persons, and to individuals the power of ruling over others in their several states.

SOCRATES: And what would you consider this to be?

GORGIAS: What is there greater than the word which persuades the judges in the courts, or the senators in the council, or the citizens in the assembly, or at any other political meeting?—if you have the power of uttering this word, you will have the physician your slave, and the trainer your slave, and the money-maker of whom you talk will be found to gather treasures, not for himself, but for you who are able to speak and to persuade the multitude.

SOCRATES: Now I think, Gorgias, that you have very accurately explained what you conceive to be the art of rhetoric; and you mean to say, if I am not mistaken, that rhetoric is the artificer of persuasion, having this and no other business, and that this is her crown and end. Do you know any other effect of rhetoric over and above that of producing persuasion?

GORGIAS: No: the definition seems to me very fair, Socrates; for persuasion is the chief end of rhetoric.

SOCRATES: Then hear me, Gorgias, for I am quite sure that if there ever was a man who entered on the discussion of a matter from a pure love of knowing the truth, I am such a one, and I should say the same of you.

GORGIAS: What is coming, Socrates?

SOCRATES: I will tell you: I am very well aware that I do not know what, according to you, is the exact nature, or what are the topics of that persuasion of which you speak, and which is given by rhetoric; although I have a suspicion about both the one and the other. And I am going to ask—what is this power of persuasion which is given by rhetoric, and about what? But why, if I have a suspicion, do I ask instead of telling you? Not for your sake, but in order that the argument may proceed in such a manner as is most likely to set forth the truth. And I would have you observe, that I am right in asking this further question: If I asked, 'What sort of a painter is Zeuxis?' and you said, 'The painter of figures,' should I not be right in asking, 'What kind of figures, and where do you find them?'

GORGIAS: Certainly.

SOCRATES: And the reason for asking this second question would be, that there are other painters besides, who paint many other figures?

GORGIAS: True.

SOCRATES: But if there had been no one but Zeuxis who painted them, then you would have answered very well?

GORGIAS: Quite so.

SOCRATES: Now I want to know about rhetoric in the same way;—is rhetoric the only art which brings persuasion, or do other arts have the same effect? I mean to say—Does he who teaches anything persuade men of that which he teaches or not?

GORGIAS: He persuades, Socrates,—there can be no mistake about that.

SOCRATES: Again, if we take the arts of which we were just now speaking:—do not arithmetic and the arithmeticians teach us the properties of number?

GORGIAS: Certainly.

SOCRATES: And therefore persuade us of them?

GORGIAS: Yes.

SOCRATES: Then arithmetic as well as rhetoric is an artificer of persuasion?

GORGIAS: Clearly.

SOCRATES: And if any one asks us what sort of persuasion, and about what,—we shall answer, persuasion which teaches the quantity of odd and even; and we shall be able to show that all the other arts of which we were just now speaking are artificers of persuasion, and of what sort, and about what.

GORGIAS: Very true.

SOCRATES: Then rhetoric is not the only artificer of persuasion?

GORGIAS: True.

SOCRATES: Seeing, then, that not only rhetoric works by persuasion, but that other arts do the same, as in the case of the painter, a question has arisen which is a very fair one: Of what persuasion is rhetoric the artificer, and about what? — is not that a fair way of putting the question?

GORGIAS: I think so.

SOCRATES: Then, if you approve the question, Gorgias, what is the answer?

GORGIAS: I answer, Socrates, that rhetoric is the art of persuasion in courts of law and other assemblies, as I was just now saying, and about the just and unjust.

SOCRATES: And that, Gorgias, was what I was suspecting to be your notion; yet I would not have you wonder if by-and-by I am found repeating a seemingly plain question; for I ask not in order to confute you, but as I was saying that the argument may proceed consecutively, and that we may not get the habit of anticipating and suspecting the meaning of one another's words; I would have you develop your own views in your own way, whatever may be your hypothesis.

GORGIAS: I think that you are quite right, Socrates.

SOCRATES: Then let me raise another question; there is such a thing as 'having learned'?

GORGIAS: Yes.

SOCRATES: And there is also 'having believed'?

GORGIAS: Yes.

SOCRATES: And is the 'having learned' the same as 'having believed,' and are learning and belief the same things?

GORGIAS: In my judgment, Socrates, they are not the same.

SOCRATES: And your judgment is right, as you may ascertain in this way:—If a person were to say to you, 'Is there, Gorgias, a false belief as well as a true?'—you would reply, if I am not mistaken, that there is.

GORGIAS: Yes.

SOCRATES: Well, but is there a false knowledge as well as a true?

GORGIAS: No.

SOCRATES: No, indeed; and this again proves that knowledge and belief differ.

GORGIAS: Very true.

SOCRATES: And yet those who have learned as well as those who have believed are persuaded?

GORGIAS: Just so.

SOCRATES: Shall we then assume two sorts of persuasion,—one which is the source of belief without knowledge, as the other is of knowledge?

GORGIAS: By all means.

SOCRATES: And which sort of persuasion does rhetoric create in courts of law and other assemblies about the just and unjust, the sort of persuasion which gives belief without knowledge, or that which gives knowledge?

GORGIAS: Clearly, Socrates, that which only gives belief.

SOCRATES: Then rhetoric, as would appear, is the artificer of a persuasion which creates belief about the just and unjust, but gives no instruction about them?

GORGIAS: True.

SOCRATES: And the rhetorician does not instruct the courts of law or other assemblies about things just and unjust, but he creates belief about them; for no one can be supposed to instruct such a vast multitude about such high matters in a short time?

GORGIAS: Certainly not.

SOCRATES: Come, then, and let us see what we really mean about rhetoric; for I do not know what my own meaning is as yet. When the assembly meets to elect a physician or a shipwright or any other craftsman, will the rhetorician be taken into counsel? Surely not. For at every election he ought to be chosen who is most skilled; and, again, when walls have to be built or harbours or docks to be constructed, not the rhetorician but the master workman will advise; or when generals have to be chosen and an order of battle arranged, or a position taken, then the military will advise and not the rhetoricians: what do you say, Gorgias? Since you profess to be a rhetorician and a maker of rhetoricians, I cannot do better than learn the nature of your art from you. And here let me assure you that I have your interest in view as well as my own. For likely enough some one or other of the young men present might desire to become your pupil, and in fact I see some, and a good many too, who have this wish, but they would be too modest to question you. And therefore when you are interrogated by me, I would have you imagine that you are interrogated by them. 'What is the use of coming to you, Gorgias?' they will say—'about what will you teach us to advise the state?—about the just and unjust only, or about those other things also which Socrates has just mentioned?' How will you answer them?

GORGIAS: I like your way of leading us on, Socrates, and I will endeavour to reveal to you the whole nature of rhetoric. You must have heard, I think, that the docks and the walls of the Athenians and the plan of the harbour were devised in accordance with the counsels, partly of Themistocles, and partly of Pericles, and not at the suggestion of the builders.

SOCRATES: Such is the tradition, Gorgias, about Themistocles; and I myself heard the speech of Pericles when he advised us about the middle wall.

GORGIAS: And you will observe, Socrates, that when a decision has to be given in such matters the rhetoricians are the advisers; they are the men who win their point.

SOCRATES: I had that in my admiring mind, Gorgias, when I asked what is the nature of rhetoric, which always appears to me, when I look at the matter in this way, to be a marvel of greatness.

GORGIAS: A marvel, indeed, Socrates, if you only knew how rhetoric comprehends and holds under her sway all the inferior arts. Let me offer you a striking example of this. On several occasions I have been with my brother Herodicus or some other physician to see one of his patients, who would not allow the physician to give him medicine, or apply a knife or hot iron to him; and I have persuaded him to do for me what he would not do for the physician just by the use of rhetoric. And I say that if a rhetorician and a physician were to go to any city, and had there to argue in the Ecclesia or any other assembly as to which of them should be elected state-physician, the physician would have no chance; but he who could speak would be chosen if he wished; and in a contest with a man of any other profession the rhetorician more than any one would have the power of getting himself chosen, for he can speak more persuasively to the multitude than any of them, and on any subject. Such is the nature and power of the art of rhetoric! And yet, Socrates, rhetoric should be used like any other competitive art, not against everybody,—the rhetorician ought not to abuse his strength any

more than a pugilist or pancratiast or other master of fence;—because
he has powers which are more than a match either for friend or enemy,
he ought not therefore to strike, stab, or slay his friends. Suppose a man
to have been trained in the palestra and to be a skilful boxer,—he in
the fulness of his strength goes and strikes his father or mother or one
of his familiars or friends; but that is no reason why the trainers or
fencing-masters should be held in detestation or banished from the
city;—surely not. For they taught their art for a good purpose, to be
used against enemies and evil-doers, in self-defence not in aggression,
and others have perverted their instructions, and turned to a bad use
their own strength and skill. But not on this account are the teachers
bad, neither is the art in fault, or bad in itself; I should rather say that
those who make a bad use of the art are to blame. And the same argument holds good of rhetoric; for the rhetorician can speak against all
men and upon any subject,—in short, he can persuade the multitude
better than any other man of anything which he pleases, but he should
not therefore seek to defraud the physician or any other artist of his reputation merely because he has the power; he ought to use rhetoric
fairly, as he would also use his athletic powers. And if after having become a rhetorician he makes a bad use of his strength and skill, his instructor surely ought not on that account to be held in detestation or
banished. For he was intended by his teacher to make a good use of his
instructions, but he abuses them. And therefore he is the person who
ought to be held in detestation, banished, and put to death, and not his
instructor.

SOCRATES: You, Gorgias, like myself, have had great experience of
disputations, and you must have observed, I think, that they do not always terminate in mutual edification, or in the definition by either
party of the subjects which they are discussing; but disagreements are
apt to arise—somebody says that another has not spoken truly or
clearly; and then they get into a passion and begin to quarrel, both par-
ties conceiving that their opponents are arguing from personal feeling
only and jealousy of themselves, not from any interest in the question
at issue. And sometimes they will go on abusing one another until the
company at last are quite vexed at themselves for ever listening to such
fellows. Why do I say this? Why, because I cannot help feeling that you
are now saying what is not quite consistent or accordant with what you
were saying at first about rhetoric. And I am afraid to point this out to
you, lest you should think that I have some animosity against you, and
that I speak, not for the sake of discovering the truth, but from jealousy
of you. Now if you are one of my sort, I should like to cross-examine
you, but if not I will let you alone. And what is my sort? you will ask. I
am one of those who are very willing to be refuted if I say anything

which is not true, and very willing to refute any one else who says what is not true, and quite as ready to be refuted as to refute; for I hold that this is the greater gain of the two, just as the gain is greater of being cured of a very great evil than of curing another. For I imagine that there is no evil which a man can endure so great as an erroneous opinion about the matters of which we are speaking; and if you claim to be one of my sort, let us have the discussion out, but if you would rather have done, no matter;—let us make an end of it.

GORGIAS: I should say, Socrates, that I am quite the man whom you indicate; but, perhaps, we ought to consider the audience, for, before you came, I had already given a long exhibition, and if we proceed the argument may run on to a great length. And therefore I think that we should consider whether we may not be detaining some part of the company when they are wanting to do something else.

CHAEREPHON: You hear the audience cheering, Gorgias and Socrates, which shows their desire to listen to you; and for myself, Heaven forbid that I should have any business on hand which would take me away from a discussion so interesting and so ably maintained.

CALLICLES: By the gods, Chaerephon, although I have been present at many discussions, I doubt whether I was ever so much delighted before, and therefore if you go on discoursing all day I shall be the better pleased.

SOCRATES: I may truly say, Callicles, that I am willing, if Gorgias is.

GORGIAS: After all this, Socrates, I should be disgraced if I refused, especially as I have promised to answer all comers; in accordance with the wishes of the company, then, do you begin, and ask of me any question which you like.

SOCRATES: Let me tell you then, Gorgias, what surprises me in your words; though I dare say that you may be right, and I may have misunderstood your meaning. You say that you can make any man, who will learn of you, a rhetorician?

GORGIAS: Yes.

SOCRATES: Do you mean that you will teach him to gain the ears of the multitude on any subject, and this not by instruction but by persuasion?

GORGIAS: Quite so.

SOCRATES: You were saying, in fact, that the rhetorician will have greater powers of persuasion than the physician even in a matter of health?

GORGIAS: Yes, with the multitude,—that is.

SOCRATES: You mean to say, with the ignorant; for with those who know he cannot be supposed to have greater powers of persuasion.

GORGIAS: Very true.

SOCRATES: But if he is to have more power of persuasion than the physician, he will have greater power than he who knows?

GORGIAS: Certainly.

SOCRATES: Although he is not a physician:—is he?

GORGIAS: No.

SOCRATES: And he who is not a physician must, obviously, be ignorant of what the physician knows.

GORGIAS: Clearly.

SOCRATES: Then, when the rhetorician is more persuasive than the physician, the ignorant is more persuasive with the ignorant than he who has knowledge?—is not that the inference?

GORGIAS: In the case supposed:—Yes.

SOCRATES: And the same holds of the relation of rhetoric to all the other arts; the rhetorician need not know the truth about things; he has only to discover some way of persuading the ignorant that he has more knowledge than those who know?

GORGIAS: Yes, Socrates, and is not this a great comfort?—not to have learned the other arts, but the art of rhetoric only, and yet to be in no way inferior to the professors of them?

SOCRATES: Whether the rhetorician is or is not inferior on this account is a question which we will hereafter examine if the enquiry is likely to be of any service to us; but I would rather begin by asking, whether he is or is not as ignorant of the just and unjust, base and honourable, good and evil, as he is of medicine and the other arts; I mean to say, does he really know anything of what is good and evil, base or honourable, just or unjust in them; or has he only a way with the ignorant of persuading them that he not knowing is to be esteemed to know more about these things than some one else who knows? Or must the pupil know these things and come to you knowing them before he can acquire the art of rhetoric? If he is ignorant, you who are the teacher of rhetoric will not teach him—it is not your business; but you will make him seem to the multitude to know them, when he does not know them; and seem to be a good man, when he is not. Or will you be unable to teach him rhetoric at all, unless he knows the truth of these things first? What is to be said about all this? By heavens, Gorgias, I wish that you would reveal to me the power of rhetoric, as you were saying that you would.

GORGIAS: Well, Socrates, I suppose that if the pupil does chance not to know them, he will have to learn of me these things as well.

SOCRATES: Say no more, for there you are right; and so he whom you make a rhetorician must either know the nature of the just and unjust already, or he must be taught by you.

GORGIAS: Certainly.

SOCRATES: Well, and is not he who has learned carpentering a carpenter?

GORGIAS: Yes.

SOCRATES: And he who has learned music a musician?

GORGIAS: Yes.

SOCRATES: And he who has learned medicine is a physician, in like manner? He who has learned anything whatever is that which his knowledge makes him.

GORGIAS: Certainly.

SOCRATES: And in the same way, he who has learned what is just is just?

GORGIAS: To be sure.

SOCRATES: And he who is just may be supposed to do what is just?

GORGIAS: Yes.

SOCRATES: And must not[1] the just man always desire to do what is just?

GORGIAS: That is clearly the inference.

SOCRATES: Surely, then, the just man will never consent to do injustice?

GORGIAS: Certainly not.

SOCRATES: And according to the argument the rhetorician must be a just man?

GORGIAS: Yes.

SOCRATES: And will therefore never be willing to do injustice?

GORGIAS: Clearly not.

SOCRATES: But do you remember saying just now that the trainer is not to be accused or banished if the pugilist makes a wrong use of his pugilistic art; and in like manner, if the rhetorician makes a bad and unjust use of his rhetoric, that is not to be laid to the charge of his teacher, who is not to be banished, but the wrong-doer himself who made a bad use of his rhetoric—he is to be banished—was not that said?

GORGIAS: Yes, it was.

SOCRATES: But now we are affirming that the aforesaid rhetorician will never have done injustice at all?

GORGIAS: True.

SOCRATES: And at the very outset, Gorgias, it was said that rhetoric treated of discourse, not (like arithmetic) about odd and even, but about just and unjust? Was not this said?

GORGIAS: Yes.

SOCRATES: I was thinking at the time, when I heard you saying so,

[1]Omitting the words τὸν ῥητορικὸν δίκαιον εἶναι and δὲ in next clause.

that rhetoric, which is always discoursing about justice, could not possibly be an unjust thing. But when you added, shortly afterwards, that the rhetorician might make a bad use of rhetoric I noted with surprise the inconsistency into which you had fallen; and I said, that if you thought, as I did, that there was a gain in being refuted, there would be an advantage in going on with the question, but if not, I would leave off. And in the course of our investigations, as you will see yourself, the rhetorician has been acknowledged to be incapable of making an unjust use of rhetoric, or of willingness to do injustice. By the dog, Gorgias, there will be a great deal of discussion, before we get at the truth of all this.

POLUS: And do even you, Socrates, seriously believe what you are now saying about rhetoric? What! because Gorgias was ashamed to deny that the rhetorician knew the just and the honourable and the good, and admitted that to any one who came to him ignorant of them he could teach them, and then out of this admission there arose a contradiction—the thing which you so dearly love, and to which not he, but you, brought the argument by your captious questions—[do you seriously believe that there is any truth in all this?] For will any one ever acknowledge that he does not know, or cannot teach, the nature of justice? The truth is, that there is great want of manners in bringing the argument to such a pass.

SOCRATES: Illustrious Polus, the reason why we provide ourselves with friends and children is, that when we get old and stumble, a younger generation may be at hand to set us on our legs again in our words and in our actions: and now, if I and Gorgias are stumbling, here are you who should raise us up; and I for my part engage to retract any error into which you may think that I have fallen—upon one condition:

POLUS: What condition?

SOCRATES: That you contract, Polus, the prolixity of speech in which you indulged at first.

POLUS: What! do you mean that I may not use as many words as I please?

SOCRATES: Only to think, my friend, that having come on a visit to Athens, which is the most free-spoken state in Hellas, you when you got there, and you alone, should be deprived of the power of speech—that would be hard indeed. But then consider my case:—shall not I be very hardly used, if, when you are making a long oration, and refusing to answer what you are asked, I am compelled to stay and listen to you, and may not go away? I say rather, if you have a real interest in the argument, or, to repeat my former expression, have any desire to set it on its legs, take back any statement which you please; and in your turn ask and answer, like myself and Gorgias—refute and be refuted: for I suppose that you would claim to know what Gorgias knows—would you not?

POLUS: Yes.

SOCRATES: And you, like him, invite any one to ask you about anything which he pleases, and you will know how to answer him?

POLUS: To be sure.

SOCRATES: And now, which will you do, ask or answer?

POLUS: I will ask; and do you answer me, Socrates, the same question which Gorgias, as you suppose, is unable to answer: What is rhetoric?

SOCRATES: Do you mean what sort of an art?

POLUS: Yes.

SOCRATES: To say the truth, Polus, it is not an art at all, in my opinion.

POLUS: Then what, in your opinion, is rhetoric?

SOCRATES: A thing which, as I was lately reading in a book of yours, you say that you have made an art.

POLUS: What thing?

SOCRATES: I should say a sort of experience.

POLUS: Does rhetoric seem to you to be an experience?

SOCRATES: That is my view, but you may be of another mind.

POLUS: An experience in what?

SOCRATES: An experience in producing a sort of delight and gratification.

POLUS: And if able to gratify others, must not rhetoric be a fine thing?

SOCRATES: What are you saying, Polus? Why do you ask me whether rhetoric is a fine thing or not, when I have not as yet told you what rhetoric is?

POLUS: Did I not hear you say that rhetoric was a sort of experience?

SOCRATES: Will you, who are so desirous to gratify others, afford a slight gratification to me?

POLUS: I will.

SOCRATES: Will you ask me, what sort of an art is cookery?

POLUS: What sort of an art is cookery?

SOCRATES: Not an art at all, Polus.

POLUS: What then?

SOCRATES: I should say an experience.

POLUS: In what? I wish that you would explain to me.

SOCRATES: An experience in producing a sort of delight and gratification, Polus.

POLUS: Then are cookery and rhetoric the same?

SOCRATES: No, they are only different parts of the same profession.

POLUS: Of what profession?

SOCRATES: I am afraid that the truth may seem discourteous; and I hesitate to answer, lest Gorgias should imagine that I am making fun of his own profession. For whether or no this is that art of rhetoric which Gorgias practises I really cannot tell:—from what he was just now saying, nothing appeared of what he thought of his art, but the rhetoric which I mean is a part of a not very creditable whole.

GORGIAS: A part of what, Socrates? Say what you mean, and never mind me.

SOCRATES: In my opinion then, Gorgias, the whole of which rhetoric is a part is not an art at all, but the habit of a bold and ready wit, which knows how to manage mankind: this habit I sum up under the word 'flattery'; and it appears to me to have many other parts, one of which is cookery, which may seem to be an art, but, as I maintain, is only an experience or routine and not an art:—another part is rhetoric, and the art of attiring and sophistry are two others: thus there are four branches, and four different things answering to them. And Polus may ask, if he likes, for he has not as yet been informed, what part of flattery is rhetoric: he did not see that I had not yet answered him when he proceeded to ask a further question: Whether I do not think rhetoric a fine thing? But I shall not tell him whether rhetoric is a fine thing or not, until I have first answered, 'What is rhetoric?' For that would not be right, Polus; but I shall be happy to answer, if you will ask me, What part of flattery is rhetoric?

POLUS: I will ask, and do you answer? What part of flattery is rhetoric?

SOCRATES: Will you understand my answer? Rhetoric, according to my view, is the ghost or counterfeit of a part of politics.

POLUS: And noble or ignoble?

SOCRATES: Ignoble, I should say, if I am compelled to answer, for I call what is bad ignoble:—though I doubt whether you understand what I was saying before.

GORGIAS: Indeed, Socrates, I cannot say that I understand myself.

SOCRATES: I do not wonder, Gorgias; for I have not as yet explained myself, and our friend Polus, colt by name and colt by nature, is apt to run away.[2]

GORGIAS: Never mind him, but explain to me what you mean by saying that rhetoric is the counterfeit of a part of politics.

SOCRATES: I will try, then, to explain my notion of rhetoric, and if I am mistaken, my friend Polus shall refute me. We may assume the existence of bodies and of souls?

This is an untranslatable play on the name 'Polus,' which means 'a colt.'

GORGIAS: Of course.

SOCRATES: You would further admit that there is a good condition of either of them?

GORGIAS: Yes.

SOCRATES: Which condition may not be really good, but good only in appearance? I mean to say, that there are many persons who appear to be in good health, and whom only a physician or trainer will discern at first sight not to be in good health.

GORGIAS: True.

SOCRATES: And this applies not only to the body, but also to the soul: in either there may be that which gives the appearance of health and not the reality?

GORGIAS: Yes, certainly.

SOCRATES: And now I will endeavour to explain to you more clearly what I mean: The soul and body being two, have two arts corresponding to them: there is the art of politics attending on the soul; and another art attending on the body, of which I know no single name, but which may be described as having two divisions, one of them gymnastic, and the other medicine. And in politics there is a legislative part, which answers to gymnastic, as justice does to medicine; and the two parts run into one another, justice having to do with the same subject as legislation, and medicine with the same subject as gymnastic, but with a difference. Now, seeing that there are these four arts, two attending on the body and two on the soul for their highest good; flattery knowing, or rather guessing their natures, has distributed herself into four shams or simulations of them; she puts on the likeness of some one or other of them, and pretends to be that which she simulates, and having no regard for men's highest interests, is ever making pleasure the bait of the unwary, and deceiving them into the belief that she is of the highest value to them. Cookery simulates the disguise of medicine, and pretends to know what food is the best for the body; and if the physician and the cook had to enter into a competition in which children were the judges, or men who had no more sense than children, as to which of them best understands the goodness or badness of food, the physician would be starved to death. A flattery I deem this to be and of an ignoble sort, Polus, for to you I am now addressing myself, because it aims at pleasure without any thought of the best. An art I do not call it, but only an experience, because it is unable to explain or to give a reason of the nature of its own applications. And I do not call any irrational thing an art; but if you dispute my words, I am prepared to argue in defence of them.

Cookery, then, I maintain to be a flattery which takes the form of medicine; and tiring, in like manner, is a flattery which takes the form of gymnastic, and is knavish, false, ignoble, illiberal, working deceitfully by the help of lines, and colours, and enamels, and garments, and making men affect a spurious beauty to the neglect of the true beauty which is given by gymnastic.

I would rather not be tedious, and therefore I will only say, after the manner of the geometricians, (for I think that by this time you will be able to follow),

as tiring:gymnastic::cookery:medicine;

or rather,

as tiring:gymnastic::sophistry:legislation;

and

as cookery:medicine::rhetoric:justice.

And this, I say, is the natural difference between the rhetorician and the sophist, but by reason of their near connection, they are apt to be jumbled up together; neither do they know what to make of themselves, nor do other men know what to make of them. For if the body presided over itself, and were not under the guidance of the soul, and the soul did not discern and discriminate between cookery and medicine, but the body was made the judge of them, and the rule of judgment was the bodily delight which was given by them, then the word of Anaxagoras, that word with which you, friend Polus, are so well acquainted, would prevail far and wide: 'Chaos' would come again, and cookery, health, and medicine would mingle in an indiscriminate mass. And now I have told you my notion of rhetoric, which is, in relation to the soul, what cookery is to the body. I may have been inconsistent in making a long speech, when I would not allow you to discourse at length. But I think that I may be excused, because you did not understand me, and could make no use of my answer when I spoke shortly, and therefore I had to enter into an explanation. And if I show an equal inability to make use of yours, I hope that you will speak at equal length; but if I am able to understand you, let me have the benefit of your brevity, as is only fair: And now you may do what you please with my answer.

POLUS: What do you mean? do you think that rhetoric is flattery?

SOCRATES: Nay, I said a part of flattery; if at your age, Polus, you cannot remember, what will you do by-and-by, when you get older?

POLUS: And are the good rhetoricians meanly regarded in states, under the idea that they are flatterers?

SOCRATES: Is that a question or the beginning of a speech?

POLUS: I am asking a question.

SOCRATES: Then my answer is, that they are not regarded at all.

POLUS: How not regarded? Have they not very great power in states?

SOCRATES: Not if you mean to say that power is a good to the possessor.

POLUS: And that is what I do mean to say.

SOCRATES: Then, if so, I think that they have the least power of all the citizens.

POLUS: What! are they not like tyrants? They kill and despoil and exile any one whom they please.

SOCRATES: By the dog, Polus, I cannot make out at each deliverance of yours, whether you are giving an opinion of your own, or asking a question of me.

POLUS: I am asking a question of you.

SOCRATES: Yes, my friend, but you ask two questions at once.

POLUS: How two questions?

SOCRATES: Why, did you not say just now that the rhetoricians are like tyrants, and that they kill and despoil or exile any one whom they please?

POLUS: I did.

SOCRATES: Well then, I say to you that here are two questions in one, and I will answer both of them. And I tell you, Polus, that rhetoricians and tyrants have the least possible power in states, as I was just now saying; for they do literally nothing which they will, but only what they think best.

POLUS: And is not that a great power?

SOCRATES: Polus has already said the reverse.

POLUS: Said the reverse! nay, that is what I assert.

SOCRATES: No, by the great—what do you call him?—not you, for you say that power is a good to him who has the power.

POLUS: I do.

SOCRATES: And would you maintain that if a fool does what he thinks best, this is a good, and would you call this great power?

POLUS: I should not.

SOCRATES: Then you must prove that the rhetorician is not a fool, and that rhetoric is an art and not a flattery—and so you will have refuted me; but if you leave me unrefuted, why, the rhetoricians who do what they think best in states, and the tyrants, will have nothing upon which to congratulate themselves, if as you say, power be indeed a good, admitting at the same time that what is done without sense is an evil.

POLUS: Yes; I admit that.

SOCRATES: How then can the rhetoricians or the tyrants have great power in states, unless Polus can refute Socrates, and prove to him that they do as they will?

POLUS: This fellow—

SOCRATES: I say that they do not do as they will;—now refute me.

POLUS: Why, have you not already said that they do as they think best?

SOCRATES: And I say so still.

POLUS: Then surely they do as they will?

SOCRATES: I deny it.

POLUS: But they do what they think best?

SOCRATES: Aye.

POLUS: That, Socrates, is monstrous and absurd.

SOCRATES: Good words, good Polus, as I may say in your own peculiar style; but if you have any questions to ask of me, either prove that I
am in error or give the answer yourself.

POLUS: Very well, I am willing to answer that I may know what you
mean.

SOCRATES: Do men appear to you to will that which they do, or to
will that further end for the sake of which they do a thing? when they
take medicine, for example, at the bidding of a physician, do they will
the drinking of the medicine which is painful, or the health for the sake
of which they drink?

POLUS: Clearly, the health.

SOCRATES: And when men go on a voyage or engage in business,
they do not will that which they are doing at the time; for who
would desire to take the risk of a voyage or the trouble of business? — But they will, to have the wealth for the sake of which they
go on a voyage.

POLUS: Certainly.

SOCRATES: And is not this universally true? If a man does something
for the sake of something else, he wills not that which he does, but that
for the sake of which he does it.

POLUS: Yes.

SOCRATES: And are not all things either good or evil, or intermediate
and indifferent?

POLUS: To be sure, Socrates.

SOCRATES: Wisdom and health and wealth and the like you would
call goods, and their opposites evils?

POLUS: I should.

SOCRATES: And the things which are neither good nor evil, and
which partake sometimes of the nature of good and at other times of
evil, or of neither, are such as sitting, walking, running, sailing; or,
again, wood, stones, and the like: — these are the things which you call
neither good nor evil?

POLUS: Exactly so.

SOCRATES: Are these indifferent things done for the sake of the good,
or the good for the sake of the indifferent?

POLUS: Clearly, the indifferent for the sake of the good.

SOCRATES: When we walk we walk for the sake of the good, and under the idea that it is better to walk, and when we stand we stand equally for the sake of the good?

POLUS: Yes.

SOCRATES: And when we kill a man we kill him or exile him or despoil him of his goods, because, as we think, it will conduce to our good?

POLUS: Certainly.

SOCRATES: Men who do any of these things do them for the sake of the good?

POLUS: Yes.

SOCRATES: And did we not admit that in doing something for the sake of something else, we do not will those things which we do, but that other thing for the sake of which we do them?

POLUS: Most true.

SOCRATES: Then we do not will simply to kill a man or to exile him or to despoil him of his goods, but we will to do that which conduces to our good, and if the act is not conducive to our good we do not will it; for we will, as you say, that which is our good, but that which is neither good nor evil, or simply evil, we do not will. Why are you silent, Polus? Am I not right?

POLUS: You are right.

SOCRATES: Hence we may infer, that if any one, whether he be a tyrant or a rhetorician, kills another or exiles another or deprives him of his property, under the idea that the act is for his own interests when really not for his own interests, he may be said to do what seems best to him?

POLUS: Yes.

SOCRATES: But does he do what he wills if he does what is evil? Why do you not answer?

POLUS: Well, I suppose not.

SOCRATES: Then if great power is a good as you allow, will such a one have great power in a state?

POLUS: He will not.

SOCRATES: Then I was right in saying that a man may do what seems good to him in a state, and not have great power, and not do what he wills?

POLUS: As though you, Socrates, would not like to have the power of doing what seemed good to you in the state, rather than not; you would not be jealous when you saw any one killing or despoiling or imprisoning whom he pleased, Oh, no!

SOCRATES: Justly or unjustly, do you mean?

POLUS: In either case is he not equally to be envied?

SOCRATES: Forbear, Polus!

POLUS: Why 'forbear'?

SOCRATES: Because you ought not to envy wretches who are not to be envied, but only to pity them.

POLUS: And are those of whom I spoke wretches?

SOCRATES: Yes, certainly they are.

POLUS: And so you think that he who slays any one whom he pleases, and justly slays him, is pitiable and wretched?

SOCRATES: No, I do not say that of him: but neither do I think that he is to be envied.

POLUS: Were you not saying just now that he is wretched?

SOCRATES: Yes, my friend, if he killed another unjustly, in which ease he is also to be pitied; and he is not to be envied if he killed him justly.

POLUS: At any rate you will allow that he who is unjustly put to death is wretched, and to be pitied?

SOCRATES: Not so much, Polus, as he who kills him, and not so much as he who is justly killed.

POLUS: How can that be, Socrates?

SOCRATES: That may very well be, inasmuch as doing injustice is the greatest of evils.

POLUS: But is it the greatest? Is not suffering injustice a greater evil?

SOCRATES: Certainly not.

POLUS: Then would you rather suffer than do injustice?

SOCRATES: I should not like either, but if I must choose between them, I would rather suffer than do.

POLUS: Then you would not wish to be a tyrant?

SOCRATES: Not if you mean by tyranny what I mean.

POLUS: I mean, as I said before, the power of doing whatever seems good to you in a state, killing, banishing, doing in all things as you like.

SOCRATES: Well then, illustrious friend, when I have said my say, do you reply to me. Suppose that I go into a crowded Agora, and take a dagger under my arm. Polus, I say to you, I have just acquired rare power, and become a tyrant; for if I think that any of these men whom you see ought to be put to death, the man whom I have a mind to kill is as good as dead; and if I am disposed to break his head or tear his garment, he will have his head broken or his garment torn in an instant. Such is my great power in this city. And if you do not believe me, and I show you the dagger, you would probably reply: Socrates, in that sort of way any one may have great power—he may burn any house which he pleases, and the docks and triremes of the Athenians, and all their other vessels, whether public or private—but can you believe that this mere doing as you think best is great power?

POLUS: Certainly not such doing as this.

SOCRATES: But can you tell me why you disapprove of such a power?

POLUS: I can.

SOCRATES: Why then?

POLUS: Why, because he who did as you say would be certain to be punished.

SOCRATES: And punishment is an evil?

POLUS: Certainly.

SOCRATES: And you would admit once more, my good sir, that great power is a benefit to a man if his actions turn out to his advantage, and that this is the meaning of great power; and if not, then his power is an evil and is no power. But let us look at the matter in another way:—do we not acknowledge that the things of which we were speaking, the infliction of death, and exile, and the deprivation of property are sometimes a good and sometimes not a good?

POLUS: Certainly.

SOCRATES: About that you and I may be supposed to agree?

POLUS: Yes.

SOCRATES: Tell me, then, when do you say that they are good and when that they are evil—what principle do you lay down?

POLUS: I would rather, Socrates, that you should answer as well as ask that question.

SOCRATES: Well, Polus, since you would rather have the answer from me, I say that they are good when they are just, and evil when they are unjust.

POLUS: You are hard of refutation, Socrates, but might not a child refute that statement?

SOCRATES: Then I shall be very grateful to the child, and equally grateful to you if you will refute me and deliver me from my foolishness. And I hope that refute me you will, and not weary of doing good to a friend.

POLUS: Yes, Socrates, and I need not go far or appeal to antiquity; events which happened only a few days ago are enough to refute you, and to prove that many men who do wrong are happy.

SOCRATES: What events?

POLUS: You see, I presume, that Archelaus the son of Perdiccas is now the ruler of Macedonia?

SOCRATES: At any rate I hear that he is.

POLUS: And do you think that he is happy or miserable?

SOCRATES: I cannot say, Polus, for I have never had any acquaintance with him.

POLUS: And cannot you tell at once, and without having an acquaintance with him, whether a man is happy?

SOCRATES: Most certainly not.

POLUS: Then clearly, Socrates, you would say that you did not even know whether the great king was a happy man?

SOCRATES: And I should speak the truth; for I do not know how he stands in the matter of education and justice.

POLUS: What! and does all happiness consist in this?

SOCRATES: Yes, indeed, Polus, that is my doctrine; the men and women who are gentle and good are also happy, as I maintain, and the unjust and evil are miserable.

POLUS: Then, according to your doctrine, the said Archelaus is miserable?

SOCRATES: Yes, my friend, if he is wicked.

POLUS: That he is wicked I cannot deny; for he had no title at all to the throne which he now occupies, he being only the son of a woman who was the slave of Alcetas the brother of Perdiccas; he himself therefore in strict right was the slave of Alcetas; and if he had meant to do rightly he would have remained his slave, and then, according to your doctrine, he would have been happy. But now he is unspeakably miserable, for he has been guilty of the greatest crimes: in the first place he invited his uncle and master, Alcetas, to come to him, under the pretence that he would restore to him the throne which Perdiccas has usurped, and after entertaining him and his son Alexander, who was his own cousin, and nearly of an age with him, and making them drunk, he threw them into a waggon and carried them off by night, and slew them, and got both of them out of the way; and when he had done all this wickedness he never discovered that he was the most miserable of all men, and was very far from repenting: shall I tell you how he showed his remorse? he had a younger brother, a child of seven years old, who was the legitimate son of Perdiccas, and to him of right the kingdom belonged; Archelaus, however, had no mind to bring him up as he ought and restore the kingdom to him; that was not his notion of happiness; but not long afterwards he threw him into a well and drowned him, and declared to his mother Cleopatra that he had fallen in while running after a goose, and had been killed. And now as he is the greatest criminal of all the Macedonians, he may be supposed to be the most miserable and not the happiest of them, and I dare say that there are many Athenians, and you would be at the head of them, who would rather be any other Macedonian than Archelaus!

SOCRATES: I praised you at first, Polus, for being a rhetorician rather than a reasoner. And this, as I suppose, is the sort of argument with which you fancy that a child might refute me, and by which I stand refuted when I say that the unjust man is not happy. But, my good friend, where is the refutation? I cannot admit a word which you have been saying.

POLUS: That is because you will not; for you surely must think as I do.

SOCRATES: Not so, my simple friend, but because you will refute me after the manner which rhetoricians practise in courts of law. For there the one party think that they refute the other when they bring forward a number of witnesses of good repute in proof of their allegations, and their adversary has only a single one or none at all. But this kind of proof is of no value where truth is the aim; a man may often be sworn down by a multitude of false witnesses who have a great air of respectability. And in this argument nearly every one, Athenian and stranger alike, would be on your side, if you should bring witnesses in disproof of my statement;—you may, if you will, summon Nicias the son of Niceratus, and let his brothers, who gave the row of tripods which stand in the precincts of Dionysus, come with him; or you may summon Aristocrates, the son of Scellius, who is the giver of that famous offering which is at Delphi; summon, if you will, the whole house of Pericles, or any other great Athenian family whom you choose;—they will all agree with you: I only am left alone and cannot agree, for you do not convince me; although you produce many false witnesses against me, in the hope of depriving me of my inheritance, which is the truth. But I consider that nothing worth speaking of will have been effected by me unless I make you the one witness of my words; nor by you, unless you make me the one witness of yours; no matter about the rest of the world. For there are two ways of refutation, one which is yours and that of the world in general; but mine is of another sort—let us compare them, and see in what they differ. For, indeed, we are at issue about matters which to know is honourable and not to know disgraceful; to know or not to know happiness and misery—that is the chief of them. And what knowledge can be nobler? or what ignorance more disgraceful than this? And therefore I will begin by asking you whether you do not think that a man who is unjust and doing injustice can be happy, seeing that you think Archelaus unjust, and yet happy? May I assume this to be your opinion?

POLUS: Certainly.

SOCRATES: But I say that this is an impossibility—here is one point about which we are at issue:—very good. And do you mean to say also that if he meets with retribution and punishment he will still be happy?

POLUS: Certainly not; in that case he will be most miserable.

SOCRATES: On the other hand, if the unjust be not punished, then, according to you, he will be happy?

POLUS: Yes.

SOCRATES: But in my opinion, Polus, the unjust or doer of unjust actions is miserable in any case,—more miserable, however, if he be not punished and does not meet with retribution, and less miserable if he be punished and meets with retribution at the hands of gods and men.

POLUS: You are maintaining a strange doctrine, Socrates.

SOCRATES: I shall try to make you agree with me, O my friend, for as a friend I regard you. Then these are the points at issue between us— are they not? I was saying that to do is worse than to suffer injustice?

POLUS: Exactly so.

SOCRATES: And you said the opposite?

POLUS: Yes.

SOCRATES: I said also that the wicked are miserable, and you refuted me?

POLUS: By Zeus, I did.

SOCRATES: In your own opinion, Polus.

POLUS: Yes, and I rather suspect that I was in the right.

SOCRATES: You further said that the wrong-doer is happy if he be un-punished?

POLUS: Certainly.

SOCRATES: And I affirm that he is most miserable, and that those who are punished are less miserable—are you going to refute this proposition also?

POLUS: A proposition which is harder of refutation than the other, Socrates.

SOCRATES: Say rather, Polus, impossible; for who can refute the truth?

POLUS: What do you mean? If a man is detected in an unjust attempt to make himself a tyrant, and when detected is racked, mutilated, has his eyes burned out, and after having had all sorts of great injuries in-flicted on him, and having seen his wife and children suffer the like, is at last impaled or tarred and burned alive, will he be happier than if he escape and become a tyrant, and continue all through life doing what he likes and holding the reins of government, the envy and admiration both of citizens and strangers? Is that the paradox which, as you say, cannot be refuted?

SOCRATES: There again, noble Polus, you are raising hobgoblins in-stead of refuting me; just now you were calling witnesses against me. But please to refresh my memory a little; did you say—'in an unjust at-tempt to make himself a tyrant'?

POLUS: Yes, I did.

SOCRATES: Then I say that neither of them will be happier than the other,—neither he who unjustly acquires a tyranny, nor he who suf-fers in the attempt, for of two miserables one cannot be the happier, but that he who escapes and becomes a tyrant is the more miserable of the two. Do you laugh, Polus? Well, this is a new kind of refutation,—when any one says anything, instead of refuting him to laugh at him.

POLUS: But do you not think, Socrates, that you have been sufficiently refuted, when you say that which no human being will allow? Ask the company.

SOCRATES: O Polus, I am not a public man, and only last year, when my tribe were serving as Prytanes, and it became my duty as their president to take the votes, there was a laugh at me, because I was unable to take them. And as I failed then, you must not ask me to count the suffrages of the company now; but if, as I was saying, you have no better argument than numbers, let me have a turn, and do you make trial of the sort of proof which, as I think, is required; for I shall produce one witness only of the truth of my words, and he is the person with whom I am arguing; his suffrage I know how to take; but with the many I have nothing to do, and do not even address myself to them. May I ask then whether you will answer in turn and have your words put to the proof? For I certainly think that I and you and every man do really believe, that to do is a greater evil than to suffer injustice: and not to be punished than to be punished.

POLUS: And I should say neither I, nor any man: would you yourself, for example, suffer rather than do injustice?

SOCRATES: Yes, and you, too; I or any man would.

POLUS: Quite the reverse; neither you, nor I, nor any man.

SOCRATES: But will you answer?

POLUS: To be sure, I will; for I am curious to hear what you can have to say.

SOCRATES: Tell me, then, and you will know, and let us suppose that I am beginning at the beginning: which of the two, Polus, in your opinion, is the worst?—to do injustice or to suffer?

POLUS: I should say that suffering was worst.

SOCRATES: And which is the greater disgrace?—Answer.

POLUS: To do.

SOCRATES: And the greater disgrace is the greater evil?

POLUS: Certainly not.

SOCRATES: I understand you to say, if I am not mistaken, that the honourable is not the same as the good, or the disgraceful as the evil?

POLUS: Certainly not.

SOCRATES: Let me ask a question of you: When you speak of beautiful things, such as bodies, colours, figures, sounds, institutions, do you not call them beautiful in reference to some standard: bodies, for example, are beautiful in proportion as they are useful, or as the sight of them gives pleasure to the spectators; can you give any other account of personal beauty?

POLUS: I cannot.

SOCRATES: And you would say of figures or colours generally that they were beautiful, either by reason of the pleasure which they give, or of their use, or of both?

POLUS: Yes, I should.

SOCRATES: And you would call sounds and music beautiful for the same reason?

POLUS: I should.

SOCRATES: Laws and institutions also have no beauty in them except in so far as they are useful or pleasant or both?

POLUS: I think not.

SOCRATES: And may not the same be said of the beauty of knowledge?

POLUS: To be sure, Socrates; and I very much approve of your measuring beauty by the standard of pleasure and utility.

SOCRATES: And deformity or disgrace may be equally measured by the opposite standard of pain and evil?

POLUS: Certainly.

SOCRATES: Then when of two beautiful things one exceeds in beauty, the measure of the excess is to be taken in one or both of these; that is to say, in pleasure or utility or both?

POLUS: Very true.

SOCRATES: And of two deformed things, that which exceeds in deformity or disgrace, exceeds either in pain or evil—must it not be so?

POLUS: Yes.

SOCRATES: But then again, what was the observation which you just now made, about doing and suffering wrong? Did you not say, that suffering wrong was more evil, and doing wrong more disgraceful?

POLUS: I did.

SOCRATES: Then, if doing wrong is more disgraceful than suffering, the more disgraceful must be more painful and must exceed in pain or in evil or both: does not that also follow?

POLUS: Of course.

SOCRATES: First, then, let us consider whether the doing of injustice exceeds the suffering in the consequent pain: Do the injurers suffer more than the injured?

POLUS: No, Socrates; certainly not.

SOCRATES: Then they do not exceed in pain?

POLUS: No.

SOCRATES: But if not in pain, then not in both?

POLUS: Certainly not.

SOCRATES: Then they can only exceed in the other?

POLUS: Yes.

SOCRATES: That is to say, in evil?

POLUS: True.

SOCRATES: Then doing injustice will have an excess of evil, and will therefore be a greater evil than suffering injustice?

POLUS: Clearly.

SOCRATES: But have not you and the world already agreed that to do injustice is more disgraceful than to suffer?

POLUS: Yes.

SOCRATES: And that is now discovered to be more evil?

POLUS: True.

SOCRATES: And would you prefer a greater evil or a greater dishonour to a less one? Answer, Polus, and fear not; for you will come to no harm if you nobly resign yourself into the healing hand of the argument as to a physician without shrinking, and either say 'Yes' or 'No' to me.

POLUS: I should say 'No.'

SOCRATES: Would any other man prefer a greater to a less evil?

POLUS: No, not according to this way of putting the case, Socrates.

SOCRATES: Then I said truly, Polus, that neither you, nor I, nor any man, would rather do than suffer injustice; for to do injustice is the greater evil of the two.

POLUS: That is the conclusion.

SOCRATES: You see, Polus, when you compare the two kinds of refutations, how unlike they are. All men, with the exception of myself, are of your way of thinking; but your single assent and witness are enough for me, — I have no need of any other, I take your suffrage, and am regardless of the rest. Enough of this, and now let us proceed to the next question; which is, Whether the greatest of evils to a guilty man is to suffer punishment, as you supposed, or whether to escape punishment is not a greater evil, as I supposed. Consider: — You would say that to suffer punishment is another name for being justly corrected when you do wrong?

POLUS: I should.

SOCRATES: And would you not allow that all just things are honourable in so far as they are just? Please to reflect, and tell me your opinion.

POLUS: Yes, Socrates, I think that they are.

SOCRATES: Consider again: — Where there is an agent, must there not also be a patient?

POLUS: I should say so.

SOCRATES: And will not the patient suffer that which the agent does, and will not the suffering have the quality of the action? I mean, for example, that if a man strikes, there must be something which is stricken?

POLUS: Yes.

SOCRATES: And if the striker strikes violently or quickly, that which is struck will be struck violently or quickly?

POLUS: True.

SOCRATES: And the suffering to him who is stricken is of the same nature as the act of him who strikes?

POLUS: Yes.

SOCRATES: And if a man burns, there is something which is burned?

POLUS: Certainly.

SOCRATES: And if he burns in excess or so as to cause pain, the thing burned will be burned in the same way?

POLUS: Truly.

SOCRATES: And if he cuts, the same argument holds—there will be something cut?

POLUS: Yes.

SOCRATES: And if the cutting be great or deep or such as will cause pain, the cut will be of the same nature?

POLUS: That is evident.

SOCRATES: Then you would agree generally to the universal proposition which I was just now asserting: that the affection of the patient answers to the affection of the agent?

POLUS: I agree.

SOCRATES: Then, as this is admitted, let me ask whether being punished is suffering or acting?

POLUS: Suffering, Socrates; there can be no doubt of that.

SOCRATES: And suffering implies an agent?

POLUS: Certainly, Socrates; and he is the punisher.

SOCRATES: And he who punishes rightly, punishes justly?

POLUS: Yes.

SOCRATES: And therefore he acts justly?

POLUS: Justly.

SOCRATES: Then he who is punished and suffers retribution, suffers justly?

POLUS: That is evident.

SOCRATES: And that which is just has been admitted to be honourable?

POLUS: Certainly.

SOCRATES: Then the punisher does what is honourable, and the punished suffers what is honourable?

POLUS: True.

SOCRATES: And if what is honourable, then what is good, for the honourable is either pleasant or useful?

POLUS: Certainly.

SOCRATES: Then he who is punished suffers what is good?

POLUS: That is true.

SOCRATES: Then he is benefited?

POLUS: Yes.

SOCRATES: Do I understand you to mean what I mean by the term 'benefited'? I mean, that if he be justly punished his soul is improved.

POLUS: Surely.

SOCRATES: Then he who is punished is delivered from the evil of his soul?

POLUS: Yes.

SOCRATES: And is he not then delivered from the greatest evil? Look at the matter in this way:—In respect of a man's estate, do you see any greater evil than poverty?

POLUS: There is no greater evil.

SOCRATES: Again, in a man's bodily frame, you would say that the evil is weakness and disease and deformity?

POLUS: I should.

SOCRATES: And do you not imagine that the soul likewise has some evil of her own?

POLUS: Of course.

SOCRATES: And this you would call injustice and ignorance and cowardice, and the like?

POLUS: Certainly.

SOCRATES: So then, in mind, body, and estate, which are three, you have pointed out three corresponding evils—injustice, disease, poverty?

POLUS: True.

SOCRATES: And which of the evils is the most disgraceful?—Is not the most disgraceful of them injustice, and in general the evil of the soul?

POLUS: By far the most.

SOCRATES: And if the most disgraceful, then also the worst?

POLUS: What do you mean, Socrates?

SOCRATES: I mean to say, that what is most disgraceful has been already admitted to be most painful or hurtful, or both.

POLUS: Certainly.

SOCRATES: And now injustice and all evil in the soul has been admitted by us to be most disgraceful?

POLUS: It has been admitted.

SOCRATES: And most disgraceful either because most painful and causing excessive pain, or most hurtful, or both?

POLUS: Certainly.

SOCRATES: And therefore to be unjust and intemperate, and cowardly and ignorant, is more painful than to be poor and sick?

POLUS: Nay, Socrates; the painfulness does not appear to me to follow from your premises.

SOCRATES: Then, if, as you would argue, not more painful, the evil of the soul is of all evils the most disgraceful; and the excess of disgrace must be caused by some preternatural greatness, or extraordinary hurtfulness of the evil.

POLUS: Clearly.

SOCRATES: And that which exceeds most in hurtfulness will be the greatest of evils?

POLUS: Yes.

SOCRATES: Then injustice and intemperance, and in general the depravity of the soul, are the greatest of evils?

POLUS: That is evident.

SOCRATES: Now, what art is there which delivers us from poverty? Does not the art of making money?

POLUS: Yes.

SOCRATES: And what art frees us from disease? Does not the art of medicine?

POLUS: Very true.

SOCRATES: And what from vice and injustice? If you are not able to answer at once, ask yourself whither we go with the sick, and to whom we take them.

POLUS: To the physicians, Socrates.

SOCRATES: And to whom do we go with the unjust and intemperate?

POLUS: To the judges, you mean.

SOCRATES: —Who are to punish them?

POLUS: Yes.

SOCRATES: And do not those who rightly punish others, punish them in accordance with a certain rule of justice?

POLUS: Clearly.

SOCRATES: Then the art of money-making frees a man from poverty; medicine from disease; and justice from intemperance and injustice?

POLUS: That is evident.

SOCRATES: Which, then, is the best of these three?

POLUS: Will you enumerate them?

SOCRATES: Money-making, medicine, and justice.

POLUS: Justice, Socrates, far excels the two others.

SOCRATES: And justice, if the best, gives the greatest pleasure or advantage or both?

POLUS: Yes.

SOCRATES: But is the being healed a pleasant thing, and are those who are being healed pleased?

POLUS: I think not.

SOCRATES: A useful thing, then?

POLUS: Yes.

SOCRATES: Yes, because the patient is delivered from a great evil; and this is the advantage of enduring the pain—that you get well?

POLUS: Certainly.

SOCRATES: And would he be the happier man in his bodily condition, who is healed, or who never was out of health?

POLUS: Clearly he who was never out of health.

SOCRATES: Yes; for happiness surely does not consist in being delivered from evils, but in never having had them.

POLUS: True.

SOCRATES: And suppose the case of two persons who have some evil in their bodies, and that one of them is healed and delivered from evil, and another is not healed, but retains the evil which of them is the most miserable?

POLUS: Clearly he who is not healed.

SOCRATES: And was not punishment said by us to be a deliverance from the greatest of evils, which is vice?

POLUS: True.

SOCRATES: And justice punishes us, and makes us more just, and is the medicine of our vice?

POLUS: True.

SOCRATES: He, then, has the first place in the scale of happiness who has never had vice in his soul; for this has been shown to be the greatest of evils.

POLUS: Clearly.

SOCRATES: And he has the second place, who is delivered from vice?

POLUS: True.

SOCRATES: That is to say, he who receives admonition and rebuke and punishment?

POLUS: Yes.

SOCRATES: Then he lives worst, who, having been unjust, has no deliverance from injustice?

POLUS: Certainly.

SOCRATES: That is, he lives worst who commits the greatest crimes, and who, being the most unjust of men, succeeds in escaping rebuke or correction or punishment; and this, as you say, has been accomplished by Archelaus and other tyrants and rhetoricians and potentates?

POLUS: True.

SOCRATES: May not their way of proceeding, my friend, be compared to the conduct of a person who is afflicted with the worst of diseases and yet contrives not to pay the penalty to the physician for his sins against his constitution, and will not be cured, because, like a child, he is afraid of the pain of being burned or cut: — Is not that a parallel case?

POLUS: Yes, truly.

SOCRATES: He would seem as if he did not know the nature of health and bodily vigour; and if we are right, Polus, in our previous conclusions, they are in a like case who strive to evade justice, which they see to be painful, but are blind to the advantage which ensues from it, not knowing how far more miserable a companion a diseased soul is than a diseased body; a soul, I say, which is corrupt and unrighteous and unholy. And hence they do all that they can to avoid punishment and to avoid being released from the greatest of evils; they provide themselves with money and friends, and cultivate to the utmost their powers of persuasion. But if we, Polus, are right, do you see what follows, or shall we draw out the consequences in form?

POLUS: If you please.

SOCRATES: Is it not a fact that injustice, and the doing of injustice, is the greatest of evils?

POLUS: That is quite clear.

SOCRATES: And further, that to suffer punishment is the way to be released from this evil?

POLUS: True.

SOCRATES: And not to suffer, is to perpetuate the evil?

POLUS: Yes.

SOCRATES: To do wrong, then, is second only in the scale of evils; but to do wrong and not to be punished, is first and greatest of all?

POLUS: That is true.

SOCRATES: Well, and was not this the point in dispute, my friend? You deemed Archelaus happy, because he was a very great criminal and unpunished: I, on the other hand, maintained that he or any other who like him has done wrong and has not been punished, is, and ought to be, the most miserable of all men; and that the doer of injustice is more miserable than the sufferer; and he who escapes punishment, more miserable than he who suffers. — Was not that what I said?

POLUS: Yes.

SOCRATES: And it has been proved to be true?

POLUS: Certainly.

SOCRATES: Well, Polus, but if this is true, where is the great use of rhetoric? If we admit what has been just now said, every man ought in every way to guard himself against doing wrong, for he will thereby suffer great evil?

POLUS: True.

SOCRATES: And if he, or any one about whom he cares, does wrong,

he ought of his own accord to go where he will be immediately punished; he will run to the judge, as he would to the physician, in order
that the disease of injustice may not be rendered chronic and become
the incurable cancer of the soul; must we not allow this consequence,
Polus, if our former admissions are to stand:—is any other inference
consistent with them?

POLUS: To that, Socrates, there can be but one answer.

SOCRATES: Then rhetoric is of no use to us, Polus, in helping a man
to excuse his own injustice, or that of his parents or friends, or children
or country; but may be of use to any one who holds that instead of ex-
cusing he ought to accuse—himself above all, and in the next degree
his family or any of his friends who may be doing wrong; he should
bring to light the iniquity and not conceal it, that so the wrong-doer
may suffer and be made whole, and he should even force himself and
others not to shrink, but with closed eyes like brave men to let the
physician operate with knife or searing iron, not regarding the pain, in
the hope of attaining the good and the honourable; let him who has
done things worthy of stripes, allow himself to be scourged, if of bonds,
to be bound, if of a fine, to be fined, if of exile, to be exiled, if of death,
to die, himself being the first to accuse himself and his own relations,
and using rhetoric to this end, that his and their unjust actions may be
made manifest, and that they themselves may be delivered from injustice, which is the greatest evil. Then, Polus, rhetoric would indeed be
useful. Do you say 'Yes' or 'No' to that?

POLUS: To me, Socrates, what you are saying appears very strange,
though probably in agreement with your premises.

SOCRATES: Is not this the conclusion, if the premises are not dis-
proven?

POLUS: Yes; it certainly is.

SOCRATES: And from the opposite point of view, if indeed it be our
duty to harm another, whether an enemy or not—I except the case of
self-defence—then I have to be upon my guard—but if my enemy in-
jures a third person, then in every sort of way, by word as well as deed,
I should try to prevent his being punished, or appearing before the
judge; and if he appears, I should contrive that he should escape, and
not suffer punishment: if he has stolen a sum of money, let him keep
what he has stolen and spend it on him and his, regardless of religion
and justice; and if he have done things worthy of death, let him not die,
but rather be immortal in his wickedness; or, if this is not possible, let
him at any rate be allowed to live as long as he can. For such purposes,
Polus, rhetoric may be useful, but is of small if of any use to him who
is not intending to commit injustice; at least, there was no such use discovered by us in the previous discussion.

CALLICLES: Tell me, Chaerephon, is Socrates in earnest, or is he joking?

CHAEREPHON: I should say, Callicles, that he is in most profound earnest; but you may well ask him.

CALLICLES: By the gods, and I will. Tell me, Socrates, are you in earnest, or only in jest? For if you are in earnest, and what you say is true, is not the whole of human life turned upside down; and are we not doing, as would appear, in everything the opposite of what we ought to be doing?

SOCRATES: O Callicles, if there were not some community of feelings among mankind, however varying in different persons—I mean to say, if every man's feelings were peculiar to himself and were not shared by the rest of his species—I do not see how we could ever communicate our impressions to one another. I make this remark because I perceive that you and I have a common feeling. For we are lovers both, and both of us have two loves apiece:—I am the lover of Alcibiades, the son of Cleinias, and of philosophy; and you of the Athenian Demus, and of Demus the son of Pyrilampes. Now, I observe that you, with all your cleverness, do not venture to contradict your favourite in any word or opinion of his; but as he changes you change, backwards and forwards. When the Athenian Demus denies anything that you are saying in the assembly, you go over to his opinion; and you do the same with Demus, the fair young son of Pyrilampes. For you have not the power to resist the words and ideas of your loves; and if a person were to express surprise at the strangeness of what you say from time to time when under their influence, you would probably reply to him, if you were honest, that you cannot help saying what your loves say unless they are prevented; and that you can only be silent when they are. Now you must understand that my words are an echo too, and therefore you need not wonder at me; but if you want to silence me, silence philosophy, who is my love, for she is always telling me what I am now telling you, my friend; neither is she capricious like my other love, for the son of Cleinias says one thing to-day and another thing to-morrow, but philosophy is always true. She is the teacher at whose words you are now wondering, and you have heard her yourself. Her you must refute, and either show, as I was saying, that to do injustice and to escape punishment is not the worst of all evils; or, if you leave her word unrefuted, by the dog the god of Egypt, I declare, O Callicles, that Callicles will never be at one with himself, but that his whole life will be a discord. And yet, my friend, I would rather that my lyre should be inharmonious, and that there should be no music in the chorus which I provided; aye, or that the whole world should be at odds with me, and oppose me, rather than that I myself should be at odds with myself, and contradict myself.

CALLICLES: O Socrates, you are a regular declaimer, and seem to be running riot in the argument. And now you are declaiming in this way because Polus has fallen into the same error himself of which he accused Gorgias:—for he said that when Gorgias was asked by you, whether, if some one came to him who wanted to learn rhetoric, and did not know justice, he would teach him justice, Gorgias in his modesty replied that he would, because he thought that mankind in general would be displeased if he answered 'No'; and then in consequence of this admission, Gorgias was compelled to contradict himself, that being just the sort of thing in which you delight. Whereupon Polus laughed at you deservedly, as I think; but now he has himself fallen into the same trap. I cannot say very much for his wit when he conceded to you that to do is more dishonourable than to suffer injustice, for this was the admission which led to his being entangled by you; and because he was too modest to say what he thought, he had his mouth stopped. For the truth is, Socrates, that you, who pretend to be engaged in the pursuit of truth, are appealing now to the popular and vulgar notions of right, which are not natural, but only conventional. Convention and nature are generally at variance with one another: and hence, if a person is too modest to say what he thinks, he is compelled to contradict himself; and you, in your ingenuity perceiving the advantage to be thereby gained, slyly ask of him who is arguing conventionally a question which is to be determined by the rule of nature; and if he is talking of the rule of nature, you slip away to custom: as, for instance, you did in this very discussion about doing and suffering injustice. When Polus was speaking of the conventionally dishonourable, you assailed him from the point of view of nature; for by the rule of nature, to suffer injustice is the greater disgrace because the greater evil; but conventionally, to do evil is the more disgraceful. For the suffering of injustice is not the part of a man, but of a slave, who indeed had better die than live; since when he is wronged and trampled upon, he is unable to help himself, or any other about whom he cares. The reason, as I conceive, is that the makers of laws are the majority who are weak; and they make laws and distribute praises and censures with a view to themselves and to their own interests; and they terrify the stronger sort of men, and those who are able to get the better of them, in order that they may not get the better of them; and they say, that dishonesty is shameful and unjust; meaning, by the word injustice, the desire of a man to have more than his neighbours; for knowing their own inferiority, I suspect that they are too glad of equality. And therefore the endeavour to have more than the many, is conventionally said to be shameful and unjust, and is called injustice (compare *Republic*), whereas nature herself intimates that it is just for the better to have more than the worse, the more powerful than the weaker; and in many ways she shows, among men as well as among animals, and indeed among whole cities and races, that justice consists in the superior ruling over and having more than the inferior. For on what principle of justice did Xerxes invade Hellas, or his father the Scythians? (not to speak of numberless other examples). Nay, but these are the men who act according to nature; yes, by Heaven, and according to the law of nature: not, perhaps, according to that artificial law, which we invent and impose upon our fellows, of whom we take the best and strongest from their youth upwards, and tame them like young lions,—charming them with the sound of the voice, and saying to them, that with equality they must be content, and that the equal is the honourable and the just. But if there were a man who had sufficient force, he would shake off and break through, and escape from all this; he would trample under foot all our formulas and spells and charms, and all our laws which are against nature: the slave would rise in rebellion and be lord over us, and the light of natural justice would shine forth. And this I take to be the sentiment of Pindar, when he says in his poem, that

'Law is the king of all, of mortals as well as of immortals';

this, as he says,

'Makes might to be right, doing violence with highest hand; as I infer from the deeds of Heracles, for without buying them—'(Fragm. Incert. 151 (Böckh).)

—I do not remember the exact words, but the meaning is, that without buying them, and without their being given to him, he carried off the oxen of Geryon, according to the law of natural right, and that the oxen and other possessions of the weaker and inferior properly belong to the stronger and superior. And this is true, as you may ascertain, if you will leave philosophy and go on to higher things: for philosophy, Socrates, if pursued in moderation and at the proper age, is an elegant accomplishment, but too much philosophy is the ruin of human life. Even if a man has good parts, still, if he carries philosophy into later life, he is necessarily ignorant of all those things which a gentleman and a person of honour ought to know; he is inexperienced in the laws of the State, and in the language which ought to be used in the dealings of man with man, whether private or public, and utterly ignorant of the pleasures and desires of mankind and of human character in general. And people of this sort, when they betake themselves to politics or business, are as ridiculous as I imagine the politicians to be, when they make their appearance in the arena of philosophy. For, as Euripides says,

'Every man shines in that and pursues that, and devotes the greatest portion of the day to that in which he most excels,' (*Antiope*, fragm. 20 (Dindorf).)

but anything in which he is inferior, he avoids and depreciates, and praises the opposite from partiality to himself, and because he thinks that he will thus praise himself. The true principle is to unite them. Philosophy, as a part of education, is an excellent thing, and there is no disgrace to a man while he is young in pursuing such a study; but when he is more advanced in years, the thing becomes ridiculous, and I feel towards philosophers as I do towards those who lisp and imitate children. For I love to see a little child, who is not of an age to speak plainly, lisping at his play; there is an appearance of grace and freedom in his utterance, which is natural to his childish years. But when I hear some small creature carefully articulating its words, I am offended; the sound is disagreeable, and has to my ears the twang of slavery. So when I hear a man lisping, or see him playing like a child, his behaviour appears to me ridiculous and unmanly and worthy of stripes. And I have the same feeling about students of philosophy; when I see a youth thus engaged,—the study appears to me to be in character, and becoming a man of liberal education, and him who neglects philosophy I regard as an inferior man, who will never aspire to anything great or noble. But if I see him continuing the study in later life, and not leaving off, I should like to beat him, Socrates; for, as I was saying, such a one, even though he have good natural parts, becomes effeminate. He flies from the busy centre and the market-place, in which, as the poet says, men become distinguished; he creeps into a corner for the rest of his life, and talks in a whisper with three or four admiring youths, but never speaks out like a freeman in a satisfactory manner. Now I, Socrates, am very well inclined towards you, and my feeling may be compared with that of Zethus towards Amphion, in the play of Euripides, whom I was mentioning just now: for I am disposed to say to you much what Zethus said to his brother, that you, Socrates, are careless about the things of which you ought to be careful; and that you

'Who have a soul so noble, are remarkable for a puerile exterior;
Neither in a court of justice could you state a case, or give any reason or proof,
Or offer valiant counsel on another's behalf.'

And you must not be offended, my dear Socrates, for I am speaking out of good-will towards you, if I ask whether you are not ashamed of being thus defenceless; which I affirm to be the condition not of you only but of all those who will carry the study of philosophy too far. For suppose that some one were to take you, or any one of your sort, off to prison, declaring that you had done wrong when you had done no wrong, you must allow that you would not know what to do:—there you would stand giddy and gaping, and not having a word to say; and when you went up before the Court, even if the accuser were a poor creature and not good for much, you would die if he were disposed to claim the penalty of death. And yet, Socrates, what is the value of

'An art which converts a man of sense into a fool,'

who is helpless, and has no power to save either himself or others, when he is in the greatest danger and is going to be despoiled by his enemies of all his goods, and has to live, simply deprived of his rights of citizenship?—he being a man who, if I may use the expression, may be boxed on the ears with impunity. Then, my good friend, take my advice, and refute no more:

'Learn the philosophy of business, and acquire the reputation of wisdom. But leave to others these niceties,'

whether they are to be described as follies or absurdities:

'For they will only
Give you poverty for the inmate of your dwelling.'

Cease, then, emulating these paltry splitters of words, and emulate only the man of substance and honour, who is well to do.

SOCRATES: If my soul, Callicles, were made of gold, should I not rejoice to discover one of those stones with which they test gold, and the very best possible one to which I might bring my soul; and if the stone and I agreed in approving of her training, then I should know that I was in a satisfactory state, and that no other test was needed by me.

CALLICLES: What is your meaning, Socrates?

SOCRATES: I will tell you; I think that I have found in you the desired touchstone.

CALLICLES: Why?

SOCRATES: Because I am sure that if you agree with me in any of the opinions which my soul forms, I have at last found the truth indeed. For I consider that if a man is to make a complete trial of the good or evil of the soul, he ought to have three qualities—knowledge, goodwill, outspokenness, which are all possessed by you. Many whom I meet are unable to make trial of me, because they are not wise as you are; others are wise, but they will not tell me the truth, because they have not the same interest in me which you have; and these two strangers, Gorgias and Polus, are undoubtedly wise men and my very good friends, but they are not outspoken enough, and they are too modest. Why, their modesty is so great that they are driven to contradict themselves, first one and then the other of them, in the face of a large company, on matters of the highest moment. But you have all the qualities in which these others are deficient, having received an excellent education; to this many Athenians can testify. And you are my friend. Shall I tell you why I think so? I know that you, Callicles, and Tisander of Aphidnae, and Andron the son of Androtion, and Nausicydes of the deme of Cholarges, studied together: there were four of you, and I once heard you advising with one another as to the extent to which the pursuit of philosophy should be carried, and, as I know, you came to the conclusion that the study should not be pushed too much into detail. You were cautioning one another not to be overwise; you were afraid that too much wisdom might unconsciously to yourselves be the ruin of you. And now when I hear you giving the same advice to me which you then gave to your most intimate friends, I have a sufficient evidence of your real good-will to me. And of the frankness of your nature and freedom from modesty I am assured by yourself, and the assurance is confirmed by your last speech. Well then, the inference in the present case clearly is, that if you agree with me in an argument about any point, that point will have been sufficiently tested by us, and will not require to be submitted to any further test. For you could not have agreed with me, either from lack of knowledge or from superfluity of modesty, nor yet from a desire to deceive me, for you are my friend, as you tell me yourself. And therefore when you and I are agreed, the result will be the attainment of perfect truth. Now there is no nobler enquiry, Callicles, than that which you censure me for making,—What ought the character of a man to be, and what his pursuits, and how far is he to go, both in maturer years and in youth? For be assured that if I err in my own conduct I do not err intentionally, but from ignorance. Do not then desist from advising me, now that you have begun, until I have learned clearly what this is which I am to practise, and how I may acquire it. And if you find me assenting to your words, and hereafter not doing that to which I assented, call me 'dolt,' and deem me unworthy of receiving further instruction. Once more, then, tell me what you and Pindar mean by natural justice: Do you not mean that the superior should take the property of the inferior by force; that the better should rule the worse, the noble have more than the mean? Am I not right in my recollection?

CALLICLES: Yes; that is what I was saying, and so I still aver.

SOCRATES: And do you mean by the better the same as the superior? for I could not make out what you were saying at the time—whether you meant by the superior the stronger, and that the weaker must obey the stronger, as you seemed to imply when you said that great cities attack small ones in accordance with natural right, because they are superior and stronger, as though the superior and stronger and better were the same; or whether the better may be also the inferior and weaker, and the superior the worse, or whether better is to be defined in the same way as superior:—this is the point which I want to have cleared up. Are the superior and better and stronger the same or different?

CALLICLES: I say unequivocally that they are the same.

SOCRATES: Then the many are by nature superior to the one, against whom, as you were saying, they make the laws?

CALLICLES: Certainly.

SOCRATES: Then the laws of the many are the laws of the superior?

CALLICLES: Very true.

SOCRATES: Then they are the laws of the better; for the superior class are far better, as you were saying?

CALLICLES: Yes.

SOCRATES: And since they are superior, the laws which are made by them are by nature good?

CALLICLES: Yes.

SOCRATES: And are not the many of opinion, as you were lately saying, that justice is equality, and that to do is more disgraceful than to suffer injustice?—is that so or not? Answer, Callicles, and let no modesty be found to come in the way;[3] do the many think, or do they not think thus?—I must beg of you to answer, in order that if you agree with me I may fortify myself by the assent of so competent an authority.

CALLICLES: Yes; the opinion of the many is what you say.

SOCRATES: Then not only custom but nature also affirms that to do is more disgraceful than to suffer injustice, and that justice is equality; so that you seem to have been wrong in your former assertion, when accusing me you said that nature and custom are opposed, and that I, knowing this, was dishonestly playing between them, appealing to custom when the argument is about nature, and to nature when the argument is about custom?

CALLICLES: This man will never cease talking nonsense. At your age, Socrates, are you not ashamed to be catching at words and chuckling over some verbal slip? do you not see—have I not told you already, that by superior I mean better: do you imagine me to say, that if a rabble of slaves and nondescripts, who are of no use except perhaps for their physical strength, get together, their ipsissima verba are laws?

SOCRATES: Ho! my philosopher, is that your line?

CALLICLES: Certainly.

SOCRATES: I was thinking, Callicles, that something of the kind must have been in your mind, and that is why I repeated the question,—

---

[3]Cf. what is said of Gorgias by Callicles at p. 64.

What is the superior? I wanted to know clearly what you meant; for you surely do not think that two men are better than one, or that your slaves are better than you because they are stronger? Then please to begin again, and tell me who the better are, if they are not the stronger; and I will ask you, great Sir, to be a little milder in your instructions, or I shall have to run away from you.

CALLICLES: You are ironical.

SOCRATES: No, by the hero Zethus, Callicles, by whose aid you were just now saying (p. 67) many ironical things against me, I am not:—tell me, then, whom you mean, by the better?

CALLICLES: I mean the more excellent.

SOCRATES: Do you not see that you are yourself using words which have no meaning and that you are explaining nothing?—will you tell me whether you mean by the better and superior the wiser, or if not, whom?

CALLICLES: Most assuredly, I do mean the wiser.

SOCRATES: Then according to you, one wise man may often be superior to ten thousand fools, and he ought to rule them, and they ought to be his subjects, and he ought to have more than they should. This is what I believe that you mean (and you must not suppose that I am word-catching), if you allow that the one is superior to the ten thousand?

CALLICLES: Yes; that is what I mean, and that is what I conceive to be natural justice—that the better and wiser should rule and have more than the inferior.

SOCRATES: Stop there, and let me ask you what you would say in this case: Let us suppose that we are all together as we are now; there are several of us, and we have a large common store of meats and drinks, and there are all sorts of persons in our company having various degrees of strength and weakness, and one of us, being a physician, is wiser in the matter of food than all the rest, and he is probably stronger than some and not so strong as others of us—will he not, being wiser, be also better than we are, and our superior in this matter of food?

CALLICLES: Certainly.

SOCRATES: Either, then, he will have a larger share of the meats and drinks, because he is better, or he will have the distribution of all of them by reason of his authority, but he will not expend or make use of a larger share of them on his own person, or if he does, he will be punished;—his share will exceed that of some, and be less than that of others, and if he be the weakest of all, he being the best of all will have the smallest share of all, Callicles:—am I not right, my friend?

CALLICLES: You talk about meats and drinks and physicians and other nonsense; I am not speaking of them.

SOCRATES: Well, but do you admit that the wiser is the better? Answer 'Yes' or 'No.'

CALLICLES: Yes.

SOCRATES: And ought not the better to have a larger share?

CALLICLES: Not of meats and drinks.

SOCRATES: I understand: then, perhaps, of coats—the skilfullest weaver ought to have the largest coat, and the greatest number of them, and go about clothed in the best and finest of them?

CALLICLES: Fudge about coats!

SOCRATES: Then the skilfullest and best in making shoes ought to have the advantage in shoes; the shoemaker, clearly, should walk about in the largest shoes, and have the greatest number of them?

CALLICLES: Fudge about shoes! What nonsense are you talking?

SOCRATES: Or, if this is not your meaning, perhaps you would say that the wise and good and true husbandman should actually have a larger share of seeds, and have as much seed as possible for his own land?

CALLICLES: How you go on, always talking in the same way, Socrates!

SOCRATES: Yes, Callicles, and also about the same things.

CALLICLES: Yes, by the Gods, you are literally always talking of cobblers and fullers and cooks and doctors, as if this had to do with our argument.

SOCRATES: But why will you not tell me in what a man must be superior and wiser in order to claim a larger share; will you neither accept a suggestion, nor offer one?

CALLICLES: I have already told you. In the first place, I mean by superiors not cobblers or cooks, but wise politicians who understand the administration of a state, and who are not only wise, but also valiant and able to carry out their designs, and not the men to faint from want of soul.

SOCRATES: See now, most excellent Callicles, how different my charge against you is from that which you bring against me, for you reproach me with always saying the same; but I reproach you with never saying the same about the same things, for at one time you were defining the better and the superior to be the stronger, then again as the wiser, and now you bring forward a new notion; the superior and the better are now declared by you to be the more courageous: I wish, my good friend, that you would tell me, once for all, whom you affirm to be the better and superior, and in what they are better?

CALLICLES: I have already told you that I mean those who are wise and courageous in the administration of a state—they ought to be the rulers of their states, and justice consists in their having more than their subjects.

SOCRATES: But whether rulers or subjects will they or will they not have more than themselves, my friend?

CALLICLES: What do you mean?

SOCRATES: I mean that every man is his own ruler; but perhaps you think that there is no necessity for him to rule himself; he is only required to rule others?

CALLICLES: What do you mean by his 'ruling over himself'?

SOCRATES: A simple thing enough; just what is commonly said, that a man should be temperate and master of himself, and ruler of his own pleasures and passions.

CALLICLES: What innocence! you mean those fools,—the temperate?

SOCRATES: Certainly:—any one may know that to be my meaning.

CALLICLES: Quite so, Socrates; and they are really fools, for how can a man be happy who is the servant of anything? On the contrary, I plainly assert, that he who would truly live ought to allow his desires to wax to the uttermost, and not to chastise them; but when they have grown to their greatest he should have courage and intelligence to minister to them and to satisfy all his longings. And this I affirm to be natural justice and nobility. To this however the many cannot attain; and they blame the strong man because they are ashamed of their own weakness, which they desire to conceal, and hence they say that intemperance is base. As I have remarked already, they enslave the nobler natures, and being unable to satisfy their pleasures, they praise temperance and justice out of their own cowardice. For if a man had been originally the son of a king, or had a nature capable of acquiring an empire or a tyranny or sovereignty, what could be more truly base or evil than temperance—to a man like him, I say, who might freely be enjoying every good, and has no one to stand in his way, and yet has admitted custom and reason and the opinion of other men to be lords over him?—must not he be in a miserable plight whom the reputation of justice and temperance hinders from giving more to his friends than to his enemies, even though he be a ruler in his city? Nay, Socrates, for you profess to be a votary of the truth, and the truth is this:—that luxury and intemperance and licence, if they be provided with means, are virtue and happiness—all the rest is a mere bauble, agreements contrary to nature, foolish talk of men, nothing worth. (Compare *Republic.*)

SOCRATES: There is a noble freedom, Callicles, in your way of approaching the argument; for what you say is what the rest of the world think, but do not like to say. And I must beg of you to persevere, that the true rule of human life may become manifest. Tell me, then:—you say, do you not, that in the rightly-developed man the passions ought not to be controlled, but that we should let them grow to the utmost and somehow or other satisfy them, and that this is virtue?

CALLICLES: Yes; I do.

SOCRATES: Then those who want nothing are not truly said to be happy?

CALLICLES: No indeed, for then stones and dead men would be the happiest of all.

SOCRATES: But surely life according to your view is an awful thing; and indeed I think that Euripides may have been right in saying,

'Who knows if life be not death and death life';

and that we are very likely dead; I have heard a philosopher say that at this moment we are actually dead, and that the body (σῶμα) is our tomb (σῆμα (compare *Phaedr.*)), and that the part of the soul which is the seat of the desires is liable to be tossed about by words and blown up and down; and some ingenious person, probably a Sicilian or an Italian, playing with the word, invented a tale in which he called the soul—because of its believing and make-believe nature—a vessel,[4] and the ignorant he called the uninitiated or leaky, and the place in the souls of the uninitiated in which the desires are seated, being the intemperate and incontinent part, he compared to a vessel full of holes, because it can never be satisfied. He is not of your way of thinking, Callicles, for he declares, that of all the souls in Hades, meaning the invisible world (ἀειδὲζ), these uninitiated or leaky persons are the most miserable, and that they pour water into a vessel which is full of holes out of a colander which is similarly perforated. The colander, as my informer assures me, is the soul, and the soul which he compares to a colander is the soul of the ignorant, which is likewise full of holes, and therefore incontinent, owing to a bad memory and want of faith. These notions are strange enough, but they show the principle which, if I can, I would fain prove to you; that you should change your mind, and, instead of the intemperate and insatiate life, choose that which is orderly and sufficient and has a due provision for daily needs. Do I make any impression on you, and are you coming over to the opinion that the orderly are happier than the intemperate? Or do I fail to persuade you, and, however many tales I rehearse to you, do you continue of the same opinion still?

CALLICLES: The latter, Socrates, is more like the truth.

SOCRATES: Well, I will tell you another image, which comes out of the same school:—Let me request you to consider how far you would accept this as an account of the two lives of the temperate and intem-

---

[4]An untranslatable pun,—διὰ τὸ πιθανόν τε καὶ πιστικὸν ὠνόμασε πίθον.

perate in a figure:—There are two men, both of whom have a number of casks; the one man has his casks sound and full, one of wine, another of honey, and a third of milk, besides others filled with other liquids, and the streams which fill them are few and scanty, and he can only obtain them with a great deal of toil and difficulty; but when his casks are once filled he has no need to feed them any more, and has no further trouble with them or care about them. The other, in like manner, can procure streams, though not without difficulty; but his vessels are leaky and unsound, and night and day he is compelled to be filling them, and if he pauses for a moment, he is in an agony of pain. Such are their respective lives:—And now would you say that the life of the intemperate is happier than that of the temperate? Do I not convince you that the opposite is the truth?

CALLICLES: You do not convince me, Socrates, for the one who has filled himself has no longer any pleasure left; and this, as I was just now saying, is the life of a stone: he has neither joy nor sorrow after he is once filled; but the pleasure depends on the superabundance of the influx.

SOCRATES: But the more you pour in, the greater the waste; and the holes must be large for the liquid to escape.

CALLICLES: Certainly.

SOCRATES: The life which you are now depicting is not that of a dead man, or of a stone, but of a cormorant; you mean that he is to be hungering and eating?

CALLICLES: Yes.

SOCRATES: And he is to be thirsting and drinking?

CALLICLES: Yes, that is what I mean; he is to have all his desires about him, and to be able to live happily in the gratification of them.

SOCRATES: Capital, excellent; go on as you have begun, and have no shame; I, too, must disencumber myself of shame: and first, will you tell me whether you include itching and scratching, provided you have enough of them and pass your life in scratching, in your notion of happiness?

CALLICLES: What a strange being you are, Socrates! a regular moborator.

SOCRATES: That was the reason, Callicles, why I scared Polus and Gorgias, until they were too modest to say what they thought; but you will not be too modest and will not be scared, for you are a brave man. And now, answer my question.

CALLICLES: I answer, that even the scratcher would live pleasantly.

SOCRATES: And if pleasantly, then also happily?

CALLICLES: To be sure.

SOCRATES: But what if the itching is not confined to the head? Shall

I pursue the question? And here, Callicles, I would have you consider how you would reply if consequences are pressed upon you, especially if in the last resort you are asked, whether the life of a catamite is not terrible, foul, miserable? Or would you venture to say, that they too are happy, if they only get enough of what they want?

CALLICLES: Are you not ashamed, Socrates, of introducing such topics into the argument?

SOCRATES: Well, my fine friend, but am I the introducer of these topics, or he who says without any qualification that all who feel pleasure in whatever manner are happy, and who admits of no distinction between good and bad pleasures? And I would still ask, whether you say that pleasure and good are the same, or whether there is some pleasure which is not a good?

CALLICLES: Well, then, for the sake of consistency, I will say that they are the same.

SOCRATES: You are breaking the original agreement, Callicles, and will no longer be a satisfactory companion in the search after truth, if you say what is contrary to your real opinion.

CALLICLES: Why, that is what you are doing too, Socrates.

SOCRATES: Then we are both doing wrong. Still, my dear friend, I would ask you to consider whether pleasure, from whatever source derived, is the good; for, if this be true, then the disagreeable consequences which have been darkly intimated must follow, and many others.

CALLICLES: That, Socrates, is only your opinion.

SOCRATES: And do you, Callicles, seriously maintain what you are saying?

CALLICLES: Indeed I do.

SOCRATES: Then, as you are in earnest, shall we proceed with the argument?

CALLICLES: By all means. (Or, 'I am in profound earnest.')

SOCRATES: Well, if you are willing to proceed, determine this question for me:—There is something, I presume, which you would call knowledge?

CALLICLES: There is.

SOCRATES: And were you not saying just now, that some courage implied knowledge?

CALLICLES: I was.

SOCRATES: And you were speaking of courage and knowledge as two things different from one another?

CALLICLES: Certainly I was.

SOCRATES: And would you say that pleasure and knowledge are the same, or not the same?

CALLICLES: Not the same, O man of wisdom.

SOCRATES: And would you say that courage differed from pleasure?

CALLICLES: Certainly.

SOCRATES: Well, then, let us remember that Callicles, the Acharnian, says that pleasure and good are the same; but that knowledge and courage are not the same, either with one another, or with the good.

CALLICLES: And what does our friend Socrates, of Foxton, say—does he assent to this, or not?

SOCRATES: He does not assent; neither will Callicles, when he sees himself truly. You will admit, I suppose, that good and evil fortune are opposed to each other?

CALLICLES: Yes.

SOCRATES: And if they are opposed to each other, then, like health and disease, they exclude one another; a man cannot have them both, or be without them both, at the same time?

CALLICLES: What do you mean?

SOCRATES: Take the case of any bodily affection:—a man may have the complaint in his eyes which is called ophthalmia?

CALLICLES: To be sure.

SOCRATES: But he surely cannot have the same eyes well and sound at the same time?

CALLICLES: Certainly not.

SOCRATES: And when he has got rid of his ophthalmia, has he got rid of the health of his eyes too? Is the final result, that he gets rid of them both together?

CALLICLES: Certainly not.

SOCRATES: That would surely be marvellous and absurd?

CALLICLES: Very.

SOCRATES: I suppose that he is affected by them, and gets rid of them in turns?

CALLICLES: Yes.

SOCRATES: And he may have strength and weakness in the same way, by fits?

CALLICLES: Yes.

SOCRATES: Or swiftness and slowness?

CALLICLES: Certainly.

SOCRATES: And does he have and not have good and happiness, and their opposites, evil and misery, in a similar alternation? (Compare *Republic*.)

CALLICLES: Certainly he has.

SOCRATES: If then there be anything which a man has and has not at the same time, clearly that cannot be good and evil—do we agree? Please not to answer without consideration.

CALLICLES: I entirely agree.

SOCRATES: Go back now to our former admissions.—Did you say that to hunger, I mean the mere state of hunger, was pleasant or painful?

CALLICLES: I said painful, but that to eat when you are hungry is pleasant.

SOCRATES: I know; but still the actual hunger is painful: am I not right?

CALLICLES: Yes.

SOCRATES: And thirst, too, is painful?

CALLICLES: Yes, very.

SOCRATES: Need I adduce any more instances, or would you agree that all wants or desires are painful?

CALLICLES: I agree, and therefore you need not adduce any more instances.

SOCRATES: Very good. And you would admit that to drink, when you are thirsty, is pleasant?

CALLICLES: Yes.

SOCRATES: And in the sentence which you have just uttered, the word 'thirsty' implies pain?

CALLICLES: Yes.

SOCRATES: And the word 'drinking' is expressive of pleasure, and of the satisfaction of the want?

CALLICLES: Yes.

SOCRATES: There is pleasure in drinking?

CALLICLES: Certainly.

SOCRATES: When you are thirsty?

SOCRATES: And in pain?

CALLICLES: Yes.

SOCRATES: Do you see the inference:—that pleasure and pain are simultaneous, when you say that being thirsty, you drink? For are they not simultaneous, and do they not affect at the same time the same part, whether of the soul or the body?—which of them is affected cannot be supposed to be of any consequence: Is not this true?

CALLICLES: It is.

SOCRATES: You said also, that no man could have good and evil fortune at the same time?

CALLICLES: Yes, I did.

SOCRATES: But you admitted, that when in pain a man might also have pleasure?

CALLICLES: Clearly.

SOCRATES: Then pleasure is not the same as good fortune, or pain the same as evil fortune, and therefore the good is not the same as the pleasant?

CALLICLES: I wish I knew, Socrates, what your quibbling means.

SOCRATES: You know, Callicles, but you affect not to know.

CALLICLES: Well, get on, and don't keep fooling: then you will know what a wiseacre you are in your admonition of me.

SOCRATES: Does not a man cease from his thirst and from his pleasure in drinking at the same time?

CALLICLES: I do not understand what you are saying.

GORGIAS: Nay, Callicles, answer, if only for our sakes;—we should like to hear the argument out.

CALLICLES: Yes, Gorgias, but I must complain of the habitual trifling of Socrates; he is always arguing about little and unworthy questions.

GORGIAS: What matter? Your reputation, Callicles, is not at stake. Let Socrates argue in his own fashion.

CALLICLES: Well, then, Socrates, you shall ask these little peddling questions, since Gorgias wishes to have them.

SOCRATES: I envy you, Callicles, for having been initiated into the great mysteries before you were initiated into the lesser. I thought that this was not allowable. But to return to our argument:—Does not a man cease from thirsting and from the pleasure of drinking at the same moment?

CALLICLES: True.

SOCRATES: And if he is hungry, or has any other desire, does he not cease from the desire and the pleasure at the same moment?

CALLICLES: Very true.

SOCRATES: Then he ceases from pain and pleasure at the same moment?

CALLICLES: Yes.

SOCRATES: But he does not cease from good and evil at the same moment, as you have admitted: do you still adhere to what you said?

CALLICLES: Yes, I do; but what is the inference?

SOCRATES: Why, my friend, the inference is that the good is not the same as the pleasant, or the evil the same as the painful; there is a cessation of pleasure and pain at the same moment; but not of good and evil, for they are different. How then can pleasure be the same as good, or pain as evil? And I would have you look at the matter in another light, which could hardly, I think, have been considered by you when you identified them: Are not the good good because they have good present with them, as the beautiful are those who have beauty present with them?

CALLICLES: Yes.

SOCRATES: And do you call the fools and cowards good men? For you were saying just now that the courageous and the wise are the good— would you not say so?

CALLICLES: Certainly.

SOCRATES: And did you never see a foolish child rejoicing?

CALLICLES: Yes, I have.

SOCRATES: And a foolish man too?

CALLICLES: Yes, certainly; but what is your drift?

SOCRATES: Nothing particular, if you will only answer.

CALLICLES: Yes, I have.

SOCRATES: And did you ever see a sensible man rejoicing or sorrowing?

CALLICLES: Yes.

SOCRATES: Which rejoice and sorrow most—the wise or the foolish?

CALLICLES: They are much upon a par, I think, in that respect.

SOCRATES: Enough: And did you ever see a coward in battle?

CALLICLES: To be sure.

SOCRATES: And which rejoiced most at the departure of the enemy, the coward or the brave?

CALLICLES: I should say 'most' of both; or at any rate, they rejoiced about equally.

SOCRATES: No matter; then the cowards, and not only the brave, rejoice?

CALLICLES: Greatly.

SOCRATES: And the foolish; so it would seem?

CALLICLES: Yes.

SOCRATES: And are only the cowards pained at the approach of their enemies, or are the brave also pained?

CALLICLES: Both are pained.

SOCRATES: And are they equally pained?

CALLICLES: I should imagine that the cowards are more pained.

SOCRATES: And are they not better pleased at the enemy's departure?

CALLICLES: I dare say.

SOCRATES: Then are the foolish and the wise and the cowards and the brave all pleased and pained, as you were saying, in nearly equal degree; but are the cowards more pleased and pained than the brave?

CALLICLES: Yes.

SOCRATES: But surely the wise and brave are the good, and the foolish and the cowardly are the bad?

CALLICLES: Yes.

SOCRATES: Then the good and the bad are pleased and pained in a nearly equal degree?

CALLICLES: Yes.

SOCRATES: Then are the good and bad good and bad in a nearly equal degree, or have the bad the advantage both in good and evil? [i.e. in having more pleasure and more pain.]

CALLICLES: I really do not know what you mean.

SOCRATES: Why, do you not remember saying that the good were good because good was present with them, and the evil because evil; and that pleasures were goods and pains evils?

CALLICLES: Yes, I remember.

SOCRATES: And are not these pleasures or goods present to those who rejoice—if they do rejoice?

CALLICLES: Certainly.

SOCRATES: Then those who rejoice are good when goods are present with them?

CALLICLES: Yes.

SOCRATES: And those who are in pain have evil or sorrow present with them?

CALLICLES: Yes.

SOCRATES: And would you still say that the evil are evil by reason of the presence of evil?

CALLICLES: I should.

SOCRATES: Then those who rejoice are good, and those who are in pain evil?

CALLICLES: Yes.

SOCRATES: The degrees of good and evil vary with the degrees of pleasure and of pain?

CALLICLES: Yes.

SOCRATES: Have the wise man and the fool, the brave and the coward, joy and pain in nearly equal degrees? or would you say that the coward has more?

CALLICLES: I should say that he has.

SOCRATES: Help me then to draw out the conclusion which follows from our admissions; for it is good to repeat and review what is good twice and thrice over, as they say. Both the wise man and the brave man we allow to be good?

CALLICLES: Yes.

SOCRATES: And the foolish man and the coward to be evil?

CALLICLES: Certainly.

SOCRATES: And he who has joy is good?

CALLICLES: Yes.

SOCRATES: And he who is in pain is evil?

CALLICLES: Certainly.

SOCRATES: The good and evil both have joy and pain, but, perhaps, the evil has more of them?

CALLICLES: Yes.

SOCRATES: Then must we not infer, that the bad man is as good and bad as the good, or, perhaps, even better?—is not this a further inference which follows equally with the preceding from the assertion that the good and the pleasant are the same:—can this be denied, Callicles?

CALLICLES: I have been listening and making admissions to you, Socrates; and I remark that if a person grants you anything in play, you, like a child, want to keep hold and will not give it back. But do you really suppose that I or any other human being denies that some pleasures are good and others bad?

SOCRATES: Alas, Callicles, how unfair you are! you certainly treat me as if I were a child, sometimes saying one thing, and then another, as if you were meaning to deceive me. And yet I thought at first that you were my friend, and would not have deceived me if you could have helped. But I see that I was mistaken; and now I suppose that I must make the best of a bad business, as they said of old, and take what I can get out of you.—Well, then, as I understand you to say, I may assume that some pleasures are good and others evil?

CALLICLES: Yes.

SOCRATES: The beneficial are good, and the hurtful are evil?

CALLICLES: To be sure.

SOCRATES: And the beneficial are those which do some good, and the hurtful are those which do some evil?

CALLICLES: Yes.

SOCRATES: Take, for example, the bodily pleasures of eating and drinking, which we were just now mentioning—you mean to say that those which promote health, or any other bodily excellence, are good, and their opposites evil?

CALLICLES: Certainly.

SOCRATES: And in the same way there are good pains and there are evil pains?

CALLICLES: To be sure.

SOCRATES: And ought we not to choose and use the good pleasures and pains?

CALLICLES: Certainly.

SOCRATES: But not the evil?

CALLICLES: Clearly.

SOCRATES: Because, if you remember, Polus and I have agreed that all our actions are to be done for the sake of the good;—and will you agree with us in saying, that the good is the end of all our actions, and that all our actions are to be done for the sake of the good, and not the good for the sake of them?—will you add a third vote to our two?

CALLICLES: I will.

SOCRATES: Then pleasure, like everything else, is to be sought for the sake of that which is good, and not that which is good for the sake of pleasure?

CALLICLES: To be sure.

SOCRATES: But can every man choose what pleasures are good and what are evil, or must he have art or knowledge of them in detail?

CALLICLES: He must have art.

SOCRATES: Let me now remind you of what I was saying to Gorgias and Polus; I was saying, as you will not have forgotten, that there were some processes which aim only at pleasure, and know nothing of a better and worse, and there are other processes which know good and evil. And I considered that cookery, which I do not call an art, but only an experience, was of the former class, which is concerned with pleasure, and that the art of medicine was of the class which is concerned with the good. And now, by the god of friendship, I must beg you, Callicles, not to jest, or to imagine that I am jesting with you; do not answer at random and contrary to your real opinion;—for you will observe that we are arguing about the way of human life; and to a man who has any sense at all, what question can be more serious than this?—whether he should follow after that way of life to which you exhort me, and act what you call the manly part of speaking in the assembly, and cultivating rhetoric, and engaging in public affairs, according to the principles now in vogue; or whether he should pursue the life of philosophy;— and in what the latter way differs from the former. But perhaps we had better first try to distinguish them, as I did before, and when we have come to an agreement that they are distinct, we may proceed to consider in what they differ from one another, and which of them we should choose. Perhaps, however, you do not even now understand what I mean?

CALLICLES: No, I do not.

SOCRATES: Then I will explain myself more clearly: seeing that you and I have agreed that there is such a thing as good, and that there is such a thing as pleasure, and that pleasure is not the same as good, and that the pursuit and process of acquisition of the one, that is pleasure, is different from the pursuit and process of acquisition of the other, which is good—I wish that you would tell me whether you agree with me thus far or not—do you agree?

CALLICLES: I do.

SOCRATES: Then I will proceed, and ask whether you also agree with me, and whether you think that I spoke the truth when I further said to Gorgias and Polus that cookery in my opinion is only an experience, and not an art at all; and that whereas medicine is an art, and attends to the nature and constitution of the patient, and has principles of action and reason in each case, cookery in attending upon pleasure never regards either the nature or reason of that pleasure to which she devotes herself, but goes straight to her end, nor ever considers or calculates anything, but works by experience and routine, and just preserves the recollection of what she has usually done when producing pleasure. And first, I would have you consider whether I have proved what I was saying, and then whether there are not other similar processes which have to do with the soul—some of them processes of art, making a provision for the soul's highest interest—others despising the interest, and, as in the previous case, considering only the pleasure of the soul, and how this may be acquired, but not considering what pleasures are good or bad, and having no other aim but to afford gratification, whether good or bad. In my opinion, Callicles, there are such processes, and this is the sort of thing which I term flattery, whether concerned with the body or the soul, or whenever employed with a view to pleasure and without any consideration of good and evil. And now I wish that you would tell me whether you agree with us in this notion, or whether you differ.

CALLICLES: I do not differ; on the contrary, I agree; for in that way I shall soonest bring the argument to an end, and shall oblige my friend Gorgias.

SOCRATES: And is this notion true of one soul, or of two or more?

CALLICLES: Equally true of two or more.

SOCRATES: Then a man may delight a whole assembly, and yet have no regard for their true interests?

CALLICLES: Yes.

SOCRATES: Can you tell me the pursuits which delight mankind—or rather, if you would prefer, let me ask, and do you answer, which of them belong to the pleasurable class, and which of them not? In the first place, what say you of flute-playing? Does not that appear to be an art which seeks only pleasure, Callicles, and thinks of nothing else?

CALLICLES: I assent.

SOCRATES: And is not the same true of all similar arts, as, for example, the art of playing the lyre at festivals?

CALLICLES: Yes.

SOCRATES: And what do you say of the choral art and of dithyrambic poetry?—are not they of the same nature? Do you imagine that Cinesias the son of Meles cares about what will tend to the moral improvement of his hearers, or about what will give pleasure to the multitude?

CALLICLES: There can be no mistake about Cinesias, Socrates.

SOCRATES: And what do you say of his father, Meles the harp-player? Did he perform with any view to the good of his hearers? Could he be said to regard even their pleasure? For his singing was an infliction to his audience. And of harp-playing and dithyrambic poetry in general, what would you say? Have they not been invented wholly for the sake of pleasure?

CALLICLES: That is my notion of them.

SOCRATES: And as for the Muse of Tragedy, that solemn and august personage—what are her aspirations? Is all her aim and desire only to give pleasure to the spectators, or does she fight against them and refuse to speak of their pleasant vices, and willingly proclaim in word and song truths welcome and unwelcome?—which in your judgment is her character?

CALLICLES: There can be no doubt, Socrates, that Tragedy has her face turned towards pleasure and the gratification of the audience.

SOCRATES: And is not that the sort of thing, Callicles, which we were just now describing as flattery?

CALLICLES: Quite true.

SOCRATES: Well now, suppose that we strip all poetry of song and rhythm and metre, there will remain speech? (Compare *Republic*.)

CALLICLES: To be sure.

SOCRATES: And this speech is addressed to a crowd of people?

CALLICLES: Yes.

SOCRATES: Then poetry is a sort of rhetoric?

CALLICLES: True.

SOCRATES: And do not the poets in the theatres seem to you to be rhetoricians?

CALLICLES: Yes.

SOCRATES: Then now we have discovered a sort of rhetoric which is addressed to a crowd of men, women, and children, freemen and slaves. And this is not much to our taste, for we have described it as having the nature of flattery.

CALLICLES: Quite true.

SOCRATES: Very good. And what do you say of that other rhetoric which addresses the Athenian assembly and the assemblies of freemen in other states? Do the rhetoricians appear to you always to aim at what is best, and do they seek to improve the citizens by their speeches, or are they too, like the rest of mankind, bent upon giving them pleasure, forgetting the public good in the thought of their own interest, playing with the people as with children, and trying to amuse them, but never considering whether they are better or worse for this?

CALLICLES: I must distinguish. There are some who have a real care of the public in what they say, while others are such as you describe.

SOCRATES: I am contented with the admission that rhetoric is of two sorts; one, which is mere flattery and disgraceful declamation; the other, which is noble and aims at the training and improvement of the souls of the citizens, and strives to say what is best, whether welcome or unwelcome, to the audience; but have you ever known such a rhetoric;

or if you have, and can point out any rhetorician who is of this stamp, who is he?

CALLICLES: But, indeed, I am afraid that I cannot tell you of any such among the orators who are at present living.

SOCRATES: Well, then, can you mention any one of a former generation, who may be said to have improved the Athenians, who found them worse and made them better, from the day that he began to make speeches? for, indeed, I do not know of such a man.

CALLICLES: What! did you never hear that Themistocles was a good man, and Cimon and Miltiades and Pericles, who is just lately dead, and whom you heard yourself?

SOCRATES: Yes, Callicles, they were good men, if, as you said at first, true virtue consists only in the satisfaction of our own desires and those of others; but if not, and if, as we were afterwards compelled to acknowledge, the satisfaction of some desires makes us better, and of others, worse, and we ought to gratify the one and not the other, and there is an art in distinguishing them, — can you tell me of any of these statesmen who did distinguish them?

CALLICLES: No, indeed, I cannot.

SOCRATES: Yet, surely, Callicles, if you look you will find such a one. Suppose that we just calmly consider whether any of these was such as I have described. Will not the good man, who says whatever he says with a view to the best, speak with a reference to some standard and not at random; just as all other artists, whether the painter, the builder, the shipwright, or any other look all of them to their own work, and do not select and apply at random what they apply, but strive to give a definite form to it? The artist disposes all things in order, and compels the one part to harmonize and accord with the other part, until he has constructed a regular and systematic whole; and this is true of all artists, and in the same way the trainers and physicians, of whom we spoke before, give order and regularity to the body: do you deny this?

CALLICLES: No; I am ready to admit it.

SOCRATES: Then the house in which order and regularity prevail is good; that in which there is disorder, evil?

CALLICLES: Yes.

SOCRATES: And the same is true of a ship?

CALLICLES: Yes.

SOCRATES: And the same may be said of the human body?

CALLICLES: Yes.

SOCRATES: And what would you say of the soul? Will the good soul be that in which disorder is prevalent, or that in which there is harmony and order?

CALLICLES: The latter follows from our previous admissions.

SOCRATES: What is the name which is given to the effect of harmony and order in the body?

CALLICLES: I suppose that you mean health and strength?

SOCRATES: Yes, I do; and what is the name which you would give to the effect of harmony and order in the soul? Try and discover a name for this as well as for the other.

CALLICLES: Why not give the name yourself, Socrates?

SOCRATES: Well, if you had rather that I should, I will; and you shall say whether you agree with me, and if not, you shall refute and answer me. 'Healthy,' as I conceive, is the name which is given to the regular order of the body, whence comes health and every other bodily excellence: is that true or not?

CALLICLES: True.

SOCRATES: And 'lawful' and 'law' are the names which are given to the regular order and action of the soul, and these make men lawful and orderly:—and so we have temperance and justice: have we not?

CALLICLES: Granted.

SOCRATES: And will not the true rhetorician who is honest and understands his art have his eye fixed upon these, in all the words which he addresses to the souls of men, and in all his actions, both in what he gives and in what he takes away? Will not his aim be to implant justice in the souls of his citizens and take away injustice, to implant temperance and take away intemperance, to implant every virtue and take away every vice? Do you not agree?

CALLICLES: I agree.

SOCRATES: For what use is there, Callicles, in giving to the body of a sick man who is in a bad state of health a quantity of the most delightful food or drink or any other pleasant thing, which may be really as bad for him as if you gave him nothing, or even worse if rightly estimated. Is not that true?

CALLICLES: I will not say No to it.

SOCRATES: For in my opinion there is no profit in a man's life if his body is in an evil plight—in that case his life also is evil: am I not right?

CALLICLES: Yes.

SOCRATES: When a man is in health the physicians will generally allow him to eat when he is hungry and drink when he is thirsty, and to satisfy his desires as he likes, but when he is sick they hardly suffer him to satisfy his desires at all: even you will admit that?

CALLICLES: Yes.

SOCRATES: And does not the same argument hold of the soul, my good sir? While she is in a bad state and is senseless and intemperate and unjust and unholy, her desires ought to be controlled, and she ought to be prevented from doing anything which does not tend to her own improvement.

CALLICLES: Yes.

SOCRATES: Such treatment will be better for the soul herself?

CALLICLES: To be sure.

SOCRATES: And to restrain her from her appetites is to chastise her?

CALLICLES: Yes.

SOCRATES: Then restraint or chastisement is better for the soul than intemperance or the absence of control, which you were just now preferring?

CALLICLES: I do not understand you, Socrates, and I wish that you would ask some one who does.

SOCRATES: Here is a gentleman who cannot endure to be improved or to subject himself to that very chastisement of which the argument speaks!

CALLICLES: I do not heed a word of what you are saying, and have only answered hitherto out of civility to Gorgias.

SOCRATES: What are we to do, then? Shall we break off in the middle?

CALLICLES: You shall judge for yourself.

SOCRATES: Well, but people say that 'a tale should have a head and not break off in the middle,' and I should not like to have the argument going about without a head (compare *Laws*); please then to go on a little longer, and put the head on.

CALLICLES: How tyrannical you are, Socrates! I wish that you and your argument would rest, or that you would get some one else to argue with you.

SOCRATES: But who else is willing?—I want to finish the argument.

CALLICLES: Cannot you finish without my help, either talking straight on, or questioning and answering yourself?

SOCRATES: Must I then say with Epicharmus, 'Two men spoke before, but now one shall be enough'? I suppose that there is absolutely no help. And if I am to carry on the enquiry by myself, I will first of all remark that not only I but all of us should have an ambition to know what is true and what is false in this matter, for the discovery of the truth is a common good. And now I will proceed to argue according to my own notion. But if any of you think that I arrive at conclusions which are untrue you must interpose and refute me, for I do not speak from any knowledge of what I am saying; I am an enquirer like yourselves, and therefore, if my opponent says anything which is of force, I shall be the first to agree with him. I am speaking on the supposition that the argument ought to be completed; but if you think otherwise let us leave off and go our ways.

GORGIAS: I think, Socrates, that we should not go our ways until you have completed the argument; and this appears to me to be the wish of the rest of the company; I myself should very much like to hear what more you have to say.

SOCRATES: I too, Gorgias, should have liked to continue the argument with Callicles, and then I might have given him an 'Amphion' in return for his 'Zethus'; but since you, Callicles, are unwilling to continue, I hope that you will listen, and interrupt me if I seem to you to be in error. And if you refute me, I shall not be angry with you as you are with me, but I shall inscribe you as the greatest of benefactors on the tablets of my soul.

CALLICLES: My good fellow, never mind me, but get on.

SOCRATES: Listen to me, then, while I recapitulate the argument:— Is the pleasant the same as the good? Not the same. Callicles and I are agreed about that. And is the pleasant to be pursued for the sake of the good? or the good for the sake of the pleasant? The pleasant is to be pursued for the sake of the good. And that is pleasant at the presence of which we are pleased, and that is good at the presence of which we are good? To be sure. And we are good, and all good things whatever are good when some virtue is present in us or them? That, Callicles, is my conviction. But the virtue of each thing, whether body or soul, instrument or creature, when given to them in the best way comes to them not by chance but as the result of the order and truth and art which are imparted to them: Am I not right? I maintain that I am. And is not the virtue of each thing dependent on order or arrangement? Yes, I say. And that which makes a thing good is the proper order inhering in each thing? Such is my view. And is not the soul which has an order of her own better than that which has no order? Certainly. And the soul which has order is orderly? Of course. And that which is orderly is temperate? Assuredly. And the temperate soul is good? No other answer can I give, Callicles dear; have you any?

CALLICLES: Go on, my good fellow.

SOCRATES: Then I shall proceed to add, that if the temperate soul is the good soul, the soul which is in the opposite condition, that is, the foolish and intemperate, is the bad soul. Very true.

And will not the temperate man do what is proper, both in relation to the gods and to men;—for he would not be temperate if he did not? Certainly he will do what is proper. In his relation to other men he will do what is just; and in his relation to the gods he will do what is holy; and he who does what is just and holy must be just and holy? Very true. And must he not be courageous? for the duty of a temperate man is not to follow or to avoid what he ought not, but what he ought, whether things or men or pleasures or pains, and patiently to endure when he ought; and therefore, Callicles, the temperate man, being, as we have described, also just and courageous and holy, cannot be other than a perfectly good man, nor can the good man do otherwise than well and perfectly whatever he does; and he who does well must of necessity be happy and blessed, and the evil man who does evil, miserable: now this latter is he whom you were applauding—the intemperate who is the opposite of the temperate. Such is my position, and these things I affirm to be true. And if they are true, then I further affirm that he who desires to be happy must pursue and practise temperance and run away from intemperance as fast as his legs will carry him: he had better order his life so as not to need punishment; but if either he or any of his friends, whether private individual or city, are in need of punishment, then justice must be done and he must suffer punishment, if he would be happy. This appears to me to be the aim which a man ought to have, and towards which he ought to direct all the energies both of himself and of the state, acting so that he may have temperance and justice present with him and be happy, not suffering his lusts to be unrestrained, and in the never-ending desire to satisfy them leading a robber's life. Such a one is the friend neither of God nor man, for he is incapable of communion, and he who is incapable of communion is also incapable of friendship. And philosophers tell us, Callicles, that communion and friendship and orderliness and temperance and justice bind together heaven and earth and gods and men, and that this universe is therefore called Cosmos or order, not disorder or misrule, my friend. But although you are a philosopher you seem to me never to have observed that geometrical equality is mighty, both among gods and men; you think that you ought to cultivate inequality or excess, and do not care about geometry.—Well, then, either the principle that the happy are made happy by the possession of justice and temperance, and the miserable miserable by the possession of vice, must be refuted, or, if it is granted, what will be the consequences? All the consequences which I drew before, Callicles, and about which you asked me whether I was in earnest when I said that a man ought to accuse himself and his son and his friend if he did anything wrong, and that to this end he should use his rhetoric—all those consequences are true. And that which you thought that Polus was led to admit out of modesty is true, viz. that, to do injustice, if more disgraceful than to suffer, is in that degree worse; and the other position, which, according to Polus, Gorgias admitted out of modesty, that he who would truly be a rhetorician ought to be just and have a knowledge of justice, has also turned out to be true.

And now, these things being as we have said, let us proceed in the next place to consider whether you are right in throwing in my teeth that I am unable to help myself or any of my friends or kinsmen, or to

save them in the extremity of danger, and that I am in the power of another like an outlaw to whom any one may do what he likes, — he may
box my ears, which was a brave saying of yours; or take away my goods
or banish me, or even do his worst and kill me; a condition which, as
you say, is the height of disgrace. My answer to you is one which has
been already often repeated, but may as well be repeated once more. I
tell you, Callicles, that to be boxed on the ears wrongfully is not the
worst evil which can befall a man, nor to have my purse or my body cut
open, but that to smite and slay me and mine wrongfully is far more disgraceful and more evil; aye, and to despoil and enslave and pillage, or
in any way at all to wrong me and mine, is far more disgraceful and evil
to the doer of the wrong than to me who am the sufferer. These truths,
which have been already set forth as I state them in the previous discussion, would seem now to have been fixed and riveted by us, if I may
use an expression which is certainly bold, in words which are like
bonds of iron and adamant; and unless you or some other still more en-
terprising hero shall break them, there is no possibility of denying what
I say. For my position has always been, that I myself am ignorant how
these things are, but that I have never met any one who could say otherwise, any more than you can, and not appear ridiculous. This is my
position still, and if what I am saying is true, and injustice is the greatest of evils to the doer of injustice, and yet there is if possible a greater
than this greatest of evils (compare *Republic*), in an unjust man not suffering retribution, what is that defence of which the want will make a
man truly ridiculous? Must not the defence be one which will avert the
greatest of human evils? And will not the worst of all defences be that
with which a man is unable to defend himself or his family or his
friends? — and next will come that which is unable to avert the next
greatest evil; thirdly that which is unable to avert the third greatest evil;
and so of other evils. As is the greatness of evil so is the honour of being
able to avert them in their several degrees, and the disgrace of not being
able to avert them. Am I not right, Callicles?

CALLICLES: Yes, quite right.

SOCRATES: Seeing then that there are these two evils, the doing injustice and the suffering injustice — and we affirm that to do injustice
is a greater, and to suffer injustice a lesser evil — by what devices can a
man succeed in obtaining the two advantages, the one of not doing and
the other of not suffering injustice? must he have the power, or only the
will to obtain them? I mean to ask whether a man will escape injustice
if he has only the will to escape, or must he have provided himself with
the power?

CALLICLES: He must have provided himself with the power; that is
clear.

SOCRATES: And what do you say of doing injustice? Is the will only sufficient, and will that prevent him from doing injustice, or must he have provided himself with power and art; and if he have not studied and practised, will he be unjust still? Surely you might say, Callicles, whether you think that Polus and I were right in admitting the conclusion that no one does wrong voluntarily, but that all do wrong against their will?

CALLICLES: Granted, Socrates, if you will only have done.

SOCRATES: Then, as would appear, power and art have to be provided in order that we may do no injustice?

CALLICLES: Certainly.

SOCRATES: And what art will protect us from suffering injustice, if not wholly, yet as far as possible? I want to know whether you agree with me; for I think that such an art is the art of one who is either a ruler or even tyrant himself, or the equal and companion of the ruling power.

CALLICLES: Well said, Socrates; and please to observe how ready I am to praise you when you talk sense.

SOCRATES: Think and tell me whether you would approve of another view of mine: To me every man appears to be most the friend of him who is most like to him—like to like, as ancient sages say: Would you not agree to this?

CALLICLES: I should.

SOCRATES: But when the tyrant is rude and uneducated, he may be expected to fear any one who is his superior in virtue, and will never be able to be perfectly friendly with him.

CALLICLES: That is true.

SOCRATES: Neither will he be the friend of any one who is greatly his inferior, for the tyrant will despise him, and will never seriously regard him as a friend.

CALLICLES: That again is true.

SOCRATES: Then the only friend worth mentioning, whom the tyrant can have, will be one who is of the same character, and has the same likes and dislikes, and is at the same time willing to be subject and subservient to him; he is the man who will have power in the state, and no one will injure him with impunity:—is not that so?

CALLICLES: Yes.

SOCRATES: And if a young man begins to ask how he may become great and formidable, this would seem to be the way—he will accustom himself, from his youth upward, to feel sorrow and joy on the same occasions as his master, and will contrive to be as like him as possible?

CALLICLES: Yes.

SOCRATES: And in this way he will have accomplished, as you and your friends would say, the end of becoming a great man and not suffering injury?

CALLICLES: Very true.

SOCRATES: But will he also escape from doing injury? Must not the very opposite be true, if he is to be like the tyrant in his injustice, and to have influence with him? Will he not rather contrive to do as much wrong as possible, and not be punished?

CALLICLES: True.

SOCRATES: And by the imitation of his master and by the power which he thus acquires will not his soul become bad and corrupted, and will not this be the greatest evil to him?

CALLICLES: You always contrive somehow or other, Socrates, to invert everything: do you not know that he who imitates the tyrant will, if he has a mind, kill him who does not imitate him and take away his goods?

SOCRATES: Excellent Callicles, I am not deaf, and I have heard that a great many times from you and from Polus and from nearly every man in the city, but I wish that you would hear me too. I dare say that he will kill him if he has a mind—the bad man will kill the good and true.

CALLICLES: And is not that just the provoking thing?

SOCRATES: Nay, not to a man of sense, as the argument shows: do you think that all our cares should be directed to prolonging life to the uttermost, and to the study of those arts which secure us from danger always; like that art of rhetoric which saves men in courts of law, and which you advise me to cultivate?

CALLICLES: Yes, truly, and very good advice too.

SOCRATES: Well, my friend, but what do you think of swimming; is that an art of any great pretensions?

CALLICLES: No, indeed.

SOCRATES: And yet surely swimming saves a man from death, and there are occasions on which he must know how to swim. And if you despise the swimmers, I will tell you of another and greater art, the art of the pilot, who not only saves the souls of men, but also their bodies and properties from the extremity of danger, just like rhetoric. Yet his art is modest and unpresuming: it has no airs or pretences of doing anything extraordinary, and, in return for the same salvation which is given by the pleader, demands only two obols, if he brings us from Aegina to Athens, or for the longer voyage from Pontus or Egypt, at the utmost two drachmae, when he has saved, as I was just now saying, the passenger and his wife and children and goods, and safely disembarked them at the Piraeus,—this is the payment which he asks in return for so great a boon; and he who is the master of the art, and has done all this, gets out and walks about on the sea-shore by his ship in an unassuming way. For he is able to reflect and is aware that he cannot tell which of his fellow-passengers he has benefited, and which of them he has injured in not allowing them to be drowned. He knows that they are just the same when he has disembarked them as when they embarked, and not a whit better either in their bodies or in their souls; and he considers that if a man who is afflicted by great and incurable bodily diseases is only to be pitied for having escaped, and is in no way benefited by him in having been saved from drowning, much less he who has great and incurable diseases, not of the body, but of the soul, which is the more valuable part of him; neither is life worth having nor of any profit to the bad man, whether he be delivered from the sea, or the law-courts, or any other devourer;—and so he reflects that such a one had better not live, for he cannot live well. (Compare *Republic*.)

And this is the reason why the pilot, although he is our saviour, is not usually conceited, any more than the engineer, who is not at all behind either the general, or the pilot, or any one else, in his saving power, for he sometimes saves whole cities. Is there any comparison between him and the pleader? And if he were to talk, Callicles, in your grandiose style, he would bury you under a mountain of words, declaring and insisting that we ought all of us to be engine-makers, and that no other profession is worth thinking about; he would have plenty to say. Nevertheless you despise him and his art, and sneeringly call him an engine-maker, and you will not allow your daughters to marry his son, or marry your son to his daughters. And yet, on your principle, what justice or reason is there in your refusal? What right have you to despise the engine-maker, and the others whom I was just now mentioning? I know that you will say, 'I am better, and better born.' But if the better is not what I say, and virtue consists only in a man saving himself and his, whatever may be his character, then your censure of the engine-maker, and of the physician, and of the other arts of salvation, is ridiculous. O my friend! I want you to see that the noble and the good may possibly be something different from saving and being saved:—May not he who is truly a man cease to care about living a certain time?—he knows, as women say, that no man can escape fate, and therefore he is not fond of life; he leaves all that with God, and considers in what way he can best spend his appointed term;—whether by assimilating himself to the constitution under which he lives, as you at this moment have to consider how you may become as like as possible to the Athenian people, if you mean to be in their good graces, and to have power in the state; whereas I want you to think and see whether this is for the interest of either of us;—I would not have us risk that which is dearest on the acquisition of this power, like the Thessalian enchantresses, who, as they say, bring down the moon from heaven at the risk of their own perdition. But if you suppose that any man will show you the art of becoming great in the city, and yet not conforming yourself to the ways of the city, whether for better or worse, then I can only say that you are mistaken, Callides; for he who would deserve to be the true natural friend of the Athenian Demus, aye, or of Pyrilampes' darling who is called after them, must be by nature like them, and not an imitator only. He, then, who will make you most like them, will make you as you desire, a statesman and orator: for every man is pleased when he is spoken to in his own language and spirit, and dislikes any other. But perhaps you, sweet Callicles, may be of another mind. What do you say?

CALLICLES: Somehow or other your words, Socrates, always appear to me to be good words; and yet, like the rest of the world, I am not quite convinced by them. (Compare *Symp.*: 1 *Alcib.*)

SOCRATES: The reason is, Callicles, that the love of Demus which abides in your soul is an adversary to me; but I dare say that if we recur to these same matters, and consider them more thoroughly, you may be convinced for all that. Please, then, to remember that there are two processes of training all things, including body and soul; in the one, as we said, we treat them with a view to pleasure, and in the other with a view to the highest good, and then we do not indulge but resist them: was not that the distinction which we drew?

CALLICLES: Very true.

SOCRATES: And the one which had pleasure in view was just a vulgar flattery:—was not that another of our conclusions?

CALLICLES: Be it so, if you will have it.

SOCRATES: And the other had in view the greatest improvement of that which was ministered to, whether body or soul?

CALLICLES: Quite true.

SOCRATES: And must we not have the same end in view in the treatment of our city and citizens? Must we not try and make them as good as possible? For we have already discovered that there is no use in imparting to them any other good, unless the mind of those who are to have the good, whether money, or office, or any other sort of power, be gentle and good. Shall we say that?

CALLICLES: Yes, certainly, if you like.

SOCRATES: Well, then, if you and I, Callicles, were intending[5] to set about some public business, and were advising one another to undertake buildings, such as walls, docks or temples of the largest size, ought we not to examine ourselves, first, as to whether we know or do not

---

[5]Reading with the majority of MSS. πράξοντες.

know the art of building, and who taught us?—would not that be necessary, Callicles?

CALLICLES: True.

SOCRATES: In the second place, we should have to consider whether we had ever constructed any private house, either of our own or for our friends, and whether this building of ours was a success or not; and if upon consideration we found that we had had good and eminent masters, and had been successful in constructing many fine buildings, not only with their assistance, but without them, by our own unaided skill—in that case prudence would not dissuade us from proceeding to the construction of public works. But if we had no master to show, and only a number of worthless buildings or none at all, then, surely, it would be ridiculous in us to attempt public works, or to advise one another to undertake them. Is not this true?

CALLICLES: Certainly.

SOCRATES: And does not the same hold in all other cases? If you and I were physicians, and were advising one another that we were competent to practise as state-physicians, should I not ask about you, and would you not ask about me, Well, but how about Socrates himself, has he good health? and was any one else ever known to be cured by him, whether slave or freeman? And I should make the same enquiries about you. And if we arrived at the conclusion that no one, whether citizen or stranger, man or woman, had ever been any the better for the medical skill of either of us, then, by Heaven, Callicles, what an absurdity to think that we or any human being should be so silly as to set up as state-physicians and advise others like ourselves to do the same, without having first practised in private, whether successfully or not, and acquired experience of the art! Is not this, as they say, to begin with the big jar when you are learning the potter's art; which is a foolish thing?

CALLICLES: True.

SOCRATES: And now, my friend, as you are already beginning to be a public character, and are admonishing and reproaching me for not being one, suppose that we ask a few questions of one another. Tell me, then, Callicles, how about making any of the citizens better? Was there ever a man who was once vicious, or unjust, or intemperate, or foolish, and became by the help of Callicles good and noble? Was there ever such a man, whether citizen or stranger, slave or freeman? Tell me, Callicles, if a person were to ask these questions of you, what would you answer? Whom would you say that you had improved by your conversation? There may have been good deeds of this sort which were done by you as a private person, before you came forward in public. Why will you not answer?

CALLICLES: You are contentious, Socrates.

SOCRATES: Nay, I ask you, not from a love of contention, but because I really want to know in what way you think that affairs should be administered among us—whether, when you come to the administration of them, you have any other aim but the improvement of the citizens? Have we not already admitted many times over that such is the duty of a public man? Nay, we have surely said so; for if you will not answer for yourself I must answer for you. But if this is what the good man ought to effect for the benefit of his own state, allow me to recall to you the names of those whom you were just now mentioning, Pericles, and Cimon, and Miltiades, and Themistocles, and ask whether you still think that they were good citizens.

CALLICLES: I do.

SOCRATES: But if they were good, then clearly each of them must have made the citizens better instead of worse?

CALLICLES: Yes.

SOCRATES: And, therefore, when Pericles first began to speak in the assembly, the Athenians were not so good as when he spoke last?

CALLICLES: Very likely.

SOCRATES: Nay, my friend, 'likely' is not the word; for if he was a good citizen, the inference is certain.

CALLICLES: And what difference does that make?

SOCRATES: None; only I should like further to know whether the Athenians are supposed to have been made better by Pericles, or, on the contrary, to have been corrupted by him; for I hear that he was the first who gave the people pay, and made them idle and cowardly, and encouraged them in the love of talk and money.

CALLICLES: You heard that, Socrates, from the laconising set who bruise their ears.

SOCRATES: But what I am going to tell you now is not mere hearsay, but well known both to you and me: that at first, Pericles was glorious and his character unimpeached by any verdict of the Athenians—this was during the time when they were not so good—yet afterwards, when they had been made good and gentle by him, at the very end of his life they convicted him of theft, and almost put him to death, clearly under the notion that he was a malefactor.

CALLICLES: Well, but how does that prove Pericles' badness?

SOCRATES: Why, surely you would say that he was a bad manager of asses or horses or oxen, who had received them originally neither kicking nor butting nor biting him, and implanted in them all these savage tricks? Would he not be a bad manager of any animals who received them gentle, and made them fiercer than they were when he received them? What do you say?

CALLICLES: I will do you the favour of saying 'yes.'

SOCRATES: And will you also do me the favour of saying whether man is an animal?

CALLICLES: Certainly he is.

SOCRATES: And was not Pericles a shepherd of men?

CALLICLES: Yes.

SOCRATES: And if he was a good political shepherd, ought not the animals who were his subjects, as we were just now acknowledging, to have become more just, and not more unjust?

CALLICLES: Quite true.

SOCRATES: And are not just men gentle, as Homer says?—or are you of another mind?

CALLICLES: I agree.

SOCRATES: And yet he really did make them more savage than he received them, and their savageness was shown towards himself; which he must have been very far from desiring.

CALLICLES: Do you want me to agree with you?

SOCRATES: Yes, if I seem to you to speak the truth.

CALLICLES: Granted then.

SOCRATES: And if they were more savage, must they not have been more unjust and inferior?

CALLICLES: Granted again.

SOCRATES: Then upon this view, Pericles was not a good statesman?

CALLICLES: That is, upon your view.

SOCRATES: Nay, the view is yours, after what you have admitted. Take the case of Cimon again. Did not the very persons whom he was serving ostracize him, in order that they might not hear his voice for ten years? and they did just the same to Themistocles, adding the penalty of exile; and they voted that Miltiades, the hero of Marathon, should be thrown into the pit of death, and he was only saved by the Prytanis. And yet, if they had been really good men, as you say, these things would never have happened to them. For the good charioteers are not those who at first keep their place, and then, when they have broken-in their horses, and themselves become better charioteers, are thrown out—that is not the way either in charioteering or in any profession.—What do you think?

CALLICLES: I should think not.

SOCRATES: Well, but if so, the truth is as I have said already, that in the Athenian State no one has ever shown himself to be a good statesman—you admitted that this was true of our present statesmen, but not true of former ones, and you preferred them to the others; yet they have turned out to be no better than our present ones; and therefore, if they were rhetoricians, they did not use the true art of rhetoric or of flattery, or they would not have fallen out of favour.

CALLICLES: But surely, Socrates, no living man ever came near any one of them in his performances.

SOCRATES: O, my dear friend, I say nothing against them regarded as the serving-men of the State; and I do think that they were certainly more serviceable than those who are living now, and better able to gratify the wishes of the State; but as to transforming those desires and not allowing them to have their way, and using the powers which they had, whether of persuasion or of force, in the improvement of their fellow citizens, which is the prime object of the truly good citizen, I do not see that in these respects they were a whit superior to our present statesmen, although I do admit that they were more clever at providing ships and walls and docks, and all that. You and I have a ridiculous way, for during the whole time that we are arguing, we are always going round and round to the same point, and constantly misunderstanding one another. If I am not mistaken, you have admitted and acknowledged more than once, that there are two kinds of operations which have to do with the body, and two which have to do with the soul: one of the two is ministerial, and if our bodies are hungry provides food for them, and if they are thirsty gives them drink, or if they are cold supplies them with garments, blankets, shoes, and all that they crave. I use the same images as before intentionally, in order that you may understand me the better. The purveyor of the articles may provide them either wholesale or retail, or he may be the maker of any of them,—the baker, or the cook, or the weaver, or the shoemaker, or the currier; and in so doing, being such as he is, he is naturally supposed by himself and every one to minister to the body. For none of them know that there is another art—an art of gymnastic and medicine which is the true minister of the body, and ought to be the mistress of all the rest, and to use their results according to the knowledge which she has and they have not, of the real good or bad effects of meats and drinks on the body. All other arts which have to do with the body are servile and menial and illiberal; and gymnastic and medicine are, as they ought to be, their mistresses. Now, when I say that all this is equally true of the soul, you seem at first to know and understand and assent to my words, and then a little while afterwards you come repeating, Has not the State had good and noble citizens? and when I ask you who they are, you reply, seemingly quite in earnest, as if I had asked, Who are or have been good trainers?—and you had replied, Thearion, the baker, Mithoecus, who wrote the Sicilian cookery-book, Sarambus, the vintner: these are ministers of the body, first-rate in their art; for the first makes admirable loaves, the second excellent dishes, and the third capital wine;—to me these appear to be the exact parallel of the statesmen whom you mention. Now you would not be altogether pleased if I said to you, My friend, you know nothing of gymnastics; those of whom you are speaking to me are only the ministers and purveyors of luxury, who have no good or noble notions of their art, and may very likely be filling and fattening men's bodies and gaining their approval, although the result is that they lose their original flesh in the long run, and become thinner than they were before; and yet they, in their simplicity, will not attribute their diseases and loss of flesh to their entertainers; but when in after years the unhealthy surfeit brings the attendant penalty of disease, he who happens to be near them at the time, and offers them advice, is accused and blamed by them, and if they could they would do him some harm; while they proceed to eulogize the men who have been the real authors of the mischief. And that, Callicles, is just what you are now doing. You praise the men who feasted the citizens and satisfied their desires, and people say that they have made the city great, not seeing that the swollen and ulcerated condition of the State is to be attributed to these elder statesmen; for they have filled the city full of harbours and docks and walls and revenues and all that, and have left no room for justice and temperance. And when the crisis of the disorder comes, the people will blame the advisers of the hour, and applaud Themistocles and Cimon and Pericles, who are the real authors of their calamities; and if you are not careful they may assail you and my friend Alcibiades, when they are losing not only their new acquisitions, but also their original possessions; not that you are the authors of these misfortunes of theirs, although you may perhaps be accessories to them. A great piece of work is always being made, as I see and am told, now as of old, about our statesmen. When the State treats any of them as malefactors, I observe that there is a great uproar and indignation at the supposed wrong which is done to them; 'after all their many services to the State, that they should unjustly perish,'—so the tale runs. But the cry is all a lie; for no statesman ever could be unjustly put to death by the city of which he is the head. The case of the professed statesman is, I believe, very much like that of the professed sophist; for the sophists, although they are wise men, are nevertheless guilty of a strange piece of folly; professing to be teachers of virtue, they will often accuse their disciples of wronging them, and defrauding them of their pay, and showing no gratitude for their services. Yet what can be more absurd than that men who have become just and good, and whose injustice has been taken away from them, and who have had justice implanted in them by their teachers, should act unjustly by reason of the injustice which is not in them? Can anything be more irrational, my friends, than this? You, Callicles, compel me to be a mob-orator, because you will not answer.

CALLICLES: And you are the man who cannot speak unless there is some one to answer?

SOCRATES: I suppose that I can; just now, at any rate, the speeches which I am making are long enough because you refuse to answer me. But I adjure you by the god of friendship, my good sir, do tell me whether there does not appear to you to be a great inconsistency in saying that you have made a man good, and then blaming him for being bad?

CALLICLES: Yes, it appears so to me.

SOCRATES: Do you never hear our professors of education speaking in this inconsistent manner?

CALLICLES: Yes, but why talk of men who are good for nothing?

SOCRATES: I would rather say, why talk of men who profess to be rulers, and declare that they are devoted to the improvement of the city, and nevertheless upon occasion declaim against the utter vileness of the city:—do you think that there is any difference between one and the other? My good friend, the sophist and the rhetorician, as I was saying to Polus, are the same, or nearly the same; but you ignorantly fancy that rhetoric is a perfect thing, and sophistry a thing to be despised; whereas the truth is, that sophistry is as much superior to rhetoric as legislation is to the practice of law, or gymnastic to medicine. The orators and sophists, as I am inclined to think, are the only class who cannot complain of the mischief ensuing to themselves from that which they teach others, without in the same breath accusing themselves of having done no good to those whom they profess to benefit. Is not this a fact?

CALLICLES: Certainly it is.

SOCRATES: If they were right in saying that they make men better, then they are the only class who can afford to leave their remuneration to those who have been benefited by them. Whereas if a man has been benefited in any other way, if, for example, he has been taught to run by a trainer, he might possibly defraud him of his pay, if the trainer left the matter to him, and made no agreement with him that he should receive money as soon as he had given him the utmost speed; for not because of any deficiency of speed do men act unjustly, but by reason of injustice.

CALLICLES: Very true.

SOCRATES: And he who removes injustice can be in no danger of being treated unjustly: he alone can safely leave the honorarium to his pupils, if he be really able to make them good—am I not right? (Compare *Protag.*)

CALLICLES: Yes.

SOCRATES: Then we have found the reason why there is no dishonour in a man receiving pay who is called in to advise about building or any other art?

CALLICLES: Yes, we have found the reason.

SOCRATES: But when the point is, how a man may become best himself, and best govern his family and state, then to say that you will give no advice gratis is held to be dishonourable?

CALLICLES: True.

SOCRATES: And why? Because only such benefits call forth a desire to requite them, and there is evidence that a benefit has been conferred when the benefactor receives a return; otherwise not. Is this true?

CALLICLES: It is.

SOCRATES: Then to which service of the State do you invite me? determine for me. Am I to be the physician of the State who will strive and struggle to make the Athenians as good as possible; or am I to be the servant and flatterer of the State? Speak out, my good friend, freely and fairly as you did at first and ought to do again, and tell me your entire mind.

CALLICLES: I say then that you should be the servant of the State.

SOCRATES: The flatterer? well, sir, that is a noble invitation.

CALLICLES: The Mysian, Socrates, or what you please. For if you refuse, the consequences will be—

SOCRATES: Do not repeat the old story—that he who likes will kill me and get my money; for then I shall have to repeat the old answer, that he will be a bad man and will kill the good, and that the money will be of no use to him, but that he will wrongly use that which he wrongly took, and if wrongly, basely, and if basely, hurtfully.

CALLICLES: How confident you are, Socrates, that you will never come to harm! you seem to think that you are living in another country, and can never be brought into a court of justice, as you very likely may be brought by some miserable and mean person.

SOCRATES: Then I must indeed be a fool, Callicles, if I do not know that in the Athenian State any man may suffer anything. And if I am brought to trial and incur the dangers of which you speak, he will be a villain who brings me to trial—of that I am very sure, for no good man would accuse the innocent. Nor shall I be surprised if I am put to death. Shall I tell you why I anticipate this?

CALLICLES: By all means.

SOCRATES: I think that I am the only or almost the only Athenian living who practises the true art of politics; I am the only politician of my time. Now, seeing that when I speak my words are not uttered with any view of gaining favour, and that I look to what is best and not to what is most pleasant, having no mind to use those arts and graces which you recommend, I shall have nothing to say in the justice court. And you might argue with me, as I was arguing with Polus:—I shall be tried just as a physician would be tried in a court of little boys at the indictment of the cook. What would he reply under such circumstances, if some one were to accuse him, saying, 'O my boys, many evil things has this man done to you: he is the death of you, especially of the younger ones among you, cutting and burning and starving and suffocating you, until you know not what to do; he gives you the bitterest potions, and compels you to hunger and thirst. How unlike the variety of meats and sweets on which I feasted you!' What do you suppose that the physician would be able to reply when he found himself in such a predicament? If he told the truth he could only say, 'All these evil things, my boys, I did for your health,' and then would there not just be a clamour among a jury like that? How they would cry out!

CALLICLES: I dare say.

SOCRATES: Would he not be utterly at a loss for a reply?

CALLICLES: He certainly would.

SOCRATES: And I too shall be treated in the same way, as I well know, if I am brought before the court. For I shall not be able to rehearse to the people the pleasures which I have procured for them, and which, although I am not disposed to envy either the procurers or enjoyers of them, are deemed by them to be benefits and advantages. And if any one says that I corrupt young men, and perplex their minds, or that I speak evil of old men, and use bitter words towards them, whether in private or public, it is useless for me to reply, as I truly might: — 'All this I do for the sake of justice, and with a view to your interest, my judges, and to nothing else.' And therefore there is no saying what may happen to me.

CALLICLES: And do you think, Socrates, that a man who is thus defenceless is in a good position?

SOCRATES: Yes, Callicles, if he have that defence, which as you have often acknowledged he should have—if he be his own defence, and have never said or done anything wrong, either in respect of gods or men; and this has been repeatedly acknowledged by us to be the best sort of defence. And if any one could convict me of inability to defend myself or others after this sort, I should blush for shame, whether I was convicted before many, or before a few, or by myself alone; and if I died from want of ability to do so, that would indeed grieve me. But if I died because I have no powers of flattery or rhetoric, I am very sure that you would not find me repining at death. For no man who is not an utter fool and coward is afraid of death itself, but he is afraid of doing wrong. For to go to the world below having one's soul full of injustice is the last and worst of all evils. And in proof of what I say, if you have no objection, I should like to tell you a story.

CALLICLES: Very well, proceed; and then we shall have done.

SOCRATES: Listen, then, as story-tellers say, to a very pretty tale, which

I dare say that you may be disposed to regard as a fable only, but which, as I believe, is a true tale, for I mean to speak the truth. Homer tells us (*Il.*), how Zeus and Poseidon and Pluto divided the empire which they inherited from their father. Now in the days of Cronos there existed a law respecting the destiny of man, which has always been, and still continues to be in Heaven,—that he who has lived all his life in justice and holiness shall go, when he is dead, to the Islands of the Blessed, and dwell there in perfect happiness out of the reach of evil; but that he who has lived unjustly and impiously shall go to the house of vengeance and punishment, which is called Tartarus. And in the time of Cronos, and even quite lately in the reign of Zeus, the judgment was given on the very day on which the men were to die; the judges were alive, and the men were alive; and the consequence was that the judgments were not well given. Then Pluto and the authorities from the Islands of the Blessed came to Zeus, and said that the souls found their way to the wrong places. Zeus said: 'I shall put a stop to this; the judgments are not well given, because the persons who are judged have their clothes on, for they are alive; and there are many who, having evil souls, are apparelled in fair bodies, or encased in wealth or rank, and, when the day of judgment arrives, numerous witnesses come forward and testify on their behalf that they have lived righteously. The judges are awed by them, and they themselves too have their clothes on when judging; their eyes and ears and their whole bodies are interposed as a veil before their own souls. All this is a hindrance to them; there are the clothes of the judges and the clothes of the judged.—What is to be done? I will tell you:—In the first place, I will deprive men of the foreknowledge of death, which they possess at present: this power which they have Prometheus has already received my orders to take from them: in the second place, they shall be entirely stripped before they are judged, for they shall be judged when they are dead; and the judge too shall be naked, that is to say, dead—he with his naked soul shall pierce into the other naked souls; and they shall die suddenly and be deprived of all their kindred, and leave their brave attire strewn upon the earth—conducted in this manner, the judgment will be just. I knew all about the matter before any of you, and therefore I have made my sons judges; two from Asia, Minos and Rhadamanthus, and one from Europe, Aeacus. And these, when they are dead, shall give judgment in the meadow at the parting of the ways, whence the two roads lead, one to the Islands of the Blessed, and the other to Tartarus. Rhadamanthus shall judge those who come from Asia, and Aeacus those who come from Europe. And to Minos I shall give the primacy, and he shall hold a court of appeal, in case either of the two others are in any doubt:—then the judgment respecting the last journey of men will be as just as possible.'

From this tale, Callicles, which I have heard and believe, I draw the following inferences: — Death, if I am right, is in the first place the separation from one another of two things, soul and body; nothing else. And after they are separated they retain their several natures, as in life; the body keeps the same habit, and the results of treatment or accident are distinctly visible in it: for example, he who by nature or training or both, was a tall man while he was alive, will remain as he was, after he is dead; and the fat man will remain fat; and so on; and the dead man, who in life had a fancy to have flowing hair, will have flowing hair. And if he was marked with the whip and had the prints of the scourge, or of wounds in him when he was alive, you might see the same in the dead body; and if his limbs were broken or misshapen when he was alive, the same appearance would be visible in the dead. And in a word, whatever was the habit of the body during life would be distinguishable after death, either perfectly, or in a great measure and for a certain time. And I should imagine that this is equally true of the soul, Callicles; when a man is stripped of the body, all the natural or acquired affections of the soul are laid open to view. — And when they come to the judge, as those from Asia come to Rhadamanthus, he places them near him and inspects them quite impartially, not knowing whose the soul is: perhaps he may lay hands on the soul of the great king, or of some other king or potentate, who has no soundness in him, but his soul is marked with the whip, and is full of the prints and scars of perjuries and crimes with which each action has stained him, and he is all crooked with falsehood and imposture, and has no straightness, because he has lived without truth. Him Rhadamanthus beholds, full of all deformity and disproportion, which is caused by licence and luxury and insolence and incontinence, and despatches him ignominiously to his prison, and there he undergoes the punishment which he deserves.

Now the proper office of punishment is twofold: he who is rightly punished ought either to become better and profit by it, or he ought to be made an example to his fellows, that they may see what he suffers, and fear and become better. Those who are improved when they are punished by gods and men, are those whose sins are curable; and they are improved, as in this world so also in another, by pain and suffering; for there is no other way in which they can be delivered from their evil. But they who have been guilty of the worst crimes, and are incurable by reason of their crimes, are made examples; for, as they are incurable, the time has passed at which they can receive any benefit. They get no good themselves, but others get good when they behold them enduring for ever the most terrible and painful and fearful sufferings as the penalty of their sins — there they are, hanging up as examples, in the prison-house of the world below, a spectacle and a warning to all unrighteous men who come thither. And among them, as I confidently affirm, will be found Archelaus, if Polus truly reports of him, and any other tyrant who is like him. Of these fearful examples, most, as I believe, are taken from the class of tyrants and kings and potentates and public men, for they are the authors of the greatest and most impious crimes, because they have the power. And Homer witnesses to the truth of this; for they are always kings and potentates whom he has described as suffering everlasting punishment in the world below: such were Tantalus and Sisyphus and Tityus. But no one ever described Thersites, or any private person who was a villain, as suffering everlasting punishment, or as incurable. For to commit the worst crimes, as I am inclined to think, was not in his power, and he was happier than those who had the power. No, Callicles, the very bad men come from the class of those who have power (compare *Republic*). And yet in that very class there may arise good men, and worthy of all admiration they are, for where there is great power to do wrong, to live and to die justly is a hard thing, and greatly to be praised, and few there are who attain to this. Such good and true men, however, there have been, and will be again, at Athens and in other states, who have fulfilled their trust righteously; and there is one who is quite famous all over Hellas, Aristeides, the son of Lysimachus. But, in general, great men are also bad, my friend.

As I was saying, Rhadamanthus, when he gets a soul of the bad kind, knows nothing about him, neither who he is, nor who his parents are; he knows only that he has got hold of a villain; and seeing this, he stamps him as curable or incurable, and sends him away to Tartarus, whither he goes and receives his proper recompense. Or, again, he looks with admiration on the soul of some just one who has lived in holiness and truth; he may have been a private man or not; and I should say, Callicles, that he is most likely to have been a philosopher who has done his own work, and not troubled himself with the doings of other men in his lifetime; him Rhadamanthus sends to the Islands of the Blessed. Aeacus does the same; and they both have sceptres, and judge; but Minos alone has a golden sceptre and is seated looking on, as Odysseus in Homer (*Odyss.*) declares that he saw him:

'Holding a sceptre of gold, and giving laws to the dead.'

Now I, Callicles, am persuaded of the truth of these things, and I consider how I shall present my soul whole and undefiled before the judge in that day. Renouncing the honours at which the world aims, I desire only to know the truth, and to live as well as I can, and, when I die, to die as well as I can. And, to the utmost of my power, I exhort all other men to do the same. And, in return for your exhortation of me, I exhort you also to take part in the great combat, which is the combat of life, and greater than every other earthly conflict. And I retort your reproach of me, and say, that you will not be able to help yourself when the day of trial and judgment, of which I was speaking, comes upon you; you will go before the judge, the son of Aegina, and, when he has got you in his grip and is carrying you off, you will gape and your head will swim round, just as mine would in the courts of this world, and very likely some one will shamefully box you on the ears, and put upon you any sort of insult.

Perhaps this may appear to you to be only an old wife's tale, which you will contemn. And there might be reason in your contemning such tales, if by searching we could find out anything better or truer: but now you see that you and Polus and Gorgias, who are the three wisest of the Greeks of our day, are not able to show that we ought to live any life which does not profit in another world as well as in this. And of all that has been said, nothing remains unshaken but the saying, that to do injustice is more to be avoided than to suffer injustice, and that the reality and not the appearance of virtue is to be followed above all things, as well in public as in private life; and that when any one has been wrong in anything, he is to be chastised, and that the next best thing to a man being just is that he should become just, and be chastised and punished; also that he should avoid all flattery of himself as well as of others, of the few or of the many: and rhetoric and any other art should be used by him, and all his actions should be done always, with a view to justice.

Follow me then, and I will lead you where you will be happy in life and after death, as the argument shows. And never mind if some one despises you as a fool, and insults you, if he has a mind; let him strike you, by Zeus, and do you be of good cheer, and do not mind the insulting blow, for you will never come to any harm in the practice of virtue, if you are a really good and true man. When we have practised virtue together, we will apply ourselves to politics, if that seems desirable, or we will advise about whatever else may seem good to us, for we shall be better able to judge then. In our present condition we ought not to give ourselves airs, for even on the most important subjects we are always changing our minds; so utterly stupid are we! Let us, then, take the argument as our guide, which has revealed to us that the best way of life is to practise justice and every virtue in life and death. This way let us go; and in this exhort all men to follow, not in the way to which you trust and in which you exhort me to follow you; for that way, Callicles, is nothing worth.

TIMAEUS

INTRODUCTION AND ANALYSIS

Of all the writings of Plato the *Timaeus* is the most obscure and repulsive to the modern reader, and has nevertheless had the greatest influence over the ancient and mediaeval world. The obscurity arises in the infancy of physical science, out of the confusion of theological, mathematical, and physiological notions, out of the desire to conceive the whole of nature without any adequate knowledge of the parts, and from a greater perception of similarities which lie on the surface than of differences which are hidden from view. To bring sense under the control of reason; to find some way through the mist or labyrinth of appearances, either the highway of mathematics, or more devious paths suggested by the analogy of man with the world, and of the world with man; to see that all things have a cause and are tending towards an end—this is the spirit of the ancient physical philosopher. He has no notion of trying an experiment and is hardly capable of observing the curiosities of nature which are 'tumbling out at his feet,' or of interpreting even the most obvious of them. He is driven back from the nearer to the more distant, from particulars to generalities, from the earth to the stars. He lifts up his eyes to the heavens and seeks to guide by their motions his erring footsteps. But we neither appreciate the conditions of knowledge to which he was subjected, nor have the ideas which fastened upon his imagination the same hold upon us. For he is hanging between matter and mind; he is under the dominion at the same time both of sense and of abstractions; his impressions are taken almost at random from the outside of nature; he sees the light, but not the objects which are revealed by the light; and he brings into juxtaposition things which to us appear wide as the poles asunder, because he finds nothing between them. He passes abruptly from persons to ideas and numbers, and from ideas and numbers to persons,—from the heavens to man, from astronomy to physiology; he confuses, or rather does not distinguish, subject and object, first and final causes, and is dreaming of geometrical figures lost in a flux of sense. He contrasts the perfect movements of the heavenly bodies with the imperfect representation of them (*Rep.* vii. 519), and he does not always require strict accuracy even in applications of number and figure (*Rep.* ix. 587D, E). His mind lingers around the forms of mythology, which he uses as symbols or translates into figures of speech. He has no implements of observation, such as the telescope or microscope; the great science of chemistry is a blank to him. It is only by an effort that the modern thinker can breathe the atmosphere of the ancient philosopher, or understand how, under such unequal conditions, he seems in many instances, by a sort of inspiration, to have anticipated the truth.

The influence which the *Timaeus* has exercised upon posterity is due partly to a misunderstanding. In the supposed depths of this dialogue the Neo-Platonists found hidden meanings and connections with the Jewish and Christian Scriptures, and out of them they elicited doctrines quite at variance with the spirit of Plato. Believing that he was inspired by the Holy Ghost, or had received his wisdom from Moses, they seemed to find in his writings the Christian Trinity, the Word, the Church, the creation of the world in a Jewish sense, as they really found the personality of God or of mind, and the immortality of the soul. All religions and philosophies met and mingled in the schools of Alexandria, and the Neo-Platonists had a method of interpretation which could elicit any meaning out of any words. They were really incapable of distinguishing between the opinions of one philosopher and another—between Aristotle and Plato, or between the serious thoughts of Plato and his passing fancies. They were absorbed in his theology and were under the dominion of his name, while that which was truly great and truly characteristic in him, his effort to realize and connect abstractions, was not understood by them at all. Yet the genius of Plato and Greek philosophy reacted upon the East, and a Greek element of thought and language overlaid and partly reduced to order the chaos of Orientalism. And kindred spirits, like St. Augustine, even though they were acquainted with his writings only through the medium of a Latin translation, were profoundly affected by them, seeming to find 'God and his word everywhere insinuated' in them (*August. Confess.* viii. c. 2).

There is no danger of the modern commentators on the *Timaeus* falling into the absurdities of the Neo-Platonists. In the present day we are well aware that an ancient philosopher is to be interpreted from himself and by the contemporary history of thought. We know that mysticism is not criticism. The fancies of the Neo-Platonists are only interesting to us because they exhibit a phase of the human mind which prevailed widely in the first centuries of the Christian era, and is not wholly extinct in our own day. But they have nothing to do with the interpretation of Plato, and in spirit they are opposed to him. They are

the feeble expression of an age which has lost the power not only of creating great works, but of understanding them. They are the spurious
birth of a marriage between philosophy and tradition, between Hellas
and the East—(εἰκὸς γεννᾶν νόθα καὶ θαῦλα) (*Rep.* vi. 496A).
Whereas the so-called mysticism of Plato is purely Greek, arising out of
his imperfect knowledge and high aspirations, and is the growth of an
age in which philosophy is not wholly separated from poetry and
mythology.

A greater danger with modern interpreters of Plato is the tendency to
regard the *Timaeus* as the centre of his system. We do not know how
Plato would have arranged his own dialogues, or whether the thought
of arranging any of them, besides the two 'Trilogies' which he has expressly connected, was ever present to his mind. But, if he had arranged
them, there are many indications that this is not the place which he
would have assigned to the *Timaeus*. We observe, first of all, that the dialogue is put into the mouth of a Pythagorean philosopher, and not of
Socrates. And this is required by dramatic propriety; for the investigation of nature was expressly renounced by Socrates in the *Phaedo*
(96ff.). Nor does Plato himself attribute any importance to his guesses
at science. He is not at all absorbed by them, as he is by the *idea* of
good. He is modest and hesitating, and confesses that his words partake
of the uncertainty of the subject (*Tim.* 29C). The dialogue is primarily
concerned with the animal creation, including under this term the
heavenly bodies, and with man only as one among the animals. But we
can hardly suppose that Plato would have preferred the study of nature
to man, or that he would have deemed the formation of the world and
the human frame to have the same interest which he ascribes to the
mystery of being and not-being, or to the great political problems
which he discusses in the *Republic* and the *Laws*. There are no speculations on physics in the other dialogues of Plato, and he himself regards the consideration of them as a rational pastime only (cf. 59D,
G.). He is beginning to feel the need of further divisions of knowledge;
and is becoming aware that besides dialectic, mathematics, and the
arts, there is another field which has been hitherto unexplored by him.
But he has not as yet defined this intermediate territory which lies
somewhere between medicine and mathematics, and he would have
felt that there was as great an impiety in ranking theories of physics first
in the order of knowledge, as in placing the body before the soul.

It is true, however, that the *Timaeus* is by no means confined to speculations on physics. The deeper foundations of the Platonic philosophy, such as the nature of God, the distinction of the sensible and intellectual, the great original conceptions of time and space, also appear
in it. They are found principally in the first half of the dialogue. The

construction of the heavens is for the most part ideal; the cyclic year serves as the connection between the world of absolute being and of generation, just as the number of population in the *Republic* (Book viii. 546) is the expression or symbol of the transition from the ideal to the actual state. In some passages we are uncertain whether we are reading a description of astronomical facts or contemplating processes of the human mind (37C), or of that divine mind (cf. *Phil.* 22D) which in Plato is hardly separable from it. The characteristics of man are transferred to the world-animal, as for example when intelligence and knowledge are said to be perfected by the circle of the Same, and true opinion by the circle of the Other; and conversely the motions of the world-animal reappear in man; its amorphous state continues in the child (44), and in both disorder and chaos are gradually succeeded by stability and order. It is not however to passages like these that Plato is referring when he speaks of the uncertainty of his subject, but rather to the composition of bodies, to the relations of colours, the nature of diseases, and the like, about which he truly feels the lamentable ignorance prevailing in his own age.

We are led by Plato himself to regard the *Timaeus*, not as the centre or inmost shrine of the edifice, but as a detached building in a different style, framed, not after the Socratic, but after some Pythagorean model. As in the Cratylus and Parmenides, we are uncertain whether Plato is expressing his own opinions, or appropriating and perhaps improving the philosophical speculations of others. In all three dialogues he is exerting his dramatic and imitative power; in the Cratylus mingling a satirical and humorous purpose with true principles of language; in the Parmenides overthrowing Megarianism by a sort of ultra-Megarianism, which discovers contradictions in the one as great as those which have been previously shown to exist in the ideas. There is a similar uncertainty about the *Timaeus*; in the first part he scales the heights of transcendentalism, in the latter part he treats in a bald and superficial manner of the functions and diseases of the human frame. He uses the thoughts and almost the words of Parmenides when he discourses of being and of essence, adopting from old religion into philosophy the conception of God, and from the Megarians the *Idea* of good. He agrees with Empedocles and the Atomists in attributing the greater differences of kinds to the figures of the elements and their movements into and out of one another. With Heracleitus, he acknowledges the perpetual flux; like Anaxagoras, he asserts the predominance of mind, although admitting an element of necessity which reason is incapable of subduing; like the Pythagoreans he supposes the mystery of the world to be contained in number. Many, if not all the elements of the Pre-Socratic philosophy are included in the *Timaeus*. It is a composite or eclectic work of imagination, in which Plato, without naming them, gathers up into a kind of system the various elements of philosophy which preceded him.

If we allow for the difference of subject, and for some growth in Plato's own mind, the discrepancy between the *Timaeus* and the other dialogues will not appear to be great. It is probable that the relation of the ideas to God or of God to the world was differently conceived by him at different times of his life. In all his later dialogues we observe a tendency in him to personify mind or God, and he therefore naturally inclines to view creation as the work of design. The creator is like a human artist who frames in his mind a plan which he executes by the help of his servants. Thus the language of philosophy which speaks of first and second causes is crossed by another sort of phraseology: 'God made the world because he was good, and the demons ministered to him.' The *Timaeus* is cast in a more theological and less philosophical mould than the other dialogues, but the same general spirit is apparent; there is the same dualism or opposition between the ideal and actual (51Bff.)—the soul is prior to the body (34C), the intelligible and unseen to the visible and corporeal (28). There is the same distinction between knowledge and opinion (37C) which occurs in the *Theaetetus* and *Republic*, the same enmity to the poets (19D), the same combination of music and gymnastics (88C). The doctrine of transmigration is still held by him (90E ff.), as in the *Phaedrus* and *Republic*; and the soul has a view of the heavens in a prior state of being (41E). The ideas also remain, but they have become types in nature, forms of men, animals, birds, fishes (39E). And the attribution of evil to physical causes (86D, E) accords with the doctrine which he maintains in the *Laws* (Book ix, 861) respecting the involuntariness of vice.

The style and plan of the *Timaeus* differ greatly from that of any other of the Platonic dialogues. The language is weighty, abrupt, and in some passages sublime. But Plato has not the same mastery over his instrument which he exhibits in the *Phaedrus* or *Symposium*. Nothing can exceed the beauty or art of the introduction, in which he is using words after his accustomed manner. But in the rest of the work the power of language seems to fail him, and the dramatic form is wholly given up. He could write in one style, but not in another, and the Greek language had not as yet been fashioned by any poet or philosopher to describe physical phenomena. The early physiologists had generally written in verse; the prose writers, like Democritus and Anaxagoras, as far as we can judge from their fragments, never attained to a periodic style. And hence we find the same sort of clumsiness in the *Timaeus* of Plato which characterizes the philosophical poem of Lucretius. There is a want of flow and often a defect of rhythm; the meaning is sometimes obscure, and there is a greater use of apposition and more of repetition than occurs in Plato's earlier writings. The sentences are less closely connected and also more involved; the antecedents of demonstrative and relative pronouns are in some cases remote and perplexing. The greater frequency of participles and of absolute constructions gives the effect of heaviness. The descriptive portion of the *Timaeus* retains traces of the first Greek prose composition; for the great master of language was speaking on a theme with which he was imperfectly acquainted, and had no words in which to express his meaning. The rugged grandeur of the opening discourse of *Timaeus* (*Tim.* 28–31) may be compared with the more harmonious beauty of a similar passage in the *Phaedrus* (245).

To the same cause we may attribute the want of plan. Plato had not the command of his materials which would have enabled him to produce a perfect work of art. Hence there are several new beginnings and resumptions and formal or artificial connexions; we miss the 'callida junctura' of the earlier dialogues. His speculations about the Eternal, his theories of creation, his mathematical anticipations, are supplemented by desultory remarks on the one immortal and the two mortal souls of man, on the functions of the bodily organs in health and disease, on sight, hearing, smell, taste, and touch. He soars into the heavens, and then, as if his wings were suddenly clipped, he walks ungracefully and with difficulty upon the earth. The greatest things in the world, and the least things in man, are brought within the compass of a short treatise. But the intermediate links are missing, and we cannot be surprised that there should be a want of unity in a work which embraces astronomy, theology, physiology, and natural philosophy in a few pages.

It is not easy to determine how Plato's cosmos may be presented to the reader in a clearer and shorter form; or how we may supply a thread of connexion to his ideas without giving greater consistency to them than they possessed in his mind, or adding on consequences which would never have occurred to him. For he has glimpses of the truth, but no comprehensive or perfect vision. There are isolated expressions about the nature of God which have a wonderful depth and power (29E ff.; 37 ff.); but we are not justified in assuming that these had any greater significance to the mind of Plato than language of a neutral and impersonal character. . . . With a view to the illustration of the *Timaeus* I propose to divide this Introduction into sections, of which the first will contain an outline of the dialogue: (2) I shall consider the aspects of nature which presented themselves to Plato and his age, and the elements of philosophy which entered into the conception of them: (3) the theology and physics of the *Timaeus*, including the soul of the world, the conception of time and space, and the composition of the elements: (4) in the fourth section I shall consider the Platonic astronomy, and the position of the earth. There will remain, (5) the psychology, (6) the physiology of Plato, and (7) his analysis of the senses to be briefly commented upon: (8) lastly, we may examine in what points Plato approaches or anticipates the discoveries of modern science.

Section 1.

Socrates begins the *Timaeus* with a summary of the *Republic*. He lightly touches upon a few points,—the division of labour and distribution of the citizens into classes, the double nature and training of the guardians, the community of property and of women and children. But he makes no mention of the second education, or of the government of philosophers.

And now he desires to see the ideal State set in motion; he would like to know how she behaved in some great struggle. But he is unable to invent such a narrative himself; and he is afraid that the poets are equally incapable; for, although he pretends to have nothing to say against them, he remarks that they are a tribe of imitators, who can only describe what they have seen. And he fears that the Sophists, who are plentifully supplied with graces of speech, in their erratic way of life having never had a city or house of their own, may through want of experience err in their conception of philosophers and statesmen. 'And therefore to you I turn, Timaeus, citizen of Locris, who are at once a philosopher and a statesman, and to you, Critias, whom all Athenians know to be similarly accomplished, and to Hermocrates, who is also fitted by nature and education to share in our discourse.' Hermocrates: 'We will do our best, and have been already preparing; for on our way home, Critias told us of an ancient tradition, which I wish, Critias, that you would repeat to Socrates.' 'I will, if Timaeus approves.' 'I approve.' Listen then, Socrates, to a tale of Solon's, who, being the friend of Dropidas my great-grandfather, told it to my grandfather Critias, and he told me. The narrative related to ancient famous actions of the Athenian people, and to one especially, which I will rehearse in honour of you and of the goddess. Critias when he told this tale of the olden time, was ninety years old, I being not more than ten. The occasion of the rehearsal was the day of the Apaturia called the Registration of Youth, at which our parents gave prizes for recitation. Some poems of Solon were recited by the boys. They had not at that time gone out of fashion, and the recital of them led some one to say, perhaps in compliment to Critias, that Solon was not only the wisest of men but also the best of poets. The old man brightened up at hearing this, and said: Had Solon only had the leisure which was required to complete the famous legend which he brought with him from Egypt he would have been as distinguished as Homer and Hesiod. 'And what was the subject of the poem?' said the person who made the remark. The subject was a very noble one; he described the most famous action in which the Athenian people were ever engaged. But the memory of their exploits has passed away owing to the lapse of time and the extinction of the actors. 'Tell us,' said the other, 'the whole story, and where Solon heard the story.' He replied—There is at the head of the Egyptian Delta, where the river Nile divides, a city and district called Sais; the city was the birthplace of King Amasis, and is under the protection of the goddess Neith or Athene. The citizens have a friendly feeling towards the Athenians, believing themselves to be related to them. Hither came Solon, and was received with honour; and here he first learnt, by conversing with the Egyptian priests, how ignorant he and his countrymen were of antiquity. Perceiving this, and with the view of eliciting information from them, he told them the tales of Phoroneus and Niobe, and also of Deucalion and Pyrrha, and he endeavoured to count the generations which had since passed. Thereupon an aged priest said to him: 'O Solon, Solon, you Hellenes are ever young, and there is no old man who is a Hellene.' 'What do you mean?' he asked. 'In mind,' replied the priest, 'I mean to say that you are children; there is no opinion or tradition of knowledge among you which is white with age; and I will tell you why. Like the rest of mankind you have suffered from convulsions of nature, which are chiefly brought about by the two great agencies of fire and water. The former is symbolized in the Hellenic tale of young Phaëthon who drove his father's horses the wrong way, and having burnt up the earth was himself burnt up by a thunderbolt. For there occurs at long intervals a derangement of the heavenly bodies, and then the earth is destroyed by fire. At such times, and when fire is the agent, those who dwell by rivers or on the seashore are safer than those who dwell upon high and dry places, who in their turn are safer when the danger is from water. Now the Nile is our saviour from fire, and as there is little rain in Egypt, we are not harmed by water; whereas in other countries, when a deluge comes, the inhabitants are swept by the rivers into the sea. The memorials which your own and other nations have once had of the famous actions of mankind perish in the waters at certain periods; and the rude survivors in the mountains begin again, knowing nothing of the world before the flood. But in Egypt the traditions of our own and other lands are by us registered for ever in our temples. The genealogies which you have recited to us out of your own annals, Solon, are a mere children's story. For in the first place, you remember one deluge only, and there were many of them, and you know nothing of that fairest and noblest race of which you are a seed or remnant. The memory of them was lost, because there was no written voice among you. For in the times before the great flood Athens was the greatest and best of cities and did the noblest deeds and had the best constitution of any under the face of heaven.' Solon marvelled, and desired to be informed of the particulars. 'You are welcome to hear them,' said the priest, 'both for your own sake and for that of the city, and above all for the sake of the goddess who is the common foundress of both our cities. Nine thousand years have elapsed since she founded yours, and eight thousand since she founded ours, as our annals record. Many laws exist among us which are the counterpart of yours as they were in the olden time. I will briefly describe them to you, and you shall read the account of them at your leisure in the sacred registers. In the first place, there was a caste of priests among the ancient Athenians, and another of artisans; also castes of shepherds, hunters, and husbandmen, and lastly of warriors, who, like the warriors of Egypt, were separated from the rest, and carried shields and spears, a custom which the goddess first taught you, and then the Asiatics, and we among Asiatics first received from her. Observe again, what care the law took in the pursuit of wisdom, searching out the deep things of the world, and applying them to the use of man. The spot of earth which the goddess chose had the best of climates, and produced the wisest men; in no other was she herself, the philosopher and warrior goddess, so likely to have votaries. And there you dwelt as became the children of the gods, excelling all men in virtue, and many famous actions are recorded of you. The most famous of them all was the overthrow of the island of Atlantis. This great island lay over against the Pillars of Heracles, in extent greater than Libya and Asia put together, and was the passage to other islands and to a great ocean of which the Mediterranean sea was only the harbour; and within the Pillars the empire of Atlantis reached in Europe to Tyrrhenia and in Libya to Egypt. This mighty power was arrayed against Egypt and Hellas and all the countries bordering on the Mediterranean. Then your city did bravely, and won renown over the whole earth. For at the peril of her own existence, and when the other Hellenes had deserted her, she repelled the invader, and of her own accord gave liberty to all the nations within the Pillars. A little while afterwards there were great earthquakes and floods, and your warrior race all sank into the earth; and the great island of Atlantis also disappeared in the sea. This is the explanation of the shallows which are found in that part of the Atlantic ocean.'

Such was the tale, Socrates, which Critias heard from Solon; and I noticed when listening to you yesterday, how close the resemblance was between your city and citizens and the ancient Athenian State. But I would not speak at the time, because I wanted to refresh my memory. I had heard the old man when I was a child, and though I could not remember the whole of our yesterday's discourse, I was able to recall every word of this, which is branded into my mind; and I am prepared, Socrates, to rehearse to you the entire narrative. The imaginary State which you were describing may be identified with the reality of Solon, and our antediluvian ancestors may be your citizens. 'That is excellent, Critias, and very appropriate to a Panathenaic festival; the truth of the story is a great advantage.' Then now let me explain to you the order of our entertainment; first, Timaeus, who is a natural philosopher, will speak of the origin of the world, going down to the creation of man, and then I shall receive the men whom he has created, and some of whom will have been educated by you, and introduce them to you as the lost Athenian citizens of whom the Egyptian record spoke. As the law of Solon prescribes, we will bring them into court and acknowledge their claims to citizenship. 'I see,' replied Socrates, 'that I shall be well entertained; and do you, Timaeus, offer up a prayer and begin.'

Tim: All men who have any right feeling, at the beginning of any enterprise, call upon the Gods; and he who is about to speak of the origin of the universe has a special need of their aid. May my words be acceptable to them, and may I speak in the manner which will be most intelligible to you and will best express my own meaning!

First, I must distinguish between that which always is and never becomes and which is apprehended by reason and reflection, and that which always becomes and never is and is conceived by opinion with the help of sense. All that becomes and is created is the work of a cause, and that is fair which the artificer makes after an eternal pattern, but whatever is fashioned after a created pattern is not fair. Is the world created or uncreated?—that is the first question. Created, I reply, being visible and tangible and having a body, and therefore sensible; and if sensible, then created; and if created, made by a cause, and the cause is the ineffable father of all things, who had before him an eternal archetype. For to imagine that the archetype was created would be blasphemy, seeing that the world is the noblest of creations, and God is the best of causes. And the world being thus created according to the eternal pattern is the copy of something; and we may assume that words are akin to the matter of which they speak. What is spoken of the unchanging or intelligible must be certain and true; but what is spoken of the created image can only be probable; being is to becoming what truth is to belief. And amid the variety of opinions which have arisen about God and the nature of the world we must be content to take probability for our rule, considering that I, who am the speaker, and you, who are the judges, are only men; to probability we may attain but no further.

Soc: Excellent, Timaeus; I like your manner of approaching the subject—proceed.

Tim: Why did the Creator make the world? . . . He was good, and therefore not jealous, and being free from jealousy he desired that all things should be like himself. Wherefore he set in order the visible world, which he found in disorder. Now he who is the best could only create the fairest; and reflecting that of visible things the intelligent is superior to the unintelligent, he put intelligence in soul and soul in body, and framed the universe to be the best and fairest work in the order of nature, and the world became a living soul through the providence of God.

In the likeness of what animal was the world made?—that is the third question . . . The form of the perfect animal was a whole, and contained all intelligible beings, and the visible animal, made after the pattern of this, included all visible creatures.

Are there many worlds or one only?—that is the fourth question. . . . One only. For if in the original there had been more than one they would have been the parts of a third, which would have been the true pattern of the world; and therefore there is, and will ever be, but one created world. Now that which is created is of necessity corporeal and visible and tangible,—visible and therefore made of fire,—tangible and therefore solid and made of earth. But two terms must be united by a third, which is a mean between them; and had the earth been a surface only, one mean would have sufficed, but two means are required to unite solid bodies. And as the world was composed of solids, between the elements of fire and earth God placed two other elements of air and water, and arranged them in a continuous proportion—

fire:air::air:water, and air:water::water:earth,

and so put together a visible and palpable heaven, having harmony and friendship in the union of the four elements; and being at unity with itself it was indissoluble except by the hand of the framer. Each of the elements was taken into the universe whole and entire; for he considered that the animal should be perfect and one, leaving no remnants out of which another animal could be created, and should also be free from old age and disease, which are produced by the action of external forces. And as he was to contain all things, he was made in the all-containing form of a sphere, round as from a lathe and every way equidistant from the centre, as was natural and suitable to him. He was finished and smooth, having neither eyes nor ears, for there was nothing without him which he could see or hear; and he had no need to carry food to his mouth, nor was there air for him to breathe; and he did not require hands, for there was nothing of which he could take hold, nor feet, with which to walk. All that he did was done rationally in and by himself, and he moved in a circle turning within himself, which is the most intellectual of motions; but the other six motions were wanting to him; wherefore the universe had no feet or legs.

And so the thought of God made a God in the image of a perfect body, having intercourse with himself and needing no other, but in every part harmonious and self-contained and truly blessed. The soul was first made by him—the elder to rule the younger; not in the order in which our wayward fancy has led us to describe them, but the soul first and afterwards the body. God took of the unchangeable and indivisible and also of the divisible and corporeal, and out of the two he made a third nature, essence, which was in a mean between them, and partook of the same and the other, the intractable nature of the other being compressed into the same. Having made a compound of all the three, he proceeded to divide the entire mass into portions related to one another in the ratios of 1, 2, 3, 4, 9, 8, 27, and proceeded to fill up the double and triple intervals thus—

$$1, \tfrac{4}{3}, \tfrac{3}{2}, \bar{2}, \tfrac{8}{3}, 3, \bar{4}, \tfrac{16}{3}, 6, \bar{8}:$$
$$\bar{1}, \tfrac{3}{2}, 2, \bar{3}, \tfrac{9}{2}, 6, \bar{9}, \tfrac{27}{2}, 18, \bar{27};$$

in which double series of numbers are two kinds of means; the one exceeds and is exceeded by equal parts of the extremes, e.g. 1, $\tfrac{4}{3}$, 2; the other kind of mean is one which is equidistant from the extremes—2, 4, 6. In this manner there were formed intervals of thirds, 3:2, of fourths, 4:3, and of ninths, 9:8. And next he filled up the intervals of a fourth with ninths, leaving a remnant which is in the ratio of 256:243. The entire compound was divided by him lengthways into two parts, which he united at the centre like the letter X, and bent them into an inner and outer circle or sphere, cutting one another again at a point over against the point at which they cross. The outer circle or sphere was named the sphere of the same—the inner, the sphere of the other or diverse; and the one revolved horizontally to the right, the other diagonally to the left. To the sphere of the same which was undivided he gave dominion, but the sphere of the other or diverse was distributed into seven unequal orbits, having intervals in ratios of twos and threes, three of either sort, and he bade the orbits move in opposite directions to one another— three of them, the Sun, Mercury, Venus, with equal swiftness, and the remaining four—the Moon, Saturn, Mars, Jupiter, with unequal swiftness to the three and to one another, but all in due proportion.

When the Creator had made the soul he made the body within her;

and the soul interfused everywhere from the centre to the circumference of heaven, herself turning in herself, began a divine life of rational and everlasting motion. The body of heaven is visible, but the soul is invisible, and partakes of reason and harmony, and is the best of creations, being the work of the best. And being composed of the same, the other, and the essence, these three, and also divided and bound in harmonical proportion, and revolving within herself—the soul when touching anything which has essence, whether divided or undivided, is stirred to utter the sameness or diversity of that and some other thing, and to tell how and when and where individuals are affected or related, whether in the world of change or of essence. When reason is in the neighbourhood of sense, and the circle of the other or diverse is moving truly, then arise true opinions and beliefs; when reason is in the sphere of thought, and the circle of the same runs smoothly, then intelligence is perfected.

When the Father who begat the world saw the image which he had made of the Eternal Gods moving and living, he rejoiced; and in his joy resolved, since the archetype was eternal, to make the creature eternal as far as this was possible. Wherefore he made an image of eternity which is time, having an uniform motion according to number, parted into months and days and years, and also having greater divisions of past, present, and future. These all apply to becoming in time, and have no meaning in relation to the eternal nature, which ever is and never was or will be; for the unchangeable is never older or younger, and when we say that he 'was' or 'will be,' we are mistaken, for these words are applicable only to becoming, and not to true being; and equally wrong are we in saying that what has become *is* become and that what becomes *is* becoming, and that the non-existent *is* non-existent. . . . These are the forms of time which imitate eternity and move in a circle measured by number.

Thus was time made in the image of the eternal nature; and it was created together with the heavens, in order that if they were dissolved, it might perish with them. And God made the sun and moon and five other wanderers, as they are called, seven in all, and to each of them he gave a body moving in an orbit, being one of the seven orbits into which the circle of the other was divided. He put the moon in the orbit which was nearest to the earth, the sun in that next, the morning star and Mercury in the orbits which move opposite to the sun but with equal swiftness—this being the reason why they overtake and are overtaken by one another. All these bodies became living creatures, and learnt their appointed tasks, and began to move, the nearer more swiftly, the remoter more slowly, according to the diagonal movement of the other. And since this was controlled by the movement of the same, the seven planets in their courses appeared to describe spirals; and that appeared fastest which was slowest, and that which overtook others appeared to be overtaken by them. And God lighted a fire in the second orbit from the earth which is called the sun, to give light over the whole heaven, and to teach intelligent beings that knowledge of number which is derived from the revolution of the same. Thus arose day and night, which are the periods of the most intelligent nature; a month is created by the revolution of the moon, a year by that of the sun. Other periods of wonderful length and complexity are not observed by men in general; there is moreover a cycle or perfect year at the completion of which they all meet and coincide. . . . To this end the stars came into being, that the created heaven might imitate the eternal nature.

Thus far the universal animal was made in the divine image, but the other animals were not as yet included in him. And God created them according to the patterns or species of them which existed in the divine original. There are four of them: one of gods, another of birds, a third of fishes, and a fourth of animals. The gods were made in the form of a circle, which is the most perfect figure and the figure of the universe. They were created chiefly of fire, that they might be bright, and were made to know and follow the best, and to be scattered over the heavens, of which they were to be the glory. Two kinds of motion were assigned to them—first, the revolution in the same and around the same, in peaceful unchanging thought of the same; and to this was added a forward motion which was under the control of the same. Thus then the fixed stars were created, being divine and eternal animals, revolving on the same spot, and the wandering stars, in their courses, were created in the manner already described. The earth, which is our nurse, clinging around the pole extended through the universe, he made to be the guardian and artificer of night and day, first and eldest of gods that are in the interior of heaven. Vain would be the labour of telling all the figures of them, moving as in dance, and their juxta-positions and approximations, and when and where and behind what other stars they appear to disappear—to tell of all this without looking at a plan of them would be labour in vain.

The knowledge of the other gods is beyond us, and we can only accept the traditions of the ancients, who were the children of the gods, as they said; for surely they must have known their own ancestors. Although they give no proof, we must believe them as is customary. They tell us that Oceanus and Tethys were the children of Earth and Heaven; that Phorcys, Cronos, and Rhea came in the next generation, and were followed by Zeus and Herè, whose brothers and children are known to everybody.

When all of them, both those who show themselves in the sky, and those who retire from view, had come into being, the Creator addressed them thus:—'Gods, sons of gods, my works, if I will, are indissoluble. That which is bound may be dissolved, but only an evil being would dissolve that which is harmonious and happy. And although you are not immortal you shall not die, for I will hold you together. Hear me, then:—Three tribes of mortal beings have still to be created, but if created by me they would be like gods. Do ye therefore make them; I will implant in them the seed of immortality, and you shall weave together the mortal and immortal, and provide food for them, and receive them again in death.' Thus he spake, and poured the remains of the elements into the cup in which he had mingled the soul of the universe. They were no longer pure as before, but diluted; and the mixture he distributed into souls equal in number to the stars, and assigned each to a star—then having mounted them, as in a chariot, he showed them the nature of the universe, and told them of their future birth and human lot. They were to be sown in the planets, and out of them was to come forth the most religious of animals, which would hereafter be called man. The souls were to be implanted in bodies, which were in a perpetual flux, whence, he said, would arise, first, sensation; secondly, love, which is a mixture of pleasure and pain; thirdly, fear and anger, and the opposite affections: and if they conquered these, they would live righteously, but if they were conquered by them, unrighteously. He who lived well would return to his native star, and would there have a blessed existence; but, if he lived ill, he would pass into the nature of a woman, and if he did not then alter his evil ways, into the likeness of some animal, until the reason which was in him reasserted her sway over the elements of fire, air, earth, water, which had engrossed her, and he regained his first and better nature. Having given this law to his creatures, that he might be guiltless of their future evil, he sowed them, some in the earth, some in the moon, and some in the other planets; and he ordered the younger gods to frame human bodies for them and to make the necessary additions to them, and to avert from them all but self-inflicted evil.

Having given these commands, the Creator remained in his own nature. And his children, receiving from him the immortal principle, borrowed from the world portions of earth, air, fire, water, hereafter to be returned, which they fastened together, not with the adamantine bonds which bound themselves, but by little invisible pegs, making each separate body out of all the elements, subject to influx and efflux, and containing the courses of the soul. These swelling and surging as in a river moved irregularly and irrationally in all the six possible ways, forwards, backwards, right, left, up and down. But violent as were the internal and alimentary fluids, the tide became still more. violent when the body came into contact with flaming fire, or the solid earth, or gliding waters, or the stormy wind; the motions produced by these impulses pass through the body to the soul and have the name of sensations. Uniting with the ever-flowing current, they shake the courses of the soul, stopping the revolution of the same and twisting in all sorts of ways the nature of the other, and the harmonical ratios of twos and threes and the mean terms which connect them, until the circles are bent and disordered and their motion becomes irregular. You may imagine a position of the body in which the head is resting upon the ground, and the legs are in the air, and the top is bottom and the left right. And something similar happens when the disordered motions of the soul come into contact with any external thing; they say the same or the other in a manner which is the very opposite of the truth, and they are false and foolish, and have no guiding principle in them. And when external impressions enter in, they are really conquered, though they seem to conquer.

By reason of these affections the soul is at first without intelligence, but as time goes on the stream of nutriment abates, and the courses of the soul regain their proper motion, and apprehend the same and the other rightly, and become rational. The soul of him who has education is whole and perfect and escapes the worst disease, but, if a man's education be neglected, he walks lamely through life and returns good for nothing to the world below. This, however, is an after-stage—at present, we are only concerned with the creation of the body and soul.

The two divine courses were encased by the gods in a sphere which is called the head, and is the god and lord of us. And to this they gave the body to be a vehicle, and the members to be instruments, having the power of flexion and extension. Such was the origin of legs and arms. In the next place, the gods gave a forward motion to the human body, because the front part of man was the more honourable and had authority. And they put in a face in which they inserted organs to minister in all things to the providence of the soul. They first contrived the eyes, into which they conveyed a light akin to the light of day, making it flow through the pupils. When the light of the eye is surrounded by the light of day, then like falls upon like, and they unite and form one body which conveys to the soul the motions of visible objects. But when the visual ray goes forth into the darkness, then unlike falls upon unlike—the eye no longer sees, and we go to sleep. The fire or light, when kept in by the eyelids, equalizes the inward motions, and there is rest accompanied by few dreams; only when the greater motions remain they engender in us corresponding visions of the night. And now we shall be able to understand the nature of reflections in mirrors. The

fires from within and from without meet about the smooth and bright
surface of the mirror; and because they meet in a manner contrary to
the usual mode, the right and left sides of the object are transposed. In
a concave mirror the top and bottom are inverted, but this is no trans-
position.

These are the second causes which God used as his ministers in fashioning the world. They are thought by many to be the prime causes,
but they are not so; for they are destitute of mind and reason, and the
lover of mind will not allow that there are any prime causes other than
the rational and invisible ones—these he investigates first, and afterwards the causes of things which are moved by others, and which work
by chance and without order. Of the second or concurrent causes of
sight I have already spoken, and I will now speak of the higher purpose
of God in giving us eyes. Sight is the source of the greatest benefits to
us; for if our eyes had never seen the sun, stars, and heavens, the words
which we have spoken would not have been uttered. The sight of them
and their revolutions has given us the knowledge of number and time,
the power of enquiry, and philosophy, which is the great blessing of
human life; not to speak of the lesser benefits which even the vulgar
can appreciate. God gave us the faculty of sight that we might behold
the order of the heavens and create a corresponding order in our own
erring minds. To the like end the gifts of speech and hearing were be-
stowed upon us; not for the sake of irrational pleasure, but in order that
we might harmonize the courses of the soul by sympathy with the harmony of sound, and cure ourselves of our irregular and graceless ways.

Thus far we have spoken of the works of mind; and there are other
works done from necessity, which we must now place beside them; for
the creation is made up of both, mind persuading necessity as far as
possible to work out good. Before the heavens there existed fire, air,
water, earth, which we suppose men to know, though no one has explained their nature, and we erroneously maintain them to be the letters or elements of the whole, although they cannot reasonably be compared even to syllables or first compounds. I am not now speaking of
the first principles of things, because I cannot discover them by our
present mode of enquiry. But as I observed the rule of probability at
first, I will begin anew, seeking by the grace of God to observe it still.

In our former discussion I distinguished two kinds of being—the unchanging or invisible, and the visible or changing. But now a third kind
is required, which I shall call the receptacle or nurse of generation.
There is a difficulty in arriving at an exact notion of this third kind, because the four elements themselves are of inexact natures and easily
pass into one another, and are too transient to be detained by any one
name; wherefore we are compelled to speak of water or fire, not as sub-

stances, but as qualities. They may be compared to images made of
gold, which are continually assuming new forms. Somebody asks what
they are; if you do not know, the safest answer is to reply that they are
gold. In like manner there is a universal nature out of which all things
are made, and which is like none of them; but they enter into and pass
out of her, and are made after patterns of the true in a wonderful and
inexplicable manner. The containing principle may be likened to a
mother, the source or spring to a father, the intermediate nature to a
child; and we may also remark that the matter which receives every variety of form must be formless, like the inodorous liquids which are prepared to receive scents, or the smooth and soft materials on which figures are impressed. In the same way space or matter is neither earth nor
fire nor air nor water, but an invisible and formless being which re
ceives all things, and in an incomprehensible manner partakes of the
intelligible. But we may say, speaking generally, that fire is that part of
this nature which is inflamed, water that which is moistened, and the
like.

Let me ask a question in which a great principle is involved: Is there
an essence of fire and the other elements, or are there only fires visible
to sense? I answer in a word: If mind is one thing and true opinion another, then there are self-existent essences; but if mind is the same with
opinion, then the visible and corporeal is most real. But they are not
the same, and they have a different origin and nature. The one comes
to us by instruction, the other by persuasion; the one is rational, the
other is irrational; the one is movable by persuasion, the other immovable; the one is possessed by every man, the other by the gods and by
very few men. And we must acknowledge that as there are two kinds of
knowledge, so there are two kinds of being corresponding to them; the
one uncreated, indestructible, immovable, which is seen by intelligence only; the other created, which is always becoming in place and
vanishing out of place, and is apprehended by opinion and sense.
There is also a third nature—that of space, which is indestructible, and
is perceived by a kind of spurious reason without the help of sense. This
is presented to us in a dreamy manner, and yet is said to be necessary,
for we say that all things must be somewhere in space. For they are the
images of other things and must therefore have a separate existence and
exist in something (i.e. in space). But true reason assures us that while
two things (i.e. the idea and the image) are different they cannot inhere
in one another, so as to be one and two at the same time.

To sum up: Being and generation and space, these three, existed before the heavens, and the nurse or vessel of generation, moistened by
water and inflamed by fire, and taking the forms of air and earth, assumed various shapes. By the motion of the vessel, the elements were

divided, and like grain winnowed by fans, the close and heavy particles settled in one place, the light and airy ones in another. At first they were without reason or measure, and had only certain faint traces of themselves, until God fashioned them by figure and number. In this, as in every other part of creation, I suppose God to have made things, as far as was possible, fair and good, out of things not fair and good.

And now I will explain to you the generation of the world by a method with which your scientific training will have made you familiar. Fire, air, earth, and water are bodies and therefore solids, and solids are contained in planes, and plane rectilinear figures are made up of triangles. Of triangles there are two kinds; one having the opposite sides equal (isosceles), the other with unequal sides (scalene). These we may fairly assume to be the original elements of fire and the other bodies; what principles are prior to these God only knows, and he of men whom God loves. Next, we must determine what are the four most beautiful figures which are unlike one another and yet sometimes capable of resolution into one another. . . . Of the two kinds of triangles the equal-sided has but one form, the unequal-sided has an infinite variety of forms; and there is none more beautiful than that which forms the half of an equilateral triangle. Let us then choose two triangles; one, the isosceles, the other, that form of scalene which has the square of the longer side three times as great as the square of the lesser side; and affirm that, out of these, fire and the other elements have been constructed.

I was wrong in imagining that all the four elements could be generated into and out of one another. For as they are formed, three of them from the triangle which has the sides unequal, the fourth from the triangle which has equal sides, three can be resolved into one another, but the fourth cannot be resolved into them nor they into it. So much for their passage into one another: I must now speak of their construction. From the triangle of which the hypothenuse is twice the lesser side the three first regular solids are formed—first, the equilateral pyramid or tetrahedron; secondly, the octahedron; thirdly, the icosahedron; and from the isosceles triangle is formed the cube. And there is a fifth figure [which is made out of twelve pentagons], the dodecahedron— this God used as a model for the twelvefold division of the Zodiac.

Let us now assign the geometrical forms to their respective elements. The cube is the most stable of them because resting on a quadrangular plane surface, and composed of isosceles triangles. To the earth then, which is the most stable of bodies and the most easily modelled of them, may be assigned the form of a cube; and the remaining forms to the other elements,—to fire the pyramid, to air the octahedron, and to water the icosahedron,—according to their degrees of lightness or

heaviness or power, or want of power, of penetration. The single particles of any of the elements are not seen by reason of their smallness;
they only become visible when collected. The ratios of their motions,
numbers, and other properties, are ordered by the God, who harmonized them as far as necessity permitted.

The probable conclusion is as follows: — Earth, when dissolved by
the more penetrating element of fire, whether acting immediately or
through the medium of air or water, is decomposed but not transformed. Water, when divided by fire or air, becomes one part fire, and
two parts air. A volume of air divided becomes two of fire. On the other
hand, when condensed, two volumes of fire make a volume of air; and
two and a half parts of air condense into one of water. Any element
which is fastened upon by fire is cut by the sharpness of the triangles,
until at length, coalescing with the fire, it is at rest; for similars are not
affected by similars. When two kinds of bodies quarrel with one another, then the tendency to decomposition continues until the smaller
either escapes to its kindred element or becomes one with its con-
queror. And this tendency in bodies to condense or escape is a source
of motion. . . . Where there is motion there must be a mover, and
where there is a mover there must be something to move. These cannot exist in what is uniform, and therefore motion is due to want of uniformity. But then why, when things are divided after their kinds, do they
not cease from motion? The answer is, that the circular motion of all
things compresses them, and as 'nature abhors a vacuum,' the finer and
more subtle particles of the lighter elements, such as fire and air, are
thrust into the interstices of the larger, each of them penetrating according to their rarity, and thus all the elements are on their way up and
down everywhere and always into their own places. Hence there is a
principle of inequality, and therefore of motion, in all time.

In the next place, we may observe that there are different kinds of
fire — (1) flame, (2) light that burns not, (3) the red heat of the embers
of fire. And there are varieties of air, as for example, the pure aether,
the opaque mist, and other nameless forms. Water, again, is of two
kinds, liquid and fusile. The liquid is composed of small and unequal
particles, the fusile of large and uniform particles and is more solid, but
nevertheless melts at the approach of fire, and then spreads upon the
earth. When the substance cools, the fire passes into the air, which is
displaced, and forces together and condenses the liquid mass. This
process is called cooling and congealment. Of the fusile kinds the
fairest and heaviest is gold; this is hardened by filtration through rock,
and is of a bright yellow colour. A shoot of gold which is darker and
denser than the rest is called adamant. Another kind is called copper,
which is harder and yet lighter because the interstices are larger than

in gold. There is mingled with it a fine and small portion of earth which comes out in the form of rust. These are a few of the conjectures which philosophy forms, when, leaving the eternal nature, she turns for innocent recreation to consider the truths of generation.

Water which is mingled with fire is called liquid because it rolls upon the earth, and soft because its bases give way. This becomes more equable when separated from fire and air, and then congeals into hail or ice, or the looser forms of hoar frost or snow. There are other waters which are called juices and are distilled through plants. Of these we may mention, first, wine, which warms the soul as well as the body; secondly, oily substances, as for example, oil or pitch; thirdly, honey, which relaxes the contracted parts of the mouth and so produces sweetness; fourthly, vegetable acid, which is frothy and has a burning quality and dissolves the flesh. Of the kinds of earth, that which is filtered through water passes into stone; the water is broken up by the earth and escapes in the form of air—this in turn presses upon the mass of earth, and the earth, compressed into an indissoluble union with the remaining water, becomes rock. Rock, when it is made up of equal particles, is fair and transparent, but the reverse when of unequal. Earth is converted into pottery when the watery part is suddenly drawn away; or if moisture remains, the earth, when fused by fire, becomes, on cooling, a stone of a black colour. When the earth is finer and of a briny nature then two half-solid bodies are formed by separating the water,—soda and salt. The strong compounds of earth and water are not soluble by water, but only by fire. Earth itself, when not consolidated, is dissolved by water; when consolidated, by fire only. The cohesion of water, when strong, is dissolved by fire only; when weak, either by air or fire, the former entering the interstices, the latter penetrating even the triangles. Air when strongly condensed is indissoluble by any power which does not reach the triangles, and even when not strongly condensed is only resolved by fire. Compounds of earth and water are unaffected by water while the water occupies the interstices in them, but begin to liquefy when fire enters into the interstices of the water. They are of two kinds, some of them, like glass, having more earth, others, like wax, having more water in them.

Having considered objects of sense, we now pass on to sensation. But we cannot explain sensation without explaining the nature of flesh and of the mortal soul; and as we cannot treat of both together, in order that we may proceed at once to the sensations we must assume the existence of body and soul.

What makes fire burn? The fineness of the sides, the sharpness of the angles, the smallness of the particles, the quickness of the motion. Moreover, the pyramid, which is the figure of fire, is more cutting than any other. The feeling of cold is produced by the larger particles of moisture outside the body trying to eject the smaller ones in the body which they compress. The struggle which arises between elements thus unnaturally brought together causes shivering. That is hard to which the flesh yields, and soft which yields to the flesh, and these two terms are also relative to one another. The yielding matter is that which has the slenderest base, whereas that which has a rectangular base is compact and repellent. Light and heavy are wrongly explained with reference to a lower and higher in place. For in the universe, which is a sphere, there is no opposition of above or below, and that which is to us above would be below to a man standing at the antipodes. The greater or less difficulty in detaching any element from its like is the real cause of heaviness or of lightness. If you draw the earth into the dissimilar air, the particles of earth cling to their native element, and you more easily detach a small portion than a large. There would be the same difficulty in moving any of the upper elements towards the lower. The smooth and the rough are severally produced by the union of evenness with compactness, and of hardness with inequality.

Pleasure and pain are the most important of the affections common to the whole body. According to our general doctrine of sensation, parts of the body which are easily moved readily transmit the motion to the mind; but parts which are not easily moved have no effect upon the patient. The bones and hair are of the latter kind, sight and hearing of the former. Ordinary affections are neither pleasant nor painful. The impressions of sight afford an example of these, and are neither violent nor sudden. But sudden replenishments of the body cause pleasure, and sudden disturbances, as for example cuttings and burnings, have the opposite effect.

From sensations common to the whole body, we proceed to those of particular parts. The affections of the tongue appear to be caused by contraction and dilation, but they have more of roughness or smoothness than is found in other affections. Earthy particles, entering into the small veins of the tongue which reach to the heart, when they melt into and dry up the little veins are astringent if they are rough; or if not so rough, they are only harsh, and if excessively abstergent, like potash and soda, bitter. Purgatives of a weaker sort are called salt and, having no bitterness, are rather agreeable. Inflammatory bodies, which by their lightness are carried up into the head, cutting all that comes in their way, are termed pungent. But when these are refined by putrefaction, and enter the narrow veins of the tongue, and meet there particles of earth and air, two kinds of globules are formed—one of earthy and impure liquid, which boils and ferments, the other of pure and transparent water, which are called bubbles; of all these affections the cause is termed acid. When, on the other hand, the composition of the deliquescent particles is congenial to the tongue, and disposes the parts according to their nature, this remedial power in them is called sweet.

Smells are not divided into kinds; all of them are transitional, and arise out of the decomposition of one element into another, for the simple air or water is without smell. They are vapours or mists, thinner than water and thicker than air: and hence in drawing in the breath, when there is an obstruction, the air passes, but there is no smell. They have no names, but are distinguished as pleasant and unpleasant, and their influence extends over the whole region from the head to the navel.

Hearing is the effect of a stroke which is transmitted through the ears by means of the air, brain, and blood to the soul, beginning at the head and extending to the liver. The sound which moves swiftly is acute; that which moves slowly is grave; that which is uniform is smooth, and the opposite is harsh. Loudness depends on the quantity of the sound. Of the harmony of sounds I will hereafter speak.

Colours are flames which emanate from all bodies, having particles corresponding to the sense of sight. Some of the particles are less and some larger, and some are equal to the parts of the sight. The equal particles appear transparent; the larger contract, and the lesser dilate the sight. White is produced by the dilation, black by the contraction, of the particles of sight. There is also a swifter motion of another sort of fire which forces a way through the passages of the eyes, and elicits from them a union of fire and water which we call tears. The inner fire flashes forth, and the outer finds a way in and is extinguished in the moisture, and all sorts of colours are generated by the mixture. This affection is termed by us dazzling, and the object which produces it is called bright. There is yet another sort of fire which mingles with the moisture of the eye without flashing, and produces a colour like blood—to this we give the name of red. A bright element mingling with red and white produces a colour which we call auburn. The law of proportion, however, according to which compound colours are formed, cannot be determined scientifically or even probably. Red, when mingled with black and white, gives a purple hue, which becomes umber when the colours are burnt and there is a larger admixture of black. Flame-colour is a mixture of auburn and dun; dun of white and black; yellow of white and auburn. White and bright meeting, and falling upon a full black, become dark blue; dark blue mingling with white becomes a light blue; the union of flame-colour and black makes leek-green. There is no difficulty in seeing how other colours are probably composed. But he who should attempt to test the truth of this by experiment, would forget the difference of the human and divine nature. God only is able to compound and resolve substances; such experiments are impossible to man.

These are the elements of necessity which the Creator received in the world of generation when he made the all-sufficient and perfect creature, using the secondary causes as his ministers, but himself fashioning the good in all things. For there are two sorts of causes, the one divine, the other necessary; and we should seek to discover the divine above all, and, for their sake, the necessary, because without them the higher cannot be attained by us.

Having now before us the causes out of which the rest of our discourse is to be framed, let us go back to the point at which we began, and add a fair ending to our tale. As I said at first, all things were originally a chaos in which there was no order or proportion. The elements of this chaos were arranged by the Creator, and out of them he made the world. Of the divine he himself was the author, but he committed to his offspring the creation of the mortal. From him they received the immortal soul, but themselves made the body to be its vehicle, and constructed within another soul which was mortal, and subject to terrible affections—pleasure, the inciter of evil; pain, which deters from good; rashness and fear, foolish counsellors; anger hard to be appeased; hope easily led astray. These they mingled with irrational sense and all daring love according to necessary laws and so framed man. And, fearing to pollute the divine element, they gave the mortal soul a separate habitation in the breast, parted off from the head by a narrow isthmus. And as in a house the women's apartments are divided from the men's, the cavity of the thorax was divided into two parts, a higher and a lower. The higher of the two, which is the seat of courage and anger, lies nearer to the head, between the midriff and the neck, and assists reason in restraining the desires. The heart is the house of guard in which all the veins meet, and through them reason sends her commands to the extremity of her kingdom. When the passions are in revolt, or danger approaches from without, then the heart beats and swells; and the creating powers, knowing this, implanted in the body the soft and bloodless substance of the lung, having a porous and springy nature like a sponge, and being kept cool by drink and air which enters through the trachea.

The part of the soul which desires meat and drink was placed between the midriff and navel, where they made a sort of manger; and here they bound it down, like a wild animal, away from the council-chamber, and leaving the better principle undisturbed to advise quietly for the good of the whole. For the Creator knew that the belly would not listen to reason, and was under the power of idols and fancies. Wherefore he framed the liver to connect with the lower nature, contriving that it should be compact, and bright, and sweet, and also bitter and smooth, in order that the power of thought which originates in the mind might there be reflected, terrifying the belly with the elements of bitterness and gall, and a suffusion of bilious colours when the liver is contracted, and causing pain and misery by twisting out of its place the lobe and closing up the vessels and gates. And the converse happens when some gentle inspiration coming from intelligence mirrors the opposite fancies, giving rest and sweetness and freedom, and at night, moderation and peace accompanied with prophetic insight, when reason and sense are asleep. For the authors of our being, in obedience to their Father's will and in order to make men as good as they could, gave to the liver the power of divination, which is never active when men are awake or in health; but when they are under the influence of some disorder or enthusiasm then they receive intimations, which have to be interpreted by others who are called prophets, but should rather be called interpreters of prophecy; after death these intimations become unintelligible. The spleen which is situated in the neighbourhood, on the left side, keeps the liver bright and clean, as a napkin does a mirror, and the evacuations of the liver are received into it; and being a hollow tissue it is for a time swollen with these impurities, but when the body is purged it returns to its natural size.

The truth concerning the soul can only be established by the word of God. Still, we may venture to assert what is probable both concerning soul and body.

The creative powers were aware of our tendency to excess. And so when they made the belly to be a receptacle for food, in order that men might not perish by insatiable gluttony, they formed the convolutions of the intestines, in this way retarding the passage of food through the body, lest mankind should be absorbed in eating and drinking, and the whole race become impervious to divine philosophy.

The creation of bones and flesh was on this wise. The foundation of these is the marrow which binds together body and soul, and the marrow is made out of such of the primary triangles as are adapted by their perfection to produce all the four elements. These God took and mingled them in due proportion, making as many kinds of marrow as there were hereafter to be kinds of souls. The receptacle of the divine soul he made round, and called that portion of the marrow brain, intending that the vessel containing this substance should be the head. The remaining part he divided into long and round figures, and to these as to anchors, fastening the mortal soul, he proceeded to make the rest of the body, first forming for both parts a covering of bone. The bone was formed by sifting pure smooth earth and wetting it with marrow. It was then thrust alternately into fire and water, and thus rendered insoluble by either. Of bone he made a globe which he placed around the brain, leaving a narrow opening, and around the marrow of the neck and spine he formed the vertebrae, like hinges, which extended from the head through the whole of the trunk. And as the bone was brittle and liable to mortify and destroy the marrow by too great rigidity and susceptibility to heat and cold, he contrived sinews and flesh—the first to give flexibility, the second to guard against heat and cold, and to be a protection against falls, containing a warm moisture, which in summer exudes and cools the body, and in winter is a defence against cold. Having this in view, the Creator mingled earth with fire and water and mixed with them a ferment of acid and salt, so as to form pulpy flesh. But the sinews he made of a mixture of bone and unfermented flesh, giving them a mean nature between the two, and a yellow colour. Hence they were more glutinous than flesh, but softer than bone. The bones which have most of the living soul within them he covered with the thinnest film of flesh, those which have least of it, he lodged deeper. At the joints he diminished the flesh in order not to impede the flexure of the limbs, and also to avoid clogging the perceptions of the mind. About the thighs and arms, which have no sense because there is little soul in the marrow, and about the inner bones, he laid the flesh thicker. For where the flesh is thicker there is less feeling, except in certain parts which the Creator has made solely of flesh, as for example, the tongue. Had the combination of solid bone and thick flesh been consistent with acute perceptions, the Creator would have given man a sinewy and fleshy head, and then he would have lived twice as long. But our creators were of opinion that a shorter life which was better was preferable to a longer which was worse, and therefore they covered the head with thin bone, and placed the sinews at the extremity of the head round the neck, and fastened the jawbones to them below the face. And they framed the mouth, having teeth and tongue and lips, with a view to the necessary and the good; for food is a necessity, and the river of speech is the best of rivers. Still, the head could not be left a bare globe of bone on account of the extremes of heat and cold, nor be allowed to become dull and senseless by an overgrowth of flesh. Wherefore it was covered by a peel or skin which met and grew by the help of the cerebral humour. The diversity of the sutures was caused by the struggle of the food against the courses of the soul. The skin of the head was pierced by fire, and out of the punctures came forth a moisture, part liquid, and part of a skinny nature, which was hardened by the pressure of the external cold and became hair. And God gave hair to the head of man to be a light covering, so that it might not interfere with his perceptions. Nails were formed by combining sinew, skin, and bone, and were made by the creators with a view to the future when, as they knew, women and other animals who would require them would be framed out of man.

The gods also mingled natures akin to that of man with other forms and perceptions. Thus trees and plants were created, which were originally wild and have been adapted by cultivation to our use. They partake of that third kind of life which is seated between the midriff and the navel, and is altogether passive and incapable of reflection.

When the creators had furnished all these natures for our sustenance, they cut channels through our bodies as in a garden, watering them with a perennial stream. Two were cut down the back, along the back bone, where the skin and flesh meet, one on the right and the other on the left, having the marrow of generation between them. In the next place, they divided the veins about the head and interlaced them with each other in order that they might form an additional link between the head and the body, and that the sensations from both sides might be diffused throughout the body. In the third place, they contrived the passage of liquids, which may be explained in this way:— Finer bodies retain coarser, but not the coarser the finer, and the belly is capable of retaining food, but not fire and air. God therefore formed a network of fire and air to irrigate the veins, having within it two lesser nets, and stretched cords reaching from both the lesser nets to the extremity of the outer net. The inner parts of the net were made by him of fire, the lesser nets and their cavities of air. The two latter he made to pass into the mouth; the one ascending by the air-pipes from the lungs, the other by the side of the air-pipes from the belly. The entrance to the first he divided into two parts, both of which he made to meet at the channels of the nose, that when the mouth was closed the passage connected with it might still be fed with air. The cavity of the network he spread around the hollows of the body, making the entire receptacle to flow into and out of the lesser nets and the lesser nets into and out of it, while the outer net found a way into and out of the pores of the body, and the internal heat followed the air to and fro. These, as we affirm, are the phenomena of respiration. And all this process takes place in order that the body may be watered and cooled and nourished, and the meat and drink digested and liquefied and carried into the veins.

The causes of respiration have now to be considered. The exhalation of the breath through the mouth and nostrils displaces the external air, and at the same time leaves a vacuum into which through the pores the air which is displaced enters. Also the vacuum which is made when the air is exhaled through the pores is filled up by the inhalation of breath through the mouth and nostrils. The explanation of this double phenomenon is as follows:— Elements move towards their natural places.

Now as every animal has within him a fountain of fire, the air which is inhaled through the mouth and nostrils, on coming into contact with this, is heated; and when heated, in accordance with the law of attraction, it escapes by the way it entered toward the place of fire. On leaving the body it is cooled and drives round the air which it displaces through the pores into the empty lungs. This again is in turn heated by the internal fire and escapes, as it entered, through the pores.

The phenomena of medical cupping-glasses, of swallowing, and of the hurling of bodies, are to be explained on a similar principle; as also sounds, which are sometimes discordant on account of the inequality of them, and again harmonious by reason of equality. The slower sounds reaching the swifter, when they begin to pause, by degrees assimilate with them: whence arises a pleasure which even the unwise feel, and which to the wise becomes a higher sense of delight, being an imitation of divine harmony in mortal motions. Streams flow, lightnings play, amber and the magnet attract, not by reason of attraction, but because 'nature abhors a vacuum,' and because things, when compounded or dissolved, move different ways, each to its own place.

I will now return to the phenomena of respiration. The fire, entering the belly, minces the food, and as it escapes, fills the veins by drawing after it the divided portions, and thus the streams of nutriment are diffused through the body. The fruits or herbs which are our daily sustenance take all sorts of colours when intermixed, but the colour of red or fire predominates, and hence the liquid which we call blood is red, being the nurturing principle of the body, whence all parts are watered and empty places filled.

The process of repletion and depletion is produced by the attraction of like to like, after the manner of the universal motion. The external elements by their attraction are always diminishing the substance of the body: the particles of blood, too, formed out of the newly digested food, are attracted towards kindred elements within the body and so fill up the void. When more is taken away than flows in, then we decay; and when less, we grow and increase.

The young of every animal has the triangles new and closely locked together, and yet the entire frame is soft and delicate, being newly made of marrow and nurtured on milk. These triangles are sharper than those which enter the body from without in the shape of food, and therefore they cut them up. But as life advances, the triangles wear out and are no longer able to assimilate food; and at length, when the bonds which unite the triangles of the marrow become undone, they in turn unloose the bonds of the soul; and if the release be according to nature, she then flies away with joy. For the death which is natural is pleasant, but that which is caused by violence is painful.

Every one may understand the origin of diseases. They may be oc-
casioned by the disarrangement or disproportion of the elements out of
which the body is framed. This is the origin of many of them, but the
worst of all owe their severity to the following causes: There is a natural
order in the human frame according to which the flesh and sinews are
made of blood, the sinews out of the fibres, and the flesh out of the congealed substance which is formed by separation from the fibres. The
glutinous matter which comes away from the sinews and the flesh, not
only binds the flesh to the bones, but nourishes the bones and waters
the marrow. When these processes take place in regular order the body
is in health.

But when the flesh wastes and returns into the veins there is discoloured blood as well as air in the veins, having acid and salt qualities,
from which is generated every sort of phlegm and bile. All things go the
wrong way and cease to give nourishment to the body, no longer preserving their natural courses, but at war with themselves and destructive to the constitution of the body. The oldest part of the flesh which
is hard to decompose blackens from long burning, and from being corroded grows bitter, and as the bitter element refines away, becomes
acid. When tinged with blood the bitter substance has a red colour,
and this when mixed with black takes the hue of grass; or again, the bitter substance has an auburn colour, when new flesh is decomposed by
the internal flame. To all which phenomena some physician or
philosopher who was able to see the one in many has given the name
of bile. The various kinds of bile have names answering to their
colours. Lymph or serum is of two kinds: first, the whey of blood, which
is gentle; secondly, the secretion of dark and bitter bile, which, when
mingled under the influence of heat with salt, is malignant and is
called acid phlegm. There is also white phlegm, formed by the decomposition of young and tender flesh, and covered with little bubbles,
separately invisible, but becoming visible when collected. The water of
tears and perspiration and similar substances is also the watery part of
fresh phlegm. All these humours become sources of disease when the
blood is replenished in irregular ways and not by food or drink. The
danger, however, is not so great when the foundation remains, for then
there is a possibility of recovery. But when the substance which unites
the flesh and bones is diseased, and is no longer renewed from the muscles and sinews, and instead of being oily and smooth and glutinous becomes rough and salt and dry, then the fleshy parts fall away and leave
the sinews bare and full of brine, and the flesh gets back again into the
circulation of the blood, and makes the previously mentioned disorders
still greater. There are other and worse diseases which are prior to
these; as when the bone through the density of the flesh does not re-

ceive sufficient air, and becomes stagnant and gangrened, and crumbling away passes into the food, and the food into the flesh, and the flesh returns again into the blood. Worst of all and most fatal is the disease of the marrow, by which the whole course of the body is reversed. There is a third class of diseases which are produced, some by wind and some by phlegm and some by bile. When the lung, which is the steward of the air, is obstructed by rheums, and in one part no air, and in another too much, enters in, then the parts which are unrefreshed by air corrode, and other parts are distorted by the excess of air; and in this manner painful diseases are produced. The most painful are caused by wind generated within the body, which gets about the great sinews of the shoulders these are termed tetanus. The cure of them is difficult, and in most cases they are relieved only by fever. White phlegm, which is dangerous if kept in, by reason of the air bubbles, is not equally dangerous if able to escape through the pores, although it variegates the body, generating divers kinds of leprosies. If, when mingled with black bile, it disturbs the courses of the head in sleep, there is not so much danger; but if it assails those who are awake, then the attack is far more dangerous, and is called epilepsy or the sacred disease. Acid and salt phlegm is the source of catarrh.

Inflammations originate in bile, which is sometimes relieved by boils and swellings, but when detained, and above all when mingled with pure blood, generates many inflammatory disorders, disturbing the position of the fibres which are scattered about in the blood in order to maintain the balance of rare and dense which is necessary to its regular circulation. If the bile, which is only stale blood, or liquefied flesh, comes in little by little, it is congealed by the fibres and produces internal cold and shuddering. But when it enters with more of a flood it overcomes the fibres by its heat and reaches the spinal marrow, and burning up the cables of the soul sets her free from the body. When on the other hand the body, though wasted, still holds out, then the bile is expelled, like an exile from a factious state, causing diarrhœas and dysenteries and similar disorders. The body which is diseased from the effects of fire is in a continual fever; when air is the agent, the fever is quotidian; when water, the fever intermits a day; when earth, which is the most sluggish element, the fever intermits three days and is with difficulty shaken off.

Of mental disorders there are two sorts, one madness, the other ignorance, and they may be justly attributed to disease. Excessive pleasures or pains are among the greatest diseases, and deprive men of their senses. When the seed about the spinal marrow is too abundant, the body has too great pleasures and pains; and during a great part of his life he who is the subject of them is more or less mad. He is often thought bad, but this is a mistake; for the truth is that the intemperance of lust is due to the fluidity of the marrow produced by the loose consistency of the bones. And this is true of vice in general, which is commonly regarded as disgraceful, whereas it is really involuntary and arises from a bad habit of the body and evil education. In like manner the soul is often made vicious by the influence of bodily pain; the briny phlegm and other bitter and bilious humours wander over the body and find no exit, but are compressed within, and mingle their own vapours with the motions of the soul, and are carried to the three places of the soul, creating infinite varieties of trouble and melancholy, of rashness and cowardice, of forgetfulness and stupidity. When men are in this evil plight of body, and evil forms of government and evil discourses are superadded, and there is no education to save them, they are corrupted through two causes; but of neither of them are they really the authors. For the planters are to blame rather than the plants, the educators and not the educated. Still, we should endeavour to attain virtue and avoid vice; but this is part of another subject.

Enough of disease—I have now to speak of the means by which the mind and body are to be preserved, a higher theme than the other. The good is the beautiful, and the beautiful is the symmetrical, and there is no greater or fairer symmetry than that of body and soul, as the contrary is the greatest of deformities. A leg or an arm too long or too short is at once ugly and unserviceable, and the same is true if body and soul are disproportionate. For a strong and impassioned soul may 'fret the pigmy body to decay,' and so produce convulsions and other evils. The violence of controversy, or the earnestness of enquiry, will often generate inflammations and rheums which are not understood, or assigned to their true cause by the professors of medicine. And in like manner the body may be too much for the soul, darkening the reason, and quickening the animal desires. The only security is to preserve the balance of the two, and to this end the mathematician or philosopher must practise gymnastics, and the gymnast must cultivate music. The parts of the body too must be treated in the same way—they should receive their appropriate exercise. For the body is set in motion when it is heated and cooled by the elements which enter in, or is dried up and moistened by external things; and, if given up to these processes when at rest, it is liable to destruction. But the natural motion, as in the world, so also in the human frame, produces harmony and divides hostile powers. The best exercise is the spontaneous motion of the body, as in gymnastics, because most akin to the motion of mind; not so good is the motion of which the source is in another, as in sailing or riding; least good when the body is at rest and the motion is in parts only, which is a species of motion imparted by physic. This should only be resorted to by men of sense in extreme cases; lesser diseases are not to be irritated by medicine. For every disease is akin to the living being and has an appointed term, just as life has, which depends on the form of the triangles, and cannot be protracted when they are worn out. And he who, instead of accepting his destiny, endeavours to prolong his life by medicine, is likely to multiply and magnify his diseases. Regimen and not medicine is the true cure, when a man has time at his disposal.

Enough of the nature of man and of the body, and of training and education. The subject is a great one and cannot be adequately treated as an appendage to another. To sum up all in a word: there are three kinds of soul located within us, and any one of them, if remaining inactive, becomes very weak; if exercised, very strong. Wherefore we should duly train and exercise all three kinds.

The divine soul God lodged in the head, to raise us, like plants which are not of earthly origin, to our kindred; for the head is nearest to heaven. He who is intent upon the gratification of his desires and cherishes the mortal soul, has all his ideas mortal, and is himself mortal in the truest sense. But he who seeks after knowledge and exercises the divine part of himself in godly and immortal thoughts, attains to truth and immortality, as far as is possible to man, and also to happiness, while he is training up within him the divine principle and indwelling power of order. There is only one way in which one person can benefit another; and that is by assigning to him his proper nurture and motion. To the motions of the soul answer the motions of the universe, and by the study of these the individual is restored to his original nature.

Thus we have finished the discussion of the universe, which, according to our original intention, has now been brought down to the creation of man. Completeness seems to require that something should be briefly said about other animals: first of women, who are probably degenerate and cowardly men. And when they degenerated, the gods implanted in men the desire of union with them, creating in man one animate substance and in woman another in the following manner: — The outlet for liquids they connected with the living principle of the spinal marrow, which the man has the desire to emit into the fruitful womb of the woman; this is like a fertile field in which the seed is quickened and matured, and at last brought to light. When this desire is unsatisfied the man is over-mastered by the power of the generative organs, and the woman is subjected to disorders from the obstruction of the passages of the breath, until the two meet and pluck the fruit of the tree.

The race of birds was created out of innocent, light-minded men, who thought to pursue the study of the heavens by sight; these were transformed into birds, and grew feathers instead of hair. The race of wild animals were men who had no philosophy, and never looked up to heaven or used the courses of the head, but followed only the influences of passion. Naturally they turned to their kindred earth, and put their forelegs to the ground, and their heads were crushed into strange oblong forms. Some of them have four feet, and some of them more than four,—the latter, who are the more senseless, drawing closer to their native element; the most senseless of all have no limbs and trail their whole body on the ground. The fourth kind are the inhabitants of the waters; these are made out of the most senseless and ignorant and impure of men, whom God placed in the uttermost parts of the world in return for their utter ignorance, and caused them to respire water instead of the pure element of air. Such are the laws by which animals pass into one another.

And so the world received animals, mortal and immortal, and was fulfilled with them, and became a visible God, comprehending the visible, made in the image of the Intellectual, being the one perfect only-begotten heaven.

Section 2.

Nature in the aspect which she presented to a Greek philosopher of the fourth century before Christ is not easily reproduced to modern eyes. The associations of mythology and poetry have to be added, and the unconscious influence of science has to be subtracted, before we can behold the heavens or the earth as they appeared to the Greek. The philosopher himself was a child and also a man—a child in the range of his attainments, but also a great intelligence having an insight into nature, and often anticipations of the truth. He was full of original thoughts, and yet liable to be imposed upon by the most obvious fallacies. He occasionally confused numbers with ideas, and atoms with numbers; his *a priori* notions were out of all proportion to his experience. He was ready to explain the phenomena of the heavens by the most trivial analogies of earth. The experiments which nature worked for him he sometimes accepted, but he never tried experiments for himself which would either prove or disprove his theories. His knowledge was unequal; while in some branches, such as medicine and astronomy, he had made considerable proficiency, there were others, such as chemistry, electricity, mechanics, of which the very names were unknown to him. He was the natural enemy of mythology, and yet mythological ideas still retained their hold over him. He was endeavouring to form a conception of principles, but these principles or ideas were regarded by him as real powers or entities, to which the world had been subjected. He was always tending to argue from what was near to what was remote, from what was known to what was unknown, from man to the universe, and back again from the universe to man. While he was arranging the world, he was arranging the forms of thought in his own mind; and the light from within and the light from without often crossed and helped to confuse one another. He might be compared to a builder engaged in some great design, who could only dig with his hands because he was unprovided with common tools; or to some poet or musician, like Tynnichus (*Ion* 534D), obliged to accommodate his lyric raptures to the limits of the tetrachord or of the flute.

The Hesiodic and Orphic cosmogonies were a phase of thought intermediate between mythology and philosophy and had a great influence on the beginnings of knowledge. There was nothing behind them; they were to physical science what the poems of Homer were to early Greek history. They made men think of the world as a whole; they carried the mind back into the infinity of past time; they suggested the first observation of the effects of fire and water on the earth's surface. To the ancient physics they stood much in the same relation which geology does to modern science. But the Greek was not, like the enquirer of the last generation, confined to a period of six thousand years; he was able to speculate freely on the effects of infinite ages in the production of physical phenomena. He could imagine cities which had existed time out of mind (*States.* 302A; *Laws* iii. 676), laws or forms of art and music which had lasted, 'not in word only, but in very truth, for ten thousand years' (*Laws* ii. 656E; cf. also vii. 799A); he was aware that natural phenomena like the Delta of the Nile might have slowly accumulated in long periods of time (cf. *Hdt.* ii. 5, 10). But he seems to have supposed that the course of events was recurring rather than progressive. To this he was probably led by the fixedness of Egyptian customs and the general observation that there were other civilisations in the world more ancient than that of Hellas.

The ancient philosophers found in mythology many ideas which, if not originally derived from nature, were easily transferred to her — such, for example, as love or hate, corresponding to attraction or repulsion; or the conception of necessity allied both to the regularity and irregularity of nature; or of chance, the nameless or unknown cause; or of justice, symbolizing the law of compensation; or of the Fates and Furies, typifying the fixed order or the extraordinary convulsions of nature. Their own interpretations of Homer and the poets were supposed by them to be the original meaning. Musing in themselves on the phenomena of nature, they were relieved at being able to utter the thoughts of their hearts in figures of speech which to them were not figures, and were already consecrated by tradition. Hesiod and the Orphic poets moved in a region of half-personification in which the meaning or principle appeared through the person. In their vaster conceptions of Chaos, Erebus, Aether, Night, and the like, the first rude attempts at generalization are dimly seen. The Gods themselves, especially the greater Gods, such as Zeus, Poseidon, Apollo, Athené, are universals as well as individuals. They were gradually becoming lost in a common conception of mind or God. They continued to exist for the purposes of ritual or of art; but from the sixth century onwards or even earlier there arose and gained strength in the minds of men the notion of 'one God, greatest among Gods and men, who was all sight, all hearing, all knowing' (Xenophanes).

Under the influence of such ideas, perhaps also deriving from the traditions of their own or of other nations scraps of medicine and astronomy, men came to the observation of nature. The Greek philosopher looked at the blue circle of the heavens and it flashed upon him that all things were one; the tumult of sense abated, and the mind found repose in the thought which former generations had been striving to realize. The first expression of this was some element, rarefied by degrees into a pure abstraction, and purged from any tincture of sense. Soon an inner world of ideas began to be unfolded, more absorbing, more overpowering, more abiding than the brightest of visible objects, which to the eye of the philosopher looking inward, seemed to pale before them, retaining only a faint and precarious existence. At the same time, the minds of men parted into the two great divisions of those who saw only a principle of motion, and of those who saw only a principle of rest, in nature and in themselves; there were born Heracliteans or Eleatics, as there have been in later ages born Aristotelians or Platonists. Like some philosophers in modern times, who are accused of making a theory first and finding their facts afterwards, the advocates of either opinion never thought of applying either to themselves or to their adversaries the criterion of fact. They were mastered by their ideas and not masters of them. Like the Heraclitean fanatics whom Plato has ridiculed in the *Theaetetus* (179E, 180), they were incapable of giving a reason of the faith that was in them, and had all the animosities of a religious sect. Yet, doubtless, there was some first impression derived from external nature, which, as in mythology, so also in philosophy, worked upon the minds of the first thinkers. Though incapable of induction or generalization in the modern sense, they caught an inspiration from the external world. The most general facts or appearances of nature, the circle of the universe, the nutritive power of water, the air which is the breath of life, the destructive force of fire, the seeming regularity of the greater part of nature and the irregularity of a remnant, the recurrence of day and night and of the seasons, the solid earth and the impalpable aether, were always present to them.

The great source of error and also the beginning of truth to them was reasoning from analogy; they could see resemblances, but not differences; and they were incapable of distinguishing illustration from argument. Analogy in modern times only points the way, and is immediately verified by experiment. The dreams and visions, which pass through the philosopher's mind, of resemblances between different classes of substances, or between the animal and vegetable world, are put into the refiner's fire, and the dross and other elements which adhere to them are purged away. But the contemporary of Plato and Socrates was incapable of resisting the power of any analogy which occurred to him, and was drawn into any consequences which seemed to follow. He had no methods of difference or of concomitant variations, by the use of which he could distinguish the accidental from the essential. He could not isolate phenomena, and he was helpless against the influence of any word which had an equivocal or double sense.

Yet without this crude use of analogy the ancient physical philosopher would have stood still; he could not have made even 'one guess among many' without comparison. The course of natural phenomena would have passed unheeded before his eyes, like fair sights or musical sounds before the eyes and ears of an animal. Even the fetichism of the savage is the beginning of reasoning; the assumption of the most fanciful of causes indicates a higher mental state than the absence of all enquiry about them. The tendency to argue from the higher to the lower, from man to the world, has led to many errors, but has also had an elevating influence on philosophy. The conception of the world as a whole, a person, an animal, has been the source of hasty generalizations; yet this general grasp of nature led also to a spirit of comprehensiveness in early philosophy, which has not increased, but rather diminished, as the fields of knowledge have become more divided. The modern physicist confines himself to one or perhaps two branches of science. But he comparatively seldom rises above his own department, and often falls under the narrowing influence which any single branch, when pursued to the exclusion of every other, has over the mind. Language, two, exercised a spell over the beginnings of physical philosophy, leading to error and sometimes to truth; for many thoughts were suggested by the double meanings of words (στοιχεῖον, συλλαβή, μουσική, ἁρμονία, κόσμος), and the accidental distinctions of words sometimes led the ancient philosopher to make corresponding differences in things (βούλεσθαι, ἐπιθυμεῖν, φόβος, δέος, αἰδώς, αἰσχύνη). 'If they are the same, why have they different names; or if they are different, why have they the same name?'—is an argument not easily answered in the infancy of knowledge. The modern philosopher has always been taught the lesson which he still imperfectly learns, that he must disengage himself from the influence of words. Nor are there wanting in Plato, who was himself too often the victim of them, impressive admonitions that we should regard not words but things (cf. *States*. 261E). But upon the whole, the ancients, though not entirely dominated by them, were much more subject to the influence of words than the moderns. They had no clear divisions of colours or substances; even the four elements were undefined; the fields of knowledge were not parted off. They were bringing order out of disorder, having a small grain of experience mingled in a confused heap of *a priori* notions. And yet, probably, their first impressions, the illusions and mirages of their fancy, created a greater intellectual activity and made a nearer approach to the truth than any patient investigation of isolated facts, for which the time had not yet come, could have accomplished.

There was one more illusion to which the ancient philosophers were subject, and against which Plato in his later dialogues seems to be struggling—the tendency to mere abstractions; not perceiving that pure abstraction is only negation, they thought that the greater the abstraction the greater the truth. Behind any pair of ideas a new idea which comprehended them—the τρίτος ἄνθρωπος, as it was technically termed—began at once to appear. Two are truer than three, one than two. The words 'being,' or 'unity,' or essence,' or 'good,' became sacred to them. They did not see that they had a word only, and in one sense the most unmeaning of words. They did not understand that the content of notions is in inverse proportion to their universality—the element which is the most widely diffused is also the thinnest; or, in the language of the common logic, the greater the extension the less the comprehension. But this vacant idea of a whole without parts, of a subject without predicates, a rest without motion, has been also the most fruitful of all ideas. It is the beginning of *a priori* thought, and indeed of thinking at all. Men were led to conceive it, not by a love of hasty generalization, but by a divine instinct, a dialectical enthusiasm, in which the human faculties seemed to yearn for enlargement. We know that 'being' is only the verb of existence, the copula, the most general symbol of relation, the first and most meagre of abstractions; but to some of the ancient philosophers this little word appeared to attain divine proportions, and to comprehend all truth. Being or essence, and similar words, represented to them a supreme or divine being, in which they thought that they found the containing and continuing principle of the universe. In a few years the human mind was peopled with abstractions; a new world was called into existence to give law and order to the old. But between them there was still a gulf, and no one could pass from the one to the other.

Number and figure were the greatest instruments of thought which were possessed by the Greek philosopher; having the same power over the mind which was exerted by abstract ideas, they were also capable of practical application. Many curious and, to the early thinker, mysterious properties of them came to light when they were compared with one another. They admitted of infinite multiplication and construction; in Pythagorean triangles or in proportions of 1:2:4:8 and 1:3:9:27, or compounds of them, the laws of the world seemed to be more than half revealed. They were also capable of infinite subdivision—a wonder and also a puzzle to the ancient thinker (cf. *Rep.* vii. 525E). They were not, like being or essence, mere vacant abstractions, but admitted of progress and growth, while at the same time they confirmed a higher sentiment of the mind, that there was order in the universe. And so there began to be a real sympathy between the world within and the world without. The numbers and figures which were present to the mind's eye became visible to the eye of sense; the truth of nature was mathematics; the other properties of objects seemed to reappear only in the light of number. Law and morality also found a natural expression in number and figure. Instruments of such power and elasticity could not fail to be 'a most gracious assistance' to the first efforts of human intelligence.

There was another reason why numbers had so great an influence over the minds of early thinkers—they were verified by experience. Every use of them, even the most trivial, assured men of their truth; they were everywhere to be found, in the least things and the greatest alike. One, two, three, counted on the fingers was a 'trivial matter' (*Rep.* vii. 522C), a little instrument out of which to create a world; but from these and by the help of these all our knowledge of nature has been developed. They were the measure of all things, and seemed to give law to all things; nature was rescued from chaos and confusion by their power; the notes of music, the motions of the stars, the forms of atoms, the evolution and recurrence of days, months, years, the military divisions of an army, the civil divisions of a state, seemed to afford a 'present witness' of them—what would have become of man or of the world if deprived of number (*Rep.* vii. 522E)? The mystery of number and the mystery of music were akin. There was a music of rhythm and of harmonious motion everywhere; and to the real connexion which existed between music and number, a fanciful or imaginary relation was superadded. There was a music of the spheres as well as of the notes of the lyre. If in all things seen there was number and figure, why should they not also pervade the unseen world, with which by their

wonderful and unchangeable nature they seemed to hold communion?

Two other points strike us in the use which the ancient philosophers
made of numbers. First, they applied to external nature the relations of
them which they found in their own minds; and where nature seemed
to be at variance with number, as for example in the case of fractions,
they protested against her (*Rep.* vii. 525; Arist. *Metaph.* i.6). Having
long meditated on the properties of 1:2:4:8, or 1:3:9:27, or of 3, 4, 5,
they discovered in them many curious correspondences and were disposed to find in them the secret of the universe. Secondly, they applied
number and figure equally to those parts of physics, such as astronomy
or mechanics, in which the modern philosopher expects to find them,
and to those in which he would never think of looking for them, such
as physiology and psychology. For the sciences were not yet divided,
and there was nothing really irrational in arguing that the same laws
which regulated the heavenly bodies were partially applied to the
erring limbs or brain of man. Astrology was the form which the lively
fancy of ancient thinkers almost necessarily gave to astronomy. The observation that the lower principle, e.g. mechanics, is always seen in the
higher, e.g. in the phenomena of life, further tended to perplex them.
Plato's doctrine of the same and the other ruling the courses of the
heavens and of the human body is not a mere vagary, but is a natural
result of the state of knowledge and thought at which he had arrived.

When in modern times we contemplate the heavens, a certain
amount of scientific truth imperceptibly blends, even with the cursory
glance of an unscientific person. He knows that the earth is revolving
round the sun, and not the sun around the earth. He does not imagine
the earth to be the centre of the universe, and he has some conception
of chemistry and the cognate sciences. A very different aspect of nature
would have been present to the mind of the early Greek philosopher.
He would have beheld the earth a surface only, not mirrored, however
faintly, in the glass of science, but indissolubly connected with some
theory of one, two, or more elements. He would have seen the world
pervaded by number and figure, animated by a principle of motion, immanent in a principle of rest. He would have tried to construct the universe on a quantitative principle, seeming to find in endless combinations of geometrical figures or in the infinite variety of their sizes a sufficient account of the multiplicity of phenomena. To these *a priori*
speculations he would add a rude conception of matter and his own
immediate experience of health and disease. His cosmos would necessarily be imperfect and unequal, being the first attempt to impress form
and order on the primaeval chaos of human knowledge. He would see
all things as in a dream.

The ancient physical philosophers have been charged by Dr. Whewell and others with wasting their fine intelligences in wrong methods of enquiry; and their progress in moral and political philosophy has been sometimes contrasted with their supposed failure in physical investigations. 'They had plenty of ideas,' says Dr. Whewell, 'and plenty of facts; but their ideas did not accurately represent the facts with which they were acquainted.' This is a very crude and misleading way of describing ancient science. It is the mistake of an uneducated person—uneducated, that is, in the higher sense of the word—who imagines every one else to be like himself and explains every other age by his own. No doubt the ancients often fell into strange and fanciful errors: the time had not yet arrived for the slower and surer path of the modern inductive philosophy. But it remains to be shown that they could have done more in their age and country; or that the contributions which they made to the sciences with which they were acquainted are not as great upon the whole as those made by their successors. There is no single step in astronomy as great as that of the nameless Pythagorean who first conceived the world to be a body moving round the sun in space: there is no truer or more comprehensive principle than the application of mathematics alike to the heavenly bodies, and to the particles of matter. The ancients had not the instruments which would have enabled them to correct or verify their anticipations, and their opportunities of observation were limited. Plato probably did more for physical science by asserting the supremacy of mathematics than Aristotle or his disciples by their collections of facts. When the thinkers of modern times, following Bacon, undervalue or disparage the speculations of ancient philosophers, they seem wholly to forget the conditions of the world and of the human mind, under which they carried on their investigations. When we accuse them of being under the influence of words, do we suppose that we are altogether free from this illusion? When we remark that Greek physics soon became stationary or extinct, may we not observe also that there have been and may be again periods in the history of modern philosophy which have been barren and unproductive? We might as well maintain that Greek art was not real or great, because it had *nihil simile aut secundum,* as say that Greek physics were a failure because they made no subsequent progress.

The charge of premature generalization which is often urged against ancient philosophers is really an anachronism. For they can hardly be said to have generalized at all. They may be said more truly to have cleared up and defined by the help of experience ideas which they already possessed. The beginnings of thought about nature must always have this character. A true method is the result of many ages of experi-

ment and observation, and is ever going on and enlarging with the
progress of science and knowledge. At first men personify nature, then
they form impressions of nature, at last they conceive 'measure' or laws
of nature. They pass out of mythology into philosophy. Early science is
not a process of discovery in the modern sense; but rather a process of
correcting by observation, and to a certain extent only, the first impressions of nature, which mankind, when they began to think, had received from poetry or language or unintelligent sense. Of all scientific
truths the greatest and simplest is the uniformity of nature; this was expressed by the ancients in many ways, as fate, or necessity, or measure,
or limit. Unexpected events, of which the cause was unknown to them,
they attributed to chance (cf. *Thucyd.* i. 140). But their conception of
nature was never that of law interrupted by exceptions,—a somewhat
unfortunate metaphysical invention of modern times, which is at variance with facts and has failed to satisfy the requirements of thought.

Section 3.

Plato's account of the soul is partly mythical or figurative, and partly
literal. Not that either he or we can draw a line between them, or say,
'This is poetry, this is philosophy'; for the transition from the one to the
other is imperceptible. Neither must we expect to find in him absolute
consistency. He is apt to pass from one level or stage of thought to another without always making it apparent that he is changing his
ground. In such passages we have to interpret his meaning by the general spirit of his writings. To reconcile his inconsistencies would be
contrary to the first principles of criticism and fatal to any true understanding of him.

There is a further difficulty in explaining this part of the *Timaeus*—
the natural order of thought is inverted. We begin with the most abstract, and proceed from the abstract to the concrete. We are searching
into things which are upon the utmost limit of human intelligence,
and then of a sudden we fall rather heavily to the earth. There are no
intermediate steps which lead from one to the other. But the abstract is
a vacant form to us until brought into relation with man and nature.
God and the world are mere names, like the Being of the Eleatics, unless some human qualities are added on to them. Yet the negation has
a kind of unknown meaning to us. The priority of God and of the
world, which he is imagined to have created, to all other existences,
gives a solemn awe to them. And as in other systems of theology and
philosophy, that of which we know least has the greatest interest to us.

There is no use in attempting to define or explain the first God in the Platonic system, who has sometimes been thought to answer to God the Father; or the world, in whom the Fathers of the Church seemed to recognize 'the firstborn of every creature.' Nor need we discuss at length how far Plato agrees in the later Jewish idea of creation, according to which God made the world out of nothing. For his original conception of matter as something which has no qualities is really a negation. Moreover in the Hebrew Scriptures the creation of the world is described, even more explicitly than in the *Timaeus*, not as a single act, but as a work or process which occupied six days. There is a chaos in both, and it would be untrue to say that the Greek, any more than the Hebrew, had any definite belief in the eternal existence of matter. The beginning of things vanished into the distance. The real creation began, not with matter, but with ideas. According to Plato in the *Timaeus*, God took of the same and the other, of the divided and undivided, of the finite and infinite, and made essence, and out of the three combined created the soul of the world. To the soul he added a body formed out of the four elements. The general meaning of these words is that God imparted determinations of thought, or, as we might say, gave law and variety to the material universe. The elements are moving in a disorderly manner before the work of creation begins (30A); and there is an eternal pattern of the world, which, like the 'idea of good,' is not the Creator himself, but not separable from him. The pattern too, though eternal, is a creation, a world of thought prior to the world of sense, which may be compared to the wisdom of God in the book of Ecclesiasticus, or to the 'God in the form of a globe' of the old Eleatic philosophers. The visible, which already exists, is fashioned in the likeness of this eternal pattern. On the other hand, there is no truth of which Plato is more firmly convinced than of the priority of the soul to the body, both in the universe and in man. So inconsistent are the forms in which he describes the works which no tongue can utter—his language, as he himself says (29C), partaking of his own uncertainty about the things of which he is speaking.

We may remark in passing, that the Platonic compared with the Jewish description of the process of creation has less of freedom or spontaneity. The Creator in Plato is still subject to a remnant of necessity which he cannot wholly overcome (cf. 35A). When his work is accomplished he remains in his own nature. Plato is more sensible than the Hebrew prophet of the existence of evil, which he seeks to put as far as possible out of the way of God (cf. 42D). And he can only suppose this to be accomplished by God retiring into himself and committing the lesser works of creation to inferior powers. (Compare, however, *Laws* X. 903 for another solution of the difficulty.)

Nor can we attach any intelligible meaning to his words when he speaks of the visible being in the image of the invisible (28). For how can that which is divided be like that which is undivided? Or that which is changing be the copy of that which is unchanging? All the old difficulties about the ideas come back upon us in an altered form. We can imagine two worlds, one of which is the mere double of the other, or one of which is an imperfect copy of the other, or one of which is the vanishing ideal of the other; but we cannot imagine an intellectual world which has no qualities—'a thing in itself'—a point which has no parts or magnitude, which is nowhere, and nothing. This cannot be the archetype according to which God made the world, and is in reality, whether in Plato or in Kant, a mere negative residuum of human thought.

There is another aspect of the same difficulty which appears to have no satisfactory solution. In what relation does the archetype stand to the Creator himself? For the idea or pattern of the world is not the thought of God, but a separate, self-existent nature, of which creation is the copy. We can only reply, (1) that to the mind of Plato subject and object were not yet distinguished; (2) that he supposes the process of creation to take place in accordance with his own theory of ideas; and as we cannot give a consistent account of the one, neither can we of the other. He means (3) to say that the creation of the world is not a material process of working with legs and arms, but ideal and intellectual; according to his own fine expression, 'the thought of God made the God that was to be.' (34A) He means (4) to draw an absolute distinction between the invisible or unchangeable which is or is the place of mind or being, and the world of sense or becoming which is visible and changing. He means (5) that the idea of the world is prior to the world, just as the other ideas are prior to sensible objects; and like them may be regarded as eternal and self-existent, and also, like the *idea* of good, may be viewed apart from the divine mind.

There are several other questions which we might ask and which can receive no answer, or at least only an answer of the same kind as the preceding. How can matter be conceived to exist without form? Or, how can the essences or forms of things be distinguished from the eternal ideas, or essence itself from the soul? Or, how could there have been motion in the chaos when as yet time was not? Or, how did chaos come into existence, if not by the will of the Creator? Or, how could there have been a time when the world was not, if time was not? Or, how could the Creator have taken portions of an indivisible same? Or, how could space or anything else have been eternal when time is only created? Or, how could the surfaces of geometrical figures have formed solids? We must reply again that we cannot follow Plato in all his inconsistencies, but that the gaps of thought are probably more apparent to us than to him. He would, perhaps, have said that 'the first things are known only to God and to him of men whom God loves.' How often have the gaps in Theology been concealed from the eye of faith! And we may say that only by an effort of metaphysical imagination can we hope to understand Plato from his own point of view; we must not ask for consistency. Everywhere we find traces of the Platonic theory of knowledge expressed in an objective form, which by us has to be translated into the subjective, before we can attach any meaning to it. And this theory is exhibited in so many different points of view, that we cannot with any certainty interpret one dialogue by another; e.g. the *Timaeus* by the *Parmenides* or *Phaedrus* or *Philebus*.

The soul of the world may also be conceived as the personification of the numbers and figures in which the heavenly bodies move. Imagine these as in a Pythagorean dream, stripped of qualitative difference and reduced to mathematical abstractions. They too conform to the principle of the same, and may be compared with the modern conception of laws of nature. They are in space, but not in time, and they are the makers of time. They are represented as constantly thinking of the same; for thought in the view of Plato is equivalent to truth or law, and need not imply a human consciousness, a conception which is familiar enough to us, but has no place, hardly even a name, in ancient Greek philosophy. To this principle of the same is opposed the principle of the other—the principle of irregularity and disorder, of necessity and chance, which is only partially impressed by mathematical laws and figures. (We may observe by the way, that the principle of the other, which is the principle of plurality and variation in the *Timaeus*, has nothing in common with the 'other' of the Sophist, which is the principle of determination.) The element of the same dominates to a certain extent over the other—the fixed stars keep the 'wanderers' of the inner circle in their courses (36C), and a similar principle of fixedness or order appears to regulate the bodily constitution of man (89A, 90D). But there still remains a rebellious seed of evil derived from the original chaos, which is the source of disorder in the world, and of vice and disease in man.

But what did Plato mean by essence, οὐσία, which is the intermediate nature compounded of the Same and the Other, and out of which, together with these two, the soul of the world is created? It is difficult to explain a process of thought so strange and unaccustomed to us, in which modern distinctions run into one another and are lost sight of. First, let us consider once more the meaning of the Same and the Other. The Same is the unchanging and indivisible, the heaven of the fixed stars, partaking of the divine nature, which, having law in itself, gives law to all besides and is the element of order and permanence in man and on the earth. It is the rational principle, mind regarded as a work, as creation—not as the creator. The old tradition of Parmenides and of the Eleatic Being, the foundation of so much in the philosophy of Greece and of the world, was lingering in Plato's mind. The Other is the variable or changing element, the residuum of disorder or chaos, which cannot be reduced to order, nor altogether banished, the source of evil, seen in the errors of man and also in the wanderings of the planets, a necessity which protrudes through nature. Of this too there was a shadow in the Eleatic philosophy in the realm of opinion, which, like a mist, seemed to darken the purity of truth in itself.—So far the words of Plato may perhaps find an intelligible meaning. But when he goes on to speak of the Essence which is compounded out of both, the track becomes fainter and we can only follow him with hesitating steps. But still we find a trace reappearing of the teaching of Anaxagoras: 'All was confusion, and then mind came and arranged things.' We have already remarked that Plato was not acquainted with the modern distinction of subject and object, and therefore he sometimes confuses mind and the things of mind—νοῦς and νοητά. By οὐσία he clearly means some conception of the intelligible and the intelligent; it belongs to the class of νοητά. Matter, being, the Same, the eternal,—for any of these terms, being almost vacant of meaning, is equally suitable to express indefinite existence,—are compared or united with the Other or Diverse, and out of the union or comparison is elicited the idea of intelligence, the 'One in many,' brighter than any Promethean fire (cf. *Phil.* 16C), which co-existing with them and so forming a new existence, is or becomes the intelligible world. . . . So we may perhaps venture to paraphrase or interpret or put into other words the parable in which Plato has wrapped up his conception of the creation of the world. The explanation may help to fill up with figures of speech the void of knowledge.

The entire compound was divided by the Creator in certain proportions and reunited; it was then cut into two strips, which were bent into an inner circle and an outer, both moving with an uniform motion around a centre, the outer circle containing the fixed, the inner the wandering stars. The soul of the world was diffused everywhere from the centre to the circumference. To this God gave a body, consisting at first of fire and earth, and afterwards receiving an addition of air and water; because solid bodies, like the world, are always connected by two middle terms and not by one. The world was made in the form of a globe, and all the material elements were exhausted in the work of creation.

The proportions in which the soul of the world as well as the human soul is divided answer to a series of numbers 1, 2, 3, 4, 9, 8, 27, composed of the two Pythagorean progressions 1, 2, 4, 8 and 1, 3, 9, 27, of which the number 1 represents a point, 2 and 3 lines, 4 and 8, 9 and 27 the squares and cubes respectively of 2 and 3. This series, of which the intervals are afterwards filled up, probably represents (1) the diatonic scale according to the Pythagoreans and Plato; (2) the order and distances of the heavenly bodies; and (3) may possibly contain an allusion to the music of the spheres, which is referred to in the myth at the end of the *Republic*. The meaning of the words that 'solid bodies are always connected by two middle terms' or mean proportionals has been much disputed. The most received explanation is that of Martin, who supposes that Plato is only speaking of surfaces and solids compounded of prime numbers (i.e. of numbers not made up of two factors, or, in other words, only measurable by unity). The square of any such number represents a surface, the cube a solid. The squares of any two such numbers (e.g. 2^2, $3^2 = 4$, 9), have always a single mean proportional (e.g. 4 and 9 have the single mean 6), whereas the cubes of primes (e.g. 3^3 and 5^3) have always two mean proportionals (e.g. 27:45:75:125). But to this explanation of Martin's it may be objected, (1) that Plato nowhere says that his proportion is to be limited to prime numbers; (2) that the limitation of surfaces to squares is also not to be found in his words; nor (3) is there any evidence to show that the distinction of prime from other numbers was known to him. What Plato chiefly intends to express is that a solid requires a stronger bond than a surface; and that the double bond which is given by two means is stronger than the single bond given by one. Having reflected on the singular numerical phenomenon of the existence of one mean proportional between two square numbers or rather perhaps only between the two lowest squares; and of two mean proportionals between two cubes, perhaps again confining his attention to the two lowest cubes, he finds in the latter symbol an expression of the relation of the elements, as in the former an image of the combination of two surfaces. Between fire and earth, the two extremes, he remarks that there are introduced, not one, but two elements, air and water, which are compared to the two mean proportionals between two cube numbers. The vagueness of his language does not allow us to determine whether anything more than this was intended by him.

Leaving the further explanation of details, which the reader will find discussed at length in Boeckh and Martin, we may now return to the main argument: Why did God make the world? Like man, he must have a purpose; and his purpose is the diffusion of that goodness or good which he himself is. The term 'goodness' is not to be understood in this passage as meaning benevolence or love, in the Christian sense of the term, but rather law, order, harmony, like the idea of good in the

Republic. The ancient mythologers, and even the Hebrew prophets, had spoken of the jealousy of God; and the Greek had imagined that there was a Nemesis always attending the prosperity of mortals. But Plato delights to think of God as the author of order in his works, who, like a father, lives over again in his children, and can never have too much of good or friendship among his creatures. Only, as there is a certain remnant of evil inherent in matter which he cannot get rid of, he detaches himself from them and leaves them to themselves, that he may be guiltless of their faults and sufferings.

Between the ideal and the sensible Plato interposes the two natures of time and space. Time is conceived by him to be only the shadow or image of eternity which ever is and never has been or will be, but is described in a figure only as past or future. This is one of the great thoughts of early philosophy, which are still as difficult to our minds as they were to the early thinkers; or perhaps more difficult, because we more distinctly see the consequences which are involved in such an hypothesis. All the objections which may be urged against Kant's doctrine of the ideality of space and time at once press upon us. If time is unreal, then all which is contained in time is unreal—the succession of human thoughts as well as the flux of sensations; there is no connecting link between φαινόμενα and ὄντα. Yet, on the other hand, we are conscious that knowledge is independent of time, that truth is not a thing of yesterday or to-morrow, but an 'eternal now.' To the 'spectator of all time and all existence' the universe remains at rest. The truths of geometry and arithmetic in all their combinations are always the same. The generations of men, like the leaves of the forest, come and go, but the mathematical laws by which the world is governed remain, and seem as if they could never change. The ever-present image of space is transferred to time—succession is conceived as extension. (We remark that Plato does away with the above and below in space, as he has done away with the absolute existence of past and future.) The course of time, unless regularly marked by divisions of number, partakes of the indefiniteness of the Heraclitean flux. By such reflections we may conceive the Greek to have attained the metaphysical conception of eternity, which to the Hebrew was gained by meditation on the Divine Being. No one saw that this objective was really a subjective, and involved the subjectivity of all knowledge. 'Non in tempore sed cum tempore finxit Deus mundum,' says St. Augustine, repeating a thought derived from the *Timaeus,* but apparently unconscious of the results to which his doctrine would have led.

The contradictions involved in the conception of time or motion, like the infinitesimal in space, were a source of perplexity to the mind of the Greek, who was driven to find a point of view above or beyond them. They had sprung up in the decline of the Eleatic philosophy and were very familiar to Plato, as we gather from the *Parmenides*. The consciousness of them had led the great Eleatic philosopher to describe the nature of God or Being under negatives. He sings of 'Being unbegotten and imperishable, unmoved and never-ending, which never was nor will be, but always is, one and continuous, which cannot spring from any other; for it cannot be said or imagined not to be.' The idea of eternity was for a great part a negation. There are regions of speculation in which the negative is hardly separable from the positive, and even seems to pass into it. Not only Buddhism, but Greek as well as Christian philosophy, show that it is quite possible that the human mind should retain an enthusiasm for mere negations. In different ages and countries there have been forms of light in which nothing could be discerned and which have nevertheless exercised a life-giving and illumining power. For the higher intelligence of man seems to require, not only something above sense, but above knowledge, which can only be described as Mind or Being or Truth or God or the unchangeable and eternal element, in the expression of which all predicates fail and fall short. Eternity or the eternal is not merely the unlimited in time but the truest of all Being, the most real of all realities, the most certain of all knowledge, which we nevertheless only see through a glass darkly. The passionate earnestness of Parmenides contrasts with the vacuity of the thought which he is revolving in his mind.

Space is said by Plato to be the 'containing vessel or nurse of generation.' Reflecting on the simplest kinds of external objects, which to the ancients were the four elements, he was led to a more general notion of a substance, more or less like themselves, out of which they were fashioned. He would not have them too precisely distinguished. Thus seems to have arisen the first dim perception of ὕλη or matter, which has played so great a part in the metaphysical philosophy of Aristotle and his followers. But besides the material out of which the elements are made, there is also a space in which they are contained. There arises thus a second nature which the senses are incapable of discerning and which can hardly be referred to the intelligible class. For it is and it is not, it is nowhere when filled, it is nothing when empty. Hence it is said to be discerned by a kind of spurious or analogous reason, partaking so feebly of existence as to be hardly perceivable, yet always reappearing as the containing mother or nurse of all things. It had not that sort of consistency to Plato which has been given to it in modern times by geometry and metaphysics. Neither of the Greek words by which it is described are so purely abstract as the English word 'space' or the Latin 'spatium.' Neither Plato nor any other Greek would have spoken of χρόνος καὶ τόπος or χώρα in the same manner as we speak of 'time' and 'space.'

Yet space is also of a very permanent or even eternal nature; and Plato seems more willing to admit of the unreality of time than of the unreality of space; because, as he says, all things must necessarily exist in space. We, on the other hand, are disposed to fancy that even if space were annihilated time might still survive. He admits indeed that our knowledge of space is of a dreamy kind, and is given by a spurious reason without the help of sense. (Compare the hypotheses and images of *Rep.* vi. 511) It is true that it does not attain to the clearness of ideas. But like them it seems to remain, even if all the objects contained in it are supposed to have vanished away. Hence it was natural for Plato to conceive of it as eternal. We must remember further that in his attempt to realize either space or matter the two abstract ideas of weight and extension, which are familiar to us, had never passed before his mind.

Thus far God, working according to an eternal pattern, out of his goodness has created the same, the other, and the essence (compare the three principles of the *Philebus*—the finite, the infinite, and the union of the two), and out of them has formed the outer circle of the fixed stars and the inner circle of the planets, divided according to certain musical intervals; he has also created time, the moving image of eternity, and space, existing by a sort of necessity and hardly distinguishable from matter. The matter out of which the world is formed is not absolutely void, but retains in the chaos certain germs or traces of the elements. These Plato, like Empedocles, supposed to be four in number—fire, air, earth, and water. They were at first mixed together; but already in the chaos, before God fashioned them by form and number, the greater masses of the elements had an appointed place. Into the confusion (μῖγμα) which preceded Plato does not attempt further to penetrate. They are called elements, but they are so far from being elements (στοιχεῖα) or letters in the higher sense that they are not even syllables or first compounds. The real elements are two triangles, the rectangular isosceles which has but one form, and the most beautiful of the many forms of scalene, which is half of an equilateral triangle. By the combination of these triangles which exist in an infinite variety of sizes, the surfaces of the four elements are constructed.

That there were only five regular solids was already known to the ancients, and out of the surfaces which he has formed Plato proceeds to generate the four first of the five. He perhaps forgets that he is only putting together surfaces and has not provided for their transformation into solids. The first solid is a regular pyramid, of which the base and sides are formed by four equilateral or twenty-four scalene triangles.

Each of the four solid angles in this figure is a little larger than the largest of obtuse angles. The second solid is composed of the same triangles, which unite as eight equilateral triangles, and make one solid angle out of four plane angles—six of these angles form a regular octahedron. The third solid is a regular icosahedron, having twenty triangular equilateral bases, and therefore 120 rectangular scalene triangles. The fourth regular solid, or cube, is formed by the combination of four isosceles triangles into one square and of six squares into a cube. The fifth regular solid, or dodecahedron, cannot be formed by a combination of either of these triangles, but each of its faces may be regarded as composed of thirty triangles of another kind. Probably Plato notices this as the only remaining regular polyhedron, which from its approximation to a globe, and possibly because, as Plutarch remarks, it is composed of 12 x 30 = 360 scalene triangles (*Platon. Quaest.* 5), representing thus the signs and degrees of the Zodiac, as well as the months and days of the year, God may be said to have 'used in the delineation of the universe.' According to Plato earth was composed of cubes, fire of regular pyramids, air of regular octahedrons, water of regular icosahedrons. The stability of the last three increases with the number of their sides.

The elements are supposed to pass into one another, but we must remember that these transformations are not the transformations of real solids, but of imaginary geometrical figures; in other words, we are composing and decomposing the faces of substances and not the substances themselves—it is a house of cards which we are pulling to pieces and putting together again (compare however *Laws* X. 894A). Yet perhaps Plato may regard these sides or faces as only the forms which are impressed on pre-existent matter. It is remarkable that he should speak of each of these solids as a possible world in itself, though upon the whole he inclines to the opinion that they form one world and not five. To suppose that there is an infinite number of worlds, as Democritus (*Hippolyt. Ref. Haer.* I. 13) had said, would be, as he satirically observes, 'the characteristic of a very indefinite and ignorant mind' (55C, D).

The twenty triangular faces of an icosahedron form the faces or sides of two regular octahedrons and of a regular pyramid (20 = 8 x 2 + 4); and therefore, according to Plato, a particle of water when decomposed is supposed to give two particles of air and one of fire. So because an octahedron gives the sides of two pyramids (8 = 4 x 2), a particle of air is resolved into two particles of fire.

The transformation is effected by the superior power or number of the conquering elements. The manner of the change is (1) a separation of portions of the elements from the masses in which they are collected; (2) a resolution of them into their original triangles; and (3) a reunion of them in new forms. Plato himself proposes the question, Why does motion continue at all when the elements are settled in their places? He answers that although the force of attraction is continually drawing similar elements to the same spot, still the revolution of the universe exercises a condensing power, and thrusts them again out of their natural places. Thus want of uniformity, the condition of motion, is produced. In all such disturbances of matter there is an alternative for the weaker element: it may escape to its kindred, or take the form of the stronger—becoming denser, if it be denser, or rarer, if rarer. This is true of fire, air, and water, which, being composed of similar triangles, are interchangeable; earth, however, which has triangles peculiar to itself, is capable of dissolution, but not of change (56D ff.). Of the interchangeable elements, fire, the rarest, can only become a denser, and water, the densest, only a rarer: but air may become a denser or a rarer. No single particle of the elements is visible, but only the aggregates of them are seen. The subordinate species depend, not upon differences of form in the original triangles, but upon differences of size. The obvious physical phenomena from which Plato has gathered his views of the relations of the elements seem to be the effect of fire upon air, water, and earth, and the effect of water upon earth. The particles are supposed by him to be in a perpetual process of circulation caused by inequality. This process of circulation does not admit of a vacuum, as he tells us in his strange account of respiration (79B).

Of the phenomena of light and heavy he speaks afterwards, when treating of sensation, but they may be more conveniently considered by us in this place. They are not, he says, to be explained by 'above' and 'below,' which in the universal globe have no existence (62D), but by the attraction of similars towards the great masses of similar substances; fire to fire, air to air, water to water, earth to earth. Plato's doctrine of attraction implies not only (1) the attraction of similar elements to one another, but also (2) of smaller bodies to larger ones. Had he confined himself to the latter he would have arrived, though, perhaps, without any further result or any sense of the greatness of the discovery, at the modern doctrine of gravitation. He does not observe that water has an equal tendency towards both water and earth. So easily did the most obvious facts which were inconsistent with his theories escape him.

The general physical doctrines of the *Timaeus* may be summed up as follows: (1) Plato supposes the greater masses of the elements to have been already settled in their places at the creation: (2) they are four in number, and are formed of rectangular triangles variously combined into regular solid figures: (3) three of them, fire, air, and water, admit of transformation into one another; the fourth, earth, cannot be similarly transformed: (4) different sizes of the same triangles form the lesser species of each element: (5) there is an attraction of like to like — smaller masses of the same kind being drawn towards greater: (6) there is no void, but the particles of matter are ever pushing one another round and round (περίωσις). Like the atomists, Plato attributes the differences between the elements to differences in geometrical figures. But he does not explain the process by which surfaces become solids; and he characteristically ridicules Democritus for not seeing that the worlds are finite and not infinite.

Section 4.

The astronomy of Plato is based on the two principles of the same and the other, which God combined in the creation of the world. The soul, which is compounded of the same, the other, and the essence, is diffused from the centre to the circumference of the heavens. We speak of a soul of the universe; but more truly regarded, the universe of the *Timaeus* is a soul, governed by mind, and holding in solution a residuum of matter or evil, which the author of the world is unable to expel, and of which Plato cannot tell us the origin. The creation, in Plato's sense, is really the creation of order; and the first step in giving order is the division of the heavens into an inner and outer circle of the other and the same, of the divisible and the indivisible, answering to the two spheres, of the planets and of the world beyond them, all together moving around the earth, which is their centre. To us there is a difficulty in apprehending how that which is at rest can also be in motion, or that which is indivisible exist in space. But the whole description is so ideal and imaginative, that we can hardly venture to attribute to many of Plato's words in the *Timaeus* any more meaning than to his mythical account of the heavens in the *Republic* and in the *Phaedrus*. (Compare his denial of the 'blasphemous opinion' that there are planets or wandering stars; all alike move in circles — *Laws* vii. 821, 2.) The stars are the habitations of the souls of men, from which they come and to which they return. In attributing to the fixed stars only the most perfect motion — that which is on the same spot or circling around the same — he might perhaps have said that to 'the spectator of all time and all existence,' to borrow once more his own grand expression, or viewed, in the language of Spinoza, 'sub specie aeternitatis,' they were still at rest, but appeared to move in order to teach men the periods of time. Although absolutely in motion, they are relatively at rest; or we may conceive of them as resting, while the space in which they are contained, or the whole *anima mundi*, revolves.

The universe revolves around a centre once in twenty-four hours, but the orbits of the fixed stars take a different direction from those of the planets. The outer and the inner sphere cross one another and meet again at a point opposite to that of their first contact; the first moving in a circle from left to right along the side of a parallelogram which is supposed to be inscribed in it, the second also moving in a circle along the diagonal of the same parallelogram from right to left; or, in other words, the first describing the path of the equator, the second, the path of the ecliptic. The motion of the second is controlled by the first, and hence the oblique line in which the planets are supposed to move becomes a spiral. The motion of the same is said to be undivided, whereas the inner motion is split into seven unequal orbits—the intervals between them being in the ratio of two and three, three of either:— the Sun, moving in the opposite direction to Mercury and Venus, but with equal swiftness; the remaining four, Moon, Saturn, Mars, Jupiter, with unequal swiftness to the former three and to one another. Thus arises the following progression:—Moon 1, Sun 2, Venus 3, Mercury 4, Mars 8, Jupiter 9, Saturn 27. This series of numbers is the compound of the two Pythagorean ratios, having the same intervals, though not in the same order, as the mixture which was originally divided in forming the soul of the world.

Plato was struck by the phenomenon of Mercury, Venus, and the Sun appearing to overtake and be overtaken by one another. The true reason of this, namely, that they lie within the circle of the earth's orbit, was unknown to him, and the reason which he gives—that the two former move in an opposite direction to the latter—is far from explaining the appearance of them in the heavens. All the planets, including the sun, are carried round in the daily motion of the circle of the fixed stars, and they have a second or oblique motion which gives the explanation of the different lengths of the sun's course in different parts of the earth. The fixed stars have also two movements—a forward movement in their orbit which is common to the whole circle; and a movement on the same spot around an axis, which Plato calls the movement of thought about the same. In this latter respect they are more perfect than the wandering stars, as Plato himself terms them in the *Timaeus*, although in the *Laws* (loc. cit.) he condemns the appellation as blasphemous.

The revolution of the world around the earth, which is accomplished in a single day and night, is described as being the most perfect or intelligent. Yet Plato also speaks of an 'annus magnus' or cyclical year, in which periods wonderful for their complexity are found to coincide in a perfect number, i.e. a number which equals the sum of its factors, as $6 = 1 + 2 + 3$. This, although not literally contradictory, is in spirit irreconcilable with the perfect revolution of twenty-four hours. The same remark may be applied to the complexity of the appearances and occultations of the stars, which, if the outer heaven is supposed to be moving around the centre once in twenty-four hours, must be confined to the effects produced by the seven planets. Plato seems to confuse the actual observation of the heavens with his desire to find in them mathematical perfection. The same spirit is carried yet further by him in the passage already quoted from the *Laws*, in which he affirms their wanderings to be an appearance only, which a little knowledge of mathematics would enable men to correct.

We have now to consider the much discussed question of the rotation or immobility of the earth. Plato's doctrine on this subject is contained in the following words:—'The earth, which is our nurse, compacted (*or* revolving) around the pole which is extended through the universe, he made to be the guardian and artificer of night and day, first and eldest of gods that are in the interior of heaven.' There is an unfortunate doubt in this passage (1) about the meaning of the word ἰλλομένην, which is translated either 'compacted' or 'revolving,' and is equally capable of both explanations. A doubt (2) may also be raised as to whether the words 'artificer of day and night' are consistent with the mere passive causation of them, produced by the immobility of the earth in the midst of the circling universe. We must admit, further, (3) that Aristotle attributed to Plato the doctrine of the rotation of the earth on its axis. On the other hand it has been urged that if the earth goes round with the outer heaven and sun in twenty-four hours, there is no way of accounting for the alternation of day and night; since the equal motion of the earth and sun would have the effect of absolute immobility. To which it may be replied that Plato never says that the earth goes round with the outer heaven and sun; although the whole question depends on the relation of earth and sun, their movements are nowhere precisely described. But if we suppose, with Mr. Grote, that the diurnal rotation of the earth on its axis and the revolution of the sun and outer heaven precisely coincide, it would be difficult to imagine that Plato was unaware of the consequence. For though he was ignorant of many things which are familiar to us, and often confused in his ideas where we have become clear, we have no right to attribute to him a childish want of reasoning about very simple facts, or an inability to understand the necessary and obvious deductions from geometrical figures or movements. Of the causes of day and night the pre-Socratic philosophers, and especially the Pythagoreans, gave various accounts, and therefore the question can hardly be imagined to have escaped him. On the other hand it may be urged that the further step, however simple and obvious, is just what Plato often seems to be ignorant of, and that as there is no limit to his insight, there is also no limit to the blindness which sometimes obscures his intelligence (compare the construction of solids out of surfaces in his account of the creation of the world, or the attraction of similars to similars). Further, Mr. Grote supposes, not that ἰλλομένην means 'revolving,' or that this is the sense in which Aristotle understood the word, but that the rotation of the earth is necessarily implied in its adherence to the cosmical axis. But (α) if, as Mr. Grote assumes, Plato did not see that the rotation of the earth on its axis and of the sun and outer heavens around the earth in equal times was inconsistent with the alternation of day and night, neither need we suppose that he would have seen the immobility of the earth to be inconsistent with the rotation of the axis. And (β) what proof is there that the axis of the world revolves at all? (γ) The comparison of the two passages quoted by Mr. Grote (see his pamphlet on 'The Rotation of the Earth') from Aristotle *De Caelo*, Book II (ἔνιοι— γέγραπται, and ἡμεῖς—μέσον) clearly shows, although this is a matter of minor importance, that Aristotle, as Proclus and Simplicius supposed, understood ἰλλεσθαι in the *Timaeus* to mean 'revolving.' For the second passage, in which motion on an axis is expressly mentioned, refers to the first, but this would be unmeaning unless ἰλλεσθαι in the first passage meant rotation on an axis. (4) The immobility of the earth is more in accordance with Plato's other writings than the opposite hypothesis. For in the *Phaedo* the earth is described as the centre of the world, and is not said to be in motion. In the *Republic* the pilgrims appear to be looking out from the earth upon the motions of the heavenly bodies; in the *Phaedrus*, Hestia, who remains immovable in the house of Zeus while the other gods go in procession, is called the first and eldest of the gods, and is probably the symbol of the earth. The silence of Plato in these and in some other passages (cf. *Laws* X. 893B) in which he might be expected to speak of the rotation of the earth, is more favourable to the doctrine of its immobility than to the opposite. If he had meant to say that the earth revolves on its axis, he would have said so in distinct words, and have explained the relation of its movements to those of the other heavenly bodies. (5) The meaning of the words 'artificer of day and night' is literally true according to Plato's view. For the alternation of day and night is not produced by the motion of the heavens alone, or by the immobility of the earth alone, but by both together; and that which has the inherent force or energy to remain at rest when all other bodies are moving, may be truly said to act, equally with them. (6) We should not lay too much stress on Aristotle, the writer of *De Caelo*, having adopted the other interpretation of the words, although Alexander of Aphrodisias thinks that he could not have been ignorant either of the doctrine of Plato or of the

sense which he intended to give to the word ἰλλομένην. For the cita-
tions of Plato in Aristotle are frequently misinterpreted by him; and he
seems hardly ever to have had in his mind the connection in which
they occur. In this instance the allusion is very slight, and there is no
reason to suppose that the diurnal revolution of the heavens was present to his mind. Hence we need not attribute to him the error from
which we are defending Plato.

After weighing one against the other all these complicated probabilities, the final conclusion at which we arrive is that there is nearly as
much to be said on the one side of the question as on the other, and
that we are not perfectly certain, whether, as Böckh and the majority of
commentators, ancient as well as modern, are inclined to believe, Plato
thought that the earth was at rest in the centre of the universe, or, as
Aristotle and Mr. Grote suppose, that it revolved on its axis. Whether
we assume the earth to be stationary in the centre of the universe, or to
revolve with the heavens, no explanation is given of the variation in the
length of days and nights at different times of the year. The relations of
the earth and heavens are so indistinct in the *Timaeus* and so figurative
in the *Phaedo*, *Phaedrus* and *Republic*, that we must give up the hope
of ascertaining how they were imagined by Plato, if he had any fixed or
scientific conception of them at all.

Section 5.

The soul of the world is framed on the analogy of the soul of man,
and many traces of anthropomorphism blend with Plato's highest
flights of idealism. The heavenly bodies are endowed with thought; the
principles of the same and other exist in the universe as well as in the
human mind. The soul of man is made out of the remains of the elements which had been used in creating the soul of the world; these remains, however, are diluted to the third degree; by this Plato expresses
the measure of the difference between the soul human and divine. The
human soul, like the cosmical, is framed before the body, as the mind
is before the soul of either (30B)—this is the order of the divine work—
and the finer parts of the body, which are more akin to the soul, such
as the spinal marrow, are prior to the bones and flesh. The brain, the
containing vessel of the divine part of the soul, is (nearly) in the form
of a globe, which is the image of the gods, who are the stars, and of the
universe.

There is, however, an inconsistency in Plato's manner of conceiving
the soul of man; he cannot get rid of the element of necessity which is
allowed to enter. He does not, like Kant, attempt to vindicate for men

a freedom out of space and time; but he acknowledges him to be subject to the influence of external causes, and leaves hardly any place for freedom of the will. The lusts of men are caused by their bodily constitution (86C), though they may be increased by bad education and bad laws, which implies that they may be decreased by good education and good laws. He appears to have an inkling of the truth that to the higher nature of man evil is involuntary. This is mixed up with the view which, while apparently agreeing with it, is in reality the opposite of it, that vice is due to physical causes (86D). In the *Timaeus*, as well as in the *Laws*, he also regards vices and crimes as simply involuntary; they are diseases analogous to the diseases of the body, and arising out of the same causes. If we draw together the opposite poles of Plato's system, we find that, like Spinoza, he combines idealism with fatalism (see infra, p. 425).

The soul of man is divided by him into three parts, answering roughly to the charioteer and steeds of the *Phaedrus*, and to the λόγος, θυμός, and ἐπιθυμία of the *Republic* and *Nicomachean Ethics*. First, there is the immortal nature of which the brain is the seat, and which is akin to the soul of the universe. This alone thinks and knows and is the ruler of the whole. Secondly, there is the higher mortal soul which, though liable to perturbations of her own, takes the side of reason against the lower appetites. The seat of this is the heart, in which courage, anger, and all the nobler affections are supposed to reside. There the veins all meet; it is their centre or house of guard whence they carry the orders of the thinking being to the extremities of his kingdom. There is also a third or appetitive soul, which receives the commands of the immortal part, not immediately but mediately, through the liver, which reflects on its surface the admonitions and threats of the reason.

The liver is imagined by Plato to be a smooth and bright substance, having a store of sweetness and also of bitterness, which reason freely uses in the execution of her mandates. In this region, as ancient superstition told, were to be found intimations of the future. But Plato is careful to observe that although such knowledge is given to the inferior parts of man, it requires to be interpreted by the superior. Reason, and not enthusiasm, is the true guide of man; he is only inspired when he is demented by some distemper or possession. The ancient saying, that 'only a man in his senses can judge of his own actions,' is approved by modern philosophy too. The same irony which appears in Plato's remark, that 'the men of old time must surely have known the gods who were their ancestors, and we should believe them as custom requires,' is also manifest in his account of divination.

The appetitive soul is seated in the belly, and there imprisoned like a wild beast, far away from the council chamber, as Plato graphically calls the head, in order that the animal passions may not interfere with the deliberations of reason. Though the soul is said by him to be prior to the body, yet we cannot help seeing that it is constructed on the model of the body—the threefold division into the rational, passionate, and appetitive corresponding to the head, heart and belly. The human soul differs from the soul of the world in this respect, that it is enveloped and finds its expression in matter, whereas the soul of the world is not only enveloped or diffused in matter, but is the element in which matter moves. The breath of man is within him, but the air or aether of heaven is the element which surrounds him and all things.

Pleasure and pain are attributed in the *Timaeus* to the suddenness of our sensations the first being a sudden restoration, the second a sudden violation, of nature (cf. *Phileb*. 31D). The sensations become conscious to us when they are exceptional. Sight is not attended either by pleasure or pain, but hunger and the appeasing of hunger are pleasant and painful because they are extraordinary.

Section 6.

I shall not attempt to connect the physiological speculations of Plato either with ancient or modern medicine. What light I can throw upon them will be derived from the comparison of them with his general system.

There is no principle so apparent in the physics of the *Timaeus*, or in ancient physics generally, as that of continuity. The world is conceived of as a whole, and the elements are formed into and out of one another; the varieties of substances and processes are hardly known or noticed. And in a similar manner the human body is conceived of as a whole, and the different substances of which, to a superficial observer, it appears to be composed—the blood, flesh, sinews—like the elements out of which they are formed, are supposed to pass into one another in regular order, while the infinite complexity of the human frame remains unobserved. And diseases arise from the opposite process—when the natural proportions of the four elements are disturbed, and the secondary substances which are formed out of them, namely, blood, flesh, sinews, are generated in an inverse order.

Plato found heat and air within the human frame, and the blood circulating in every part. He assumes in language almost unintelligible to us that a network of fire and air envelopes the greater part of the body. This outer net contains two lesser nets, one corresponding to the stomach, the other to the lungs; and the entrance to the latter is forked or divided into two passages which lead to the nostrils and to the mouth.

In the process of respiration the external net is said to find a way in and out of the pores of the skin: while the interior of it and the lesser nets move alternately into each other. The whole description is figurative, as Plato himself implies (79D) when he speaks of a 'fountain of fire *which we compare* to the network of a creel.' He really means by this what we should describe as a state of heat or temperature in the interior of the body. The 'fountain of fire' or heat is also in a figure the circulation of the blood. The passage is partly imagination, partly fact.

He has a singular theory of respiration for which he accounts solely by the movement of the air in and out of the body; he does not attribute any part of the process to the action of the body itself. The air has a double ingress and a double exit, through the mouth or nostrils, and through the skin. When exhaled through the mouth or nostrils, it leaves a vacuum which is filled up by other air finding a way in through the pores, this air being thrust out of its place by the exhalation from the mouth and nostrils. There is also a corresponding process of inhalation through the mouth or nostrils, and of exhalation through the pores. The inhalation through the pores appears to take place nearly at the same time as the exhalation through the mouth; and conversely. The internal fire is in either case the propelling cause outwards—the inhaled air, when heated by it, having a natural tendency to move out of the body to the place of fire; while the impossibility of a vacuum is the propelling cause inwards.

Thus we see that this singular theory is dependent on two principles largely employed by Plato in explaining the operations of nature, the impossibility of a vacuum and the attraction of like to like. To these there has to be added a third principle, which is the condition of the action of the other two,—the interpenetration of particles in proportion to their density or rarity. It is this which enables fire and air to permeate the flesh.

Plato's account of digestion and the circulation of the blood is closely connected with his theory of respiration. Digestion is supposed to be effected by the action of the internal fire, which in the process of respiration moves into the stomach and minces the food. As the fire returns to its place, it takes with it the minced food or blood; and in this way the veins are replenished. Plato does not enquire how the blood is separated from the faeces.

Of the anatomy and functions of the body he knew very little,—e.g. of the uses of the nerves in conveying motion and sensation, which he supposed to be communicated by the bones and veins; he was also ignorant of the distinction between veins and arteries;—the latter term he applies to the vessels which conduct air from the mouth to the lungs;—he supposes the lung to be hollow and bloodless; the spinal marrow he conceives to be the seed of generation; he confuses the parts of the body with the states of the body—the network of fire and air is spoken of as a bodily organ; he has absolutely no idea of the phenomena of respiration, which he attributes to a law of equalization in nature, the air which is breathed out displacing other air which finds a way in; he is wholly unacquainted with the process of digestion. Except the general divisions into the spleen, the liver, the belly, and the lungs, and the obvious distinctions of flesh, bones, and the limbs of the body, we find nothing that reminds us of anatomical facts. But we find much which is derived from his theory of the universe, and transferred to man, as there is much also in his theory of the universe which is suggested by man. The microcosm of the human body is the lesser image of the macrocosm. The courses of the same and the other affect both; they are made of the same elements and therefore in the same proportions. Both are intelligent natures endued with the power of self-motion, and the same equipoise is maintained in both. The animal is a sort of 'world' to the particles of the blood which circulate in it. All the four elements entered into the original composition of the human frame; the bone was formed out of smooth earth; liquids of various kinds pass to and fro; the network of fire and air irrigates the veins. Infancy and childhood is the chaos or first turbid flux of sense prior to the establishment of order; the intervals of time which may be observed in some intermittent fevers correspond to the density of the elements. The spinal marrow, including the brain, is formed out of the finest sorts of triangles, and is the connecting link between body and mind. Health is only to be preserved by imitating the motions of the world in space, which is the mother and nurse of generation. The work of digestion is carried on by the superior sharpness of the triangles forming the substances of the human body to those which are introduced into it in the shape of food. The freshest and acutest forms of triangles are those that are found in children, but they become more obtuse with advancing years; and when they finally wear out and fall to pieces, old age and death supervene.

As in the *Republic*, Plato is still the enemy of the purgative treatment of physicians, which, except in extreme cases, no man of sense will ever adopt. For, as he adds, with an insight into the truth, 'every disease is akin to the nature of the living being and is only irritated by stimulants.' He is of opinion that nature should be left to herself, and is inclined to think that physicians are in vain (cf. *Laws* vi. 761C—where he says that warm baths would be more beneficial to the limbs of the aged rustic than the prescriptions of a not over-wise doctor). If he seems to be extreme in his condemnation of medicine and to rely too much on diet and exercise, he might appeal to nearly all the best physicians of our own age in support of his opinions, who often speak to their patients of the worthlessness of drugs. For we ourselves are sceptical about medicine, and very unwilling to submit to the purgative treatment of physicians. May we not claim for Plato an anticipation of modern ideas as about some questions of astronomy and physics, so also about medicine? As in the *Charmides* (156, 7) he tells us that the body cannot be cured without the soul, so in the *Timaeus* he strongly asserts the sympathy of soul and body; any defect of either is the occasion of the greatest discord and disproportion in the other. Here too may be a presentiment that in the medicine of the future the interdependence of mind and body will be more fully recognized, and that the influence of the one over the other may be exerted in a manner which is not now thought possible.

Section 7.

In Plato's explanation of sensation we are struck by the fact that he has not the same distinct conception of organs of sense which is familiar to ourselves. The senses are not instruments, but rather passages, through which external objects strike upon the mind. The eye is the aperture through which the stream of vision passes, the ear is the aperture through which the vibrations of sound pass. But that the complex structure of the eye or the ear is in any sense the cause of sight and hearing he seems hardly to be aware.

The process of sight is the most complicated (cf. *Rep.* vi. 507, 508), and consists of three elements—the light which is supposed to reside within the eye, the light of the sun, and the light emitted from external objects. When the light of the eye meets the light of the sun, and both together meet the light issuing from an external object, this is the simple act of sight. When the particles of light which proceed from the object are exactly equal to the particles of the visual ray which meet them from within, then the body is transparent. If they are larger and contract the visual ray, a black colour is produced; if they are smaller and dilate it, a white. Other phenomena are produced by the variety and motion of light. A sudden flash of fire at once elicits light and moisture from the eye, and causes a bright colour. A more subdued light, on mingling with the moisture of the eye, produces a red colour. Out of these elements all other colours are derived. All of them are combinations of bright and red with white and black. Plato himself tells us that he does not know in what proportions they combine, and he is of opinion that such knowledge is granted to the gods only. To have seen the affinity of them to each other and their connection with light, is not a bad basis for a the-

ory of colours. We must remember that they were not distinctly defined
to his, as they are to our eyes; he saw them, not as they are divided in the
prism, or artificially manufactured for the painter's use, but as they exist
in nature, blended and confused with one another.

We can hardly agree with him when he tells us that smells do not
admit of kinds. He seems to think that no definite qualities can attach
to bodies which are in a state of transition or evaporation; he also makes
the subtle observation that smells must be denser than air, though thinner than water, because when there is an obstruction to the breathing,
air can penetrate, but not smell.

The affections peculiar to the tongue are of various kinds, and, like
many other affections, are caused by contraction and dilation. Some of
them are produced by rough, others by abstergent, others by inflammatory substances,—these act upon the testing instruments of the
tongue, and produce a more or less disagreeable sensation, while other
particles congenial to the tongue soften and harmonize them. The instruments of taste reach from the tongue to the heart. Plato has a lively
sense of the manner in which sensation and motion are communicated
from one part of the body to the other, though he confuses the affections with the organs. Hearing is a blow which passes through the ear
and ends in the region of the liver, being transmitted by means of the
air, the brain, and the blood to the soul. The swifter sound is acute, the
sound which moves slowly is grave. A great body of sound is loud, the
opposite is low. Discord is produced by the swifter and slower motions
of two sounds, and is converted into harmony when the swifter motions
begin to pause and are overtaken by the slower.

The general phenomena of sensation are partly internal, but the
more violent are caused by conflict with external objects. Proceeding
by a method of superficial observation, Plato remarks that the more
sensitive parts of the human frame are those which are least covered by
flesh, as is the case with the head and the elbows. Man, if his head had
been covered with a thicker pulp of flesh, might have been a longer-
lived animal than he is, but could not have had as quick perceptions.
On the other hand, the tongue is one of the most sensitive of organs;
but then this is made, not to be a covering to the bones which contain
the marrow or source of life, but with an express purpose, and in a separate mass (75A).

Section 8.

We have now to consider how far in any of these speculations Plato
approximated to the discoveries of modern science. The modern phys-

ical philosopher is apt to dwell exclusively on the absurdities of ancient ideas about science, on the hap-hazard fancies and *a priori* assumptions of ancient teachers, on their confusion of facts and ideas, on their inconsistency and blindness to the most obvious phenomena. He measures them not by what preceded them, but by what has followed them. He does not consider that ancient physical philosophy was not a free enquiry, but a growth, in which the mind was passive rather than active, and was incapable of resisting the impressions which flowed in upon it. He hardly allows to the notions of the ancients the merit of being the stepping-stones by which he has himself risen to a higher knowledge. He never reflects, how great a thing it was to have formed a conception, however imperfect, either of the human frame as a whole, or of the world as a whole. According to the view taken in these volumes the errors of ancient physicists were not separable from the intellectual conditions under which they lived. Their genius was their own; and they were not the rash and hasty generalizers which, since the days of Bacon, we have been apt to suppose them. The thoughts of men widened to receive experience; at first they seemed to know all things as in a dream: after a while they look at them closely and hold them in their hands. They begin to arrange them in classes and to connect causes with effects. General notions are necessary to the apprehension of particular facts, the metaphysical to the physical. Before men can observe the world, they must be able to conceive it.

To do justice to the subject, we should consider the physical philosophy of the ancients as a whole; we should remember, (1) that the nebular theory was the received belief of several of the early physicists; (2) that the development of animals out of fishes who came to land, and of man out of the animals, was held by Anaximander in the sixth century before Christ (cf. Plut. *Symp. Quaest* viii. 8. 4; *Plac. Phil.* v. 19. I); (3) that even by Philolaus and the early Pythagoreans, the earth was held to be a body like the other stars revolving in space around the sun or a central fire; (4) that the beginnings of chemistry are discernible in the 'similar particles' of Anaxagoras. Also they knew or thought (5) that there was a sex in plants as well as in animals; (6) they were aware that musical notes depended on the relative length or tension of the strings from which they were emitted, and were measured by ratios of number; (7) that mathematical laws pervaded the world; and even qualitative differences were supposed to have their origin in number and figure; (8) the annihilation of matter was denied by several of them, and the seeming disappearance of it held to be a transformation only. For, although one of these discoveries might have been supposed to be a happy guess, taken together they seem to imply a great advance and almost maturity of natural knowledge.

We should also remember, when we attribute to the ancients hasty generalizations and delusions of language, that physical philosophy and metaphysical too have been guilty of similar fallacies in quite recent times. We by no means distinguish clearly between mind and body, between ideas and facts. Have not many discussions arisen about the Atomic theory in which a point has been confused with a material atom? Have not the natures of things been explained by imaginary entities, such as life or phlogiston, which exist in the mind only? Has not disease been regarded, like sin, sometimes as a negative and necessary, sometimes as a positive or malignant principle? The 'idols' of Bacon are nearly as common now as ever; they are inherent in the human mind, and when they have the most complete dominion over us, we are least able to perceive them. We recognize them in the ancients, but we fail to see them in ourselves.

Such reflections, although this is not the place in which to dwell upon them at length, lead us to take a favourable view of the speculations of the *Timaeus*. We should consider not how much Plato actually knew, but how far he has contributed to the general ideas of physics, or supplied the notions which, whether true or false, have stimulated the minds of later generations in the path of discovery. Some of them may seem old-fashioned, but may nevertheless have had a great influence in promoting system and assisting enquiry, while in others we hear the latest word of physical or metaphysical philosophy. There is also an intermediate class, in which Plato falls short of the truths of modern science, though he is not wholly unacquainted with them. (1) To the first class belongs the teleological theory of creation. Whether all things in the world can be explained as the result of natural laws, or whether we must not admit of tendencies and marks of design also, has been a question much disputed of late years. Even if all phenomena are the result of natural forces, we must admit that there are many things in heaven and earth which are as well expressed under the image of mind or design as under any other. At any rate, the language of Plato has been the language of natural theology down to our own time, nor can any description of the world wholly dispense with it. The notion of first and second or co-operative causes, which originally appears in the *Timaeus*, has likewise survived to our own day, and has been a great peace-maker between theology and science. Plato also approaches very near to our doctrine of the primary and secondary qualities of matter (61ff). (2) Another popular notion which is found in the *Timaeus*, is the feebleness of the human intellect — 'God knows the original qualities of things; man can only hope to attain to probability.' We speak in almost the same words of human intelligence, but not in the same manner of the uncertainty of our knowledge of nature. The reason is that the latter is assured to us by experiment, and is not contrasted with the certainty of ideal or mathematical knowledge. But the ancient philosopher never experimented: in the *Timaeus* Plato seems to have thought that there would be impiety in making the attempt; he, for example, who tried experiments in colours would 'forget the difference of the human and divine natures' (68D). Their indefiniteness is probably the reason why he singles them out, as especially incapable of being tested by experiment. (Compare the saying of Anaxagoras—*Sext. Pyrrh.* i.33—that since snow is made of water and water is black, snow ought to be black.)

The greatest 'divination' of the ancients was the supremacy which they assigned to mathematics in all the realms of nature; for in all of them there is a foundation of mechanics. Even physiology partakes of figure and number; and Plato is not wrong in attributing them to the human frame, but in the omission to observe how little could be explained by them. Thus we may remark in passing that the most fanciful of ancient philosophies is also the most nearly verified in fact. The fortunate guess that the world is a sum of numbers and figures has been the most fruitful of anticipations. The 'diatonic' scale of the Pythagoreans and Plato suggested to Kepler that the secret of the distances of the planets from one another was to be found in mathematical proportions. The doctrine that the heavenly bodies all move in a circle is known by us to be erroneous; but without such an error how could the human mind have comprehended the heavens? Astronomy, even in modern times, has made far greater progress by the high *a priori* road than could have been attained by any other. Yet, strictly speaking—and the remark applies to ancient physics generally—this high *a priori* road was based upon a *posteriori* grounds. For there were no facts of which the ancients were so well assured by experience as facts of number. Having observed that they held good in a few instances, they applied them everywhere; and in the complexity, of which they were capable, found the explanation of the equally complex phenomena of the universe. They seemed to see them in the least things as well as in the greatest; in atoms, as well as in suns and stars; in the human body as well as in external nature. And now a favourite speculation of modern chemistry is the explanation of qualitative difference by quantitative, which is at present verified to a certain extent and may hereafter be of far more universal application. What is this but the atoms of Democritus and the triangles of Plato? The ancients should not be wholly deprived of the credit of their guesses because they were unable to prove them. May they not have had, like the animals, an instinct of something more than they knew?

Besides general notions we seem to find in the *Timaeus* some more precise approximations to the discoveries of modern physical science. First, the doctrine of equipoise. Plato affirms, almost in so many words, that nature abhors a vacuum. Whenever a particle is displaced, the rest push and thrust one another until equality is restored. We must remember that these ideas were not derived from any definite experiment, but were the original reflections of man, fresh from the first observation of nature. The latest word of modern philosophy is continuity and development, but to Plato this is the beginning and foundation of science; there is nothing that he is so strongly persuaded of as that the world is one, and that all the various existences which are contained in it are only the transformations of the same soul of the world acting on the same matter. He would have readily admitted that out of the protoplasm all things were formed by the gradual process of creation; but he would have insisted that mind and intelligence—not meaning by this, however, a conscious mind or person—were prior to them, and could alone have created them. Into the workings of this eternal mind or intelligence he does not enter further; nor would there have been any use in attempting to investigate the things which no eye has seen nor any human language can express.

Lastly, there remain two points in which he seems to touch great discoveries of modern times—the law of gravitation, and the circulation of the blood.

(1) The law of gravitation, according to Plato, is a law, not only of the attraction of lesser bodies to larger ones, but of similar bodies to similar, having a magnetic power as well as a principle of gravitation. He observed that earth, water, and air had settled down to their places, and he imagined fire or the exterior aether to have a place beyond air. When air seemed to go upwards and fire to pierce through air—when water and earth fell downward, they were seeking their native elements. He did not remark that his own explanation did not suit all phenomena; and the simpler explanation, which assigns to bodies degrees of heaviness and lightness proportioned to the mass and distance of the bodies which attract them, never occurred to him. Yet the affinities of similar substances have some effect upon the composition of the world, and of this Plato may be thought to have had an anticipation. He may be described as confusing the attraction of gravitation with the attraction of cohesion. The influence of such affinities and the chemical action of one body upon another in long periods of time have become a recognized principle of geology.

(2) Plato is perfectly aware—and he could hardly be ignorant—that blood is a fluid in constant motion. He also knew that blood is partly a solid substance consisting of several elements, which, as he might have observed in the use of 'cupping-glasses,' decompose and die, when no

longer in motion. But the specific discovery that the blood flows out on one side of the heart through the arteries and returns through the veins on the other, which is commonly called the circulation of the blood, was absolutely unknown to him.

A further study of the *Timaeus* suggests some after-thoughts which may be conveniently brought together in this place. The topics which I propose briefly to reconsider are (*a*) the relation of the *Timaeus* to the other dialogues of Plato and to the previous philosophy; (*b*) the nature of God and of creation (*c*) the morality of the *Timaeus*:—

(*a*) The *Timaeus* is more imaginative and less scientific than any other of the Platonic dialogues. It is conjectural astronomy, conjectural natural philosophy, conjectural medicine. The writer himself is constantly repeating that he is speaking what is probable only. The dialogue is put into the mouth of *Timaeus*, a Pythagorean philosopher, and therefore here, as in the *Parmenides*, we are in doubt how far Plato is expressing his own sentiments. Hence the connexion with the other dialogues is comparatively slight. We may fill up the lacunae of the *Timaeus* by the help of the *Republic* or *Phaedrus*: we may identify the same and other with the πέρας and ἄπειρον of the *Philebus*. We may find in the *Laws* or in the *Statesman* parallels with the account of creation and of the first origin of man. It would be possible to frame a scheme in which all these various elements might have a place. But such a mode of proceeding would be unsatisfactory, because we have no reason to suppose that Plato intended his scattered thoughts to be collected in a system. There is a common spirit in his writings, and there are certain general principles, such as the opposition of the sensible and intellectual, and the priority of mind, which run through all of them; but he has no definite forms of words in which he consistently expresses himself. While the determinations of human thought are in process of creation he is necessarily tentative and uncertain. And there is least of definiteness, whenever either in describing the beginning or the end of the world, he has recourse to myths. These are not the fixed modes in which spiritual truths are revealed to him, but the efforts of imagination, by which at different times and in various manners he seeks to embody his conceptions. The clouds of mythology are still resting upon him, and he has not yet pierced 'to the heaven of the fixed stars' which is beyond them. It is safer then to admit the inconsistencies of the *Timaeus*, or to endeavour to fill up what is wanting from our own imagination, inspired by a study of the dialogue, than to refer to other Platonic writings,—and still less should we refer to the successors of Plato,—for the elucidation of it.

More light is thrown upon the *Timaeus* by a comparison of the pre-

vious philosophies. For the physical science of the ancients was tradi-
tional, descending through many generations of Ionian and
Pythagorean philosophers. Plato does not look out upon the heavens
and describe what he sees in them, but he builds upon the foundations
of others, adding something out of the 'depths of his own self-
consciousness.' Socrates had already spoken of God the creator, who
made all things for the best. While he ridiculed the superficial explanations of phenomena which were current in his age, he recognised
the marks both of benevolence and of design in the frame of man and
in the world. The apparatus of winds and waters is contemptuously re-
jected by him in the *Phaedo*, but he thinks that there is a power greater
than that of any Atlas in the 'Best' (*Phaedo* 97ff.; cf. Arist. *Met.* i. 4, 5).
Plato, following his master, affirms this principle of the best, but he acknowledges that the best is limited by the conditions of matter. In the
generation before Socrates, Anaxagoras had brought together 'Chaos'
and 'Mind'; and these are connected by Plato in the *Timaeus*, but in
accordance with his own mode of thinking he has interposed between
them the idea or pattern according to which mind worked. The circular impulse (περίωσις) of the one philosopher answers to the circular
movement (περιχώρησις) of the other. But unlike Anaxagoras, Plato
made the sun and stars living beings and not masses of earth or metal.
The Pythagoreans again had framed a world out of numbers, which
they constructed into figures. Plato adopted their speculations and improved upon them by a more exact knowledge of geometry. The
Atomists too made the world, if not out of geometrical figures, at least
out of different forms of atoms, and these atoms resembled the triangles
of Plato in being too small to be visible. But though the physiology of
the *Timaeus* is partly borrowed from them, they are either ignored by
Plato or referred to with a secret contempt and dislike. He looks with
more favour on the Pythagoreans, whose intervals of number applied to
the distances of the planets reappear in the *Timaeus*. It is probable that
among the Pythagoreans living in the fourth century B.C., there were
already some who, like Plato, made the earth their centre. Whether he
obtained his circles of the Same and Other from any previous thinker
is uncertain. The four elements are taken from Empedocles; the interstices of the *Timaeus* may also be compared with his πόροι. The passage of one element into another is common to Heracleitus and several
of the Ionian philosophers. So much of a syncretist is Plato, though not
after the manner of the Neoplatonists. For the elements which he bor-
rows from others are fused and transformed by his own genius. On the
other hand we find fewer traces in Plato of early Ionic or Eleatic speculation. He does not imagine the world of sense to be made up of opposites or to be in a perpetual flux, but to vary within certain limits

which are controlled by what he calls the principle of the same. Unlike the Eleatics, who relegated the world to the sphere of not-being, he admits creation to have an existence which is real and even eternal, although dependent on the will of the creator (41A, B). Instead of maintaining the doctrine that the void has a necessary place in the existence of the world, he rather affirms the modern thesis that nature abhors a vacuum, as in the Sophist he also denies the reality of not-being (cf. *Aristot. Metaph.* i. 4, §9). But though in these respects he differs from them, he is deeply penetrated by the spirit of their philosophy; he differs from them with reluctance, and gladly recognizes the 'generous depth' of Parmenides (*Theaet.* 183E).

There is a similarity between the *Timaeus* and the fragments of Philolaus, which by some has been thought to be so great as to create a suspicion that they are derived from it. Philolaus is known to us from the *Phaedo* of Plato as a Pythagorean philosopher residing at Thebes in the latter half of the fifth century B.C., after the dispersion of the original Pythagorean society. He was the teacher of Simmias and Cebes, who became disciples of Socrates. We have hardly any other information about him. The story that Plato had purchased three books of his writings from a relation is not worth repeating; it is only a fanciful way in which an ancient biographer dresses up the fact that there was supposed to be a resemblance between the two writers. Similar gossiping stories are told about the sources of the *Republic* and the *Phaedo*. That there really existed in antiquity a work passing under the name of Philolaus there can be no doubt. Fragments of this work are preserved to us, chiefly in Stobaeus, a few in Boethius and other writers. They remind us of the *Timaeus*, as well as of the *Phaedrus* and *Philebus*. When the writer says (Stob. *Eclog.* i. 22, 7) that all things are either finite (definite) or infinite (indefinite), or a union of the two, and that this antithesis and synthesis pervades all art and nature, we are reminded of the *Philebus* (23ff.). When he calls the centre of the world ἑστία, we have a parallel to the *Phaedrus* (247A). His distinction between the world of order, to which the sun and moon and the stars belong, and the world of disorder, which lies in the region between the moon and the earth, approximates to Plato's sphere of the Same and of the Other. Like Plato (*Tim.* 62C ff.), he denied the above and below in space, and said that all things were the same in relation to a centre. He speaks also of the world as one and indestructible: 'for neither from within nor from without does it admit of destruction' (cf. *Tim.* 33). He mentions ten heavenly bodies, including the sun and moon, the earth and the counter-earth (ἀντίχθων), and in the midst of them all he places the central fire, around which they are moving—this is hidden from the earth by the counter-earth. Of neither is there any trace in Plato, who

makes the earth the centre of his system. Philolaus magnifies the
virtues of particular numbers, especially of the number 10 (Stob. *Eclog.*
i.2, 3), and descants upon odd and even numbers, after the manner of
the later Pythagoreans. It is worthy of remark that these mystical fancies
are nowhere to be found in the writings of Plato, although the importance of number as a form and also an instrument of thought is ever
present to his mind. Both Philolaus and Plato agree in making the
world move in certain numerical ratios according to a musical scale:
though Böckh is of opinion that the two scales, of Philolaus and of the
Timaeus, do not correspond. . . . We appear not to be sufficiently acquainted with the early Pythagoreans to know how far the statements
contained in these fragments corresponded with their doctrines; and
we therefore cannot pronounce, either in favour of the genuineness of
the fragments, with Böckh and Zeller, or, with Valentine Rose and
Schaarschmidt, against them. But it is clear that they throw but little
light upon the *Timaeus,* and that their resemblance to it has been exaggerated.

That there is a degree of confusion and indistinctness in Plato's account both of man and of the universe has been already acknowledged.
We cannot tell (nor could Plato himself have told) where the figure or
myth ends and the philosophical truth begins; we cannot explain (nor
could Plato himself have explained to us) the relation of the ideas to appearance, of which one is the copy of the other, and yet of all things in
the world they are the most opposed and unlike. This opposition is presented to us in many forms, as the antithesis of the one and many, of
the finite and infinite, of the intelligible and sensible, of the unchangeable and the changing, of the indivisible and the divisible, of the
fixed stars and the planets, of the creative mind and the primeval chaos.
These pairs of opposites are so many aspects of the great opposition between ideas and phenomena—they easily pass into one another; and
sometimes the two members of the relation differ in kind, sometimes
only in degree. As in Aristotle's matter and form, the connexion between them is really inseparable; for if we attempt to separate them
they become devoid of content and therefore indistinguishable; there
is no difference between the idea of which nothing can be predicated,
and the chaos or matter which has no perceptible qualities—between
Being in the abstract and Nothing. Yet we are frequently told that the
one class of them is the reality and the other appearance; and one is
often spoken of as the double or reflection of the other. For Plato never
clearly saw that both elements had an equal place in mind and in nature; and hence, especially when we argue from isolated passages in his
writings, or attempt to draw what appear to us to be the natural inferences from them, we are full of perplexity. There is a similar confusion

about necessity and free-will, and about the state of the soul after death. Also he sometimes supposes that God is immanent in the world, sometimes that he is transcendent. And having no distinction of objective and subjective, he passes imperceptibly from one to the other; from intelligence to soul, from eternity to time. These contradictions may·be softened or concealed by a judicious use of language, but they cannot be wholly got rid of. That an age of intellectual transition must also be one of inconsistency; that the creative is opposed to the critical or defining habit of mind or time, has been often repeated by us. But, as Plato would say, 'there is no harm in repeating twice or thrice' (*Laws* vi. 754C) what is important for the understanding of a great author.

It has not, however, been observed, that the confusion partly arises out of the elements of opposing philosophies which are preserved in him. He holds these in solution, he brings them into relation with one another, but he does not perfectly harmonize them. They are part of his own mind, and he is incapable of placing himself outside of them and criticizing them. They grow as he grows; they are a kind of composition with which his own philosophy is overlaid. In early life he fancies that he has mastered them: but he is also mastered by them; and in language (cf. *Sophist*, 243B) which may be compared with the hesitating tone of the *Timaeus*, he confesses in his later years that they are full of obscurity to him. He attributes new meanings to the words of *Parmenides* and *Heracleitus*; but at times the old Eleatic philosophy appears to go beyond him; then the world of phenomena disappears, but the doctrine of ideas is also reduced to nothingness. All of them are nearer to one another than they themselves supposed, and nearer to him than he supposed. All of them are antagonistic to sense and have an affinity to number and measure and a presentiment of ideas. Even in Plato they still retain their contentious or controversial character, which was developed by the growth of dialectic. He is never able to reconcile the first causes of the pre-Socratic philosophers with the final causes of Socrates himself. There is no intelligible account of the relation of numbers to the universal ideas, or of universals to the idea of good. He found them all three, in the Pythagorean philosophy and in the teaching of Socrates and of the Megarians respectively; and, because they all furnished modes of explaining and arranging phenomena, he is unwilling to give up any of them, though he is unable to unite them in a consistent whole.

Lastly, Plato, though an idealist philosopher, is Greek and not Oriental in spirit and feeling. He is no mystic or ascetic; he is not seeking in vain to get rid of matter or to find absorption in the divine nature, or in the Soul of the universe. And therefore we are not surprised to find that his philosophy in the *Timaeus* returns at last to a worship of the heavens, and that to him, as to other Greeks, nature, though containing a remnant of evil, is still glorious and divine. He takes away or drops the veil of mythology, and presents her to us in what appears to him to be the form—fairer and truer far—of mathematical figures. It is this element in the *Timaeus*, no less than its affinity to certain Pythagorean speculations, which gives it a character not wholly in accordance with the other dialogues of Plato.

(b) The *Timaeus* contains an assertion perhaps more distinct than is found in any of the other dialogues (cf. *Rep.* ii. 379A; *Laws* x. 901, 2) of the goodness of God. 'He was good himself, and he fashioned the good everywhere.' He was not 'a jealous God,' and therefore he desired that all other things should be equally good. He is the *idea* of good who has now become a person, and speaks and is spoken of as God. Yet his personality seems to appear only in the act of creation. In so far as he works with his eye fixed upon an eternal pattern he is like the human artificer in the *Republic* (vi. 501B; x. 597). Here the theory of Platonic ideas intrudes upon us. God, like man, is supposed to have an ideal of which Plato is unable to tell us the origin. He may be said, in the language of modern philosophy, to resolve the divine mind into subject and object.

The first work of creation is perfected, the second begins under the direction of inferior ministers. The supreme God is withdrawn from the world and returns to his own accustomed nature (*Tim.* 42E). As in the *Statesman* (272E), he retires to his place of view. So early did the Epicurean doctrine take possession of the Greek mind, and so natural is it to the heart of man, when he has once passed out of the stage of mythology into that of rational religion. For he sees the marks of design in the world; but he no longer sees or fancies that he sees God walking in the garden or haunting stream or mountain. He feels also that he must put God as far as possible out of the way of evil, and therefore he banishes him from an evil world. Plato is sensible of the difficulty; and he often shows that he is desirous of justifying the ways of God to man. Yet on the other hand, in the Tenth Book of the *Laws* (899, 900 ff.) he passes a censure on those who say that the Gods have no care of human things.

The creation of the world is the impression of order on a previously existing chaos. The formula of Anaxagoras—'all things were in chaos or confusion, and then mind came and disposed them'—is a summary of the first part of the *Timaeus*. It is true that of a chaos without differences no idea could be formed. All was not mixed but one; and therefore it was not difficult for the later Platonists to draw inferences by which they were enabled to reconcile the narrative of the *Timaeus* with the Mosaic account of the creation. Neither when we speak of mind or intelligence, do we seem to get much further in our conception than circular motion, which was deemed to be the most perfect. Plato, like Anaxagoras, while commencing his theory of the universe with ideas of mind and of the best, is compelled in the execution of his design to condescend to the crudest physics.

(c) The morality of the *Timaeus* is singular, and it is difficult to adjust the balance between the two elements of it. The difficulty which Plato feels, is that which all of us feel, and which is increased in our own day by the progress of physical science, how the responsibility of man is to be reconciled with his dependence on natural causes. And sometimes, like other men, he is more impressed by one aspect of human life, sometimes by the other. In the *Republic* he represents man as freely choosing his own lot in a state prior to birth—a conception which, if taken literally, would still leave him subject to the dominion of necessity in his after life; in the *Statesman* he supposes the human race to be preserved in the world only by a divine interposition; while in the *Timaeus* the supreme God commissions the inferior deities to avert from him all but self-inflicted evils—words which imply that all the evils of men are really self-inflicted. And here, like Plato (54B;— the insertion of a note in the text of an ancient writer is a literary curiosity worthy of remark), we may take occasion to correct an error. For we too hastily said that Plato in the *Timaeus* regarded all 'vices and crimes as involuntary.' But the fact is that he is inconsistent with himself; in one and the same passage (86) vice is attributed to the relaxation of the bodily frame, and yet we are exhorted to avoid it and pursue virtue. It is also admitted that good and evil conduct are to be attributed respectively to good and evil laws and institutions. These cannot be given by individuals to themselves; and therefore human actions, in so far as they are dependent upon them, are regarded by Plato as involuntary rather than voluntary. Like other writers on this subject, he is unable to escape from some degree of self-contradiction. He had learned from Socrates that vice is ignorance, and suddenly the doctrine seems to him to be confirmed by observing how much of the good and bad in human character depends on the bodily constitution. So in modern times the speculative doctrine of necessity has often been supported by physical facts.

The *Timaeus* also contains an anticipation of the stoical life according to nature. Man contemplating the heavens is to regulate his erring life according to them. He is to partake of the repose of nature and of the order of nature, to bring the variable principle in himself into harmony with the principle of the same. The ethics of the *Timaeus* may be summed up in the single idea of 'law.' To feel habitually that he is part of the order of the universe, is one of the highest ethical motives of which man is capable. Something like this is what Plato means when he speaks of the soul 'moving about the same in unchanging thought of the same.' He does not explain how man is acted upon by the lesser influences of custom or of opinion; or how the commands of the soul watching in the citadel are conveyed to the bodily organs. But this perhaps, to use once more expressions of his own, 'is part of another subject' (87B) or 'may be more suitably discussed on some other occasion' (38B).

There is no difficulty, by the help of Aristotle and later writers, in criticizing the *Timaeus* of Plato, in pointing out the inconsistencies of the work, in dwelling on the ignorance of anatomy displayed by the author, in showing the fancifulness or unmeaningness of some of his reasons. But the *Timaeus* still remains the greatest effort of the human mind to conceive the world as a whole which the genius of antiquity has bequeathed to us.

One more aspect of the *Timaeus* remains to be considered—the mythological or geographical. Is it not a wonderful thing that a few pages of one of Plato's dialogues have grown into a great legend, not confined to Greece only, but spreading far and wide over the nations of Europe and reaching even to Egypt and Asia? Like the tale of Troy, or the legend of the Ten Tribes (Ewald, *Hist. of Isr.*, Vol. v.), which perhaps originated in a few verses of II Esdras, it has become famous, because it has coincided with a great historical fact. Like the romance of King Arthur, which has had so great a charm, it has found a way over the seas from one country and language to another. It inspired the navigators of the fifteenth and sixteenth centuries; it foreshadowed the discovery of America. It realized the fiction so natural to the human mind, because it answered the enquiry about the origin of the arts, that there had somewhere existed an ancient primitive civilization. It might find a place wherever men chose to look for it; in North, South, East, or West; in the Islands of the Blest; before the entrance of the Straits of Gibraltar, in Sweden or in Palestine. It mattered little whether the description in Plato agreed with the locality assigned to it or not. It was a legend so adapted to the human mind that it made a habitation for itself in any country. It was an island in the clouds, which might be seen anywhere by the eye of faith. It was a subject especially congenial to the ponderous industry of certain French and Swedish writers, who delighted in heaping up learning of all sorts but were incapable of using it.

M. Martin has written a valuable dissertation on the opinions entertained respecting the Island of Atlantis in ancient and modern times. It is a curious chapter in the history of the human mind. The tale of Atlantis is the fabric of a vision, but it has never ceased to interest mankind. It was variously regarded by the ancients themselves. The stronger heads among them, like Strabo and Longinus, were as little disposed to believe in the truth of it as the modern reader in Gulliver or Robinson Crusoe. On the other hand there is no kind or degree of absurdity or fancy in which the more foolish writers, both of antiquity and of modern times, have not indulged respecting it. The Neo-Platonists, loyal to their master, like some commentators on the Christian Scriptures, sought to give an allegorical meaning to what they also believed to be an historical fact. It was as if some one in our own day were to convert the poems of Homer into an allegory of the Christian religion, at the same time maintaining them to be an exact and veritable history. In the Middle Ages the legend seems to have been half-forgotten until revived by the discovery of America. It helped to form the Utopia of Sir Thomas More and the New Atlantis of Bacon, although probably neither of those great men were at all imposed upon by the fiction. It was most prolific in the seventeenth or in the early part of the eighteenth century, when the human mind, seeking for Utopias or inventing them, was glad to escape out of the dulness of the present into the romance of the past or some ideal of the future. The later forms of such narratives contained features taken from the Edda, as well as from the Old and New Testament; also from the tales of missionaries and the experiences of travellers and of colonists.

The various opinions respecting the Island of Atlantis have no interest for us except in so far as they illustrate the extravagances of which men are capable. But this is a real interest and a serious lesson, if we remember that now as formerly the human mind is liable to be imposed upon by the illusions of the past, which are ever assuming some new form.

When we have shaken off the rubbish of ages, there remain one or two questions of which the investigation has a permanent value:—

i. Did Plato derive the legend of Atlantis from an Egyptian source? It may be replied that there is no such legend in any writer previous to Plato; neither in Homer, nor in Pindar, nor in Herodotus is there any mention of an Island of Atlantis, nor any reference to it in Aristotle, nor any citation of an earlier writer by a later one in which it is to be found. Nor have any traces been discovered hitherto in Egyptian monuments of a connexion between Greece and Egypt older than the eighth or ninth century B.C. It is true that Proclus, writing in the fifth century after Christ, tells us of stones and columns in Egypt on which the history of the Island of Atlantis was engraved. The statement may be false—there are similar tales about columns set up 'by the Canaanites whom Joshua drove out' (*Procop.*); but even if true, it would only show that the legend, 800 years after the time of Plato, had been transferred to Egypt, and inscribed, not, like other forgeries, in books, but on stone. Probably in the Alexandrian age, when Egypt had ceased to have a history and began to appropriate the legends of other nations, many such monuments were to be found of events which had become famous in that or other countries. The oldest witness to the story is said to be Crantor, a Stoic philosopher who lived a generation later than Plato, and therefore may have borrowed it from him. The statement is found in Proclus; but we require better assurance than Proclus can give us before we accept this or any other statement which he makes.

Secondly, passing from the external to the internal evidence, we may remark that the story is far more likely to have been invented by Plato than to have been brought by Solon from Egypt. That is another part of his legend which Plato also seeks to impose upon us. The verisimilitude which he has given to the tale is a further reason for suspecting it; for he could easily 'invent Egyptian or any other tales' (*Phaedrus* 275B). Are not the words, 'The truth of the story is a great advantage,' if we read between the lines, an indication of the fiction? It is only a legend that Solon went to Egypt, and if he did he could not have conversed with Egyptian priests or have read records in their temples. The truth is that the introduction is a mosaic work of small touches which, partly by their minuteness, and also by their seeming probability, win the confidence of the reader. Who would desire better evidence than that of Critias, who had heard the narrative in youth when the memory is strongest (26B) at the age of ten from his grandfather Critias, an old man of ninety, who in turn had heard it from Solon himself? Is not the famous expression—'You Hellenes are ever children and there is no knowledge among you hoary with age,' really a compliment to the Athenians who are described in these words as 'ever young'? And is the thought expressed in them to be attributed to the learning of the Egyptian priest, and not rather to the genius of Plato? Or when the Egyptian says—'Hereafter at our leisure we will take up the written documents and examine in detail the exact truth about these things'—what is this but a literary trick by which Plato sets off his narrative? Could any war between Athens and the Island of Atlantis have really coincided with the struggle between the Greeks and Persians, as is sufficiently hinted though not expressly stated in the narrative of Plato? And whence came the tradition to Egypt? or in what does the story consist except in the war between the two rival powers and the submersion of both of them? And how was the tale transferred to the poem of Solon? 'It is not improbable,' says Mr. Grote, 'that Solon did leave an unfinished Egyptian poem' (*Plato*, vol. iii. p. 295). But are probabilities for which there is not a tittle of evidence, and which are without any parallel, to be deemed worthy of attention by the critic? How came the poem of Solon to disappear in antiquity? or why did Plato, if the whole narrative was known to him, break off almost at the beginning of it?

While therefore admiring the diligence and erudition of M. Martin, we cannot for a moment suppose that the tale was told to Solon by an Egyptian priest, nor can we believe that Solon wrote a poem upon the theme which was thus suggested to him—a poem which disappeared in antiquity; or that the Island of Atlantis or the antediluvian Athens ever had any existence except in the imagination of Plato. Martin is of opinion that Plato would have been terrified if he could have foreseen the endless fancies to which his Island of Atlantis has given occasion. Rather he would have been infinitely amused if he could have known that his gift of invention would have deceived M. Martin himself into the belief that the tradition was brought from Egypt by Solon and made the subject of a poem by him (Tome i. p. 323). M. Martin may also be gently censured for citing without sufficient discrimination ancient authors having very different degrees of authority and value.

ii. It is an interesting and not unimportant question which is touched upon by Martin, whether the Atlantis of Plato in any degree held out a guiding light to the early navigators. He is inclined to think that there is no real connexion between them. But surely the discovery of the New World was preceded by a prophetic anticipation of it, which, like the hope of a Messiah, was entering into the hearts of men? And this hope was nursed by ancient tradition, which had found expression from time to time in the celebrated lines of Seneca and in many other places. This tradition was sustained by the great authority of Plato, and therefore the legend of the Island of Atlantis, though not closely connected with the voyages of the early navigators, may be truly said to have contributed indirectly to the great discovery.

The *Timaeus* of Plato, like the *Protagoras* and several portions of the *Phaedrus* and *Republic*, was translated by Cicero into Latin. About a fourth, comprehending with lacunae the first portion of the dialogue, is preserved in several MSS. These generally agree, and therefore may be supposed to be derived from a single original. The version is very faithful, and is a remarkable monument of Cicero's skill in managing the difficult and intractable Greek. In his treatise *De Naturâ Deorum* i. 8, 12, ii. 12, he also refers to the *Timaeus*, which, speaking in the person of Velleius the Epicurean, he severely criticises.

The commentary of Proclus (fl. c. 440 A.D.) on the *Timaeus* is a wonderful monument of the silliness and prolixity of the Alexandrian Age. It extends to about thirty pages of the book, and is thirty times the length of the original. It is surprising that this voluminous work should have found a translator (Thomas Taylor, a kindred spirit, who was himself a Neo-Platonist, after the fashion, not of the fifth or sixteenth, but of the nineteenth century A.D.). The commentary is of little or no value, either in a philosophical or philological point of view. The writer is unable to explain particular passages in any precise manner, and he is equally incapable of grasping the whole. He does not take words in their simple meaning or sentences in their natural connexion. He is thinking, not of the context in Plato, but of the contemporary Pythagorean philosophers and their wordy strife. He finds nothing in the text which he does not bring to it. He is full of Porphyry, Iamblichus and Plotinus, of misapplied logic, of misunderstood grammar, and of the Orphic theology.

Although such a work can contribute little or nothing to the understanding of Plato, it throws an interesting light on the Alexandrian times; it realizes how a philosophy made up of words only may create a deep and widespread enthusiasm, how the forms of logic and rhetoric may usurp the place of reason and truth, how all philosophies grow faded and discoloured, and are patched and made up again like worn-out garments, and retain only a second-hand existence. He who would study this degeneracy of philosophy and of the Greek mind in the original cannot do better than devote a few of his days and nights to the commentary of Proclus on the *Timaeus*.

A very different account must be given of the short work entitled 'Timaeus Locrus,' which is a brief but clear analysis of the *Timaeus* of Plato, omitting the introduction or dialogue and making a few small additions. It does not allude to the original from which it is taken; it is quite free from mysticism and Neo-Platonism. In length it does not exceed a fifth part of the *Timaeus*. It is written in the Doric dialect, and contains several words which do not occur in classical Greek. No other indication of its date, except this uncertain one of language, appears in it. In several places the writer has simplified the language of Plato, in a few others he has embellished and exaggerated it. He generally preserves the thought of the original, but does not copy the words. On the whole this little tract faithfully reflects the meaning and spirit of the *Timaeus*.

From the garden of the *Timaeus*, as from the other dialogues of Plato, we may still gather a few flowers and present them at parting to the reader. There is nothing in Plato grander and simpler than the conversation between Solon and the Egyptian priest, in which the youthfulness of Hellas is contrasted with the antiquity of Egypt. Here are to be found the famous words, 'O Solon, Solon, you Hellenes are ever young, and there is not an old man among you'—which may be compared to the lively saying of Hegel, that 'Greek history began with the youth Achilles and left off with the youth Alexander.' The numerous arts of verisimilitude by which Plato insinuates into the mind of the reader the truth of his narrative have been already referred to. Here occur a sentence or two not wanting in Platonic irony (φωνᾶντα συνετοῖσι—a word to the wise). 40D ff.: 'To know or tell the origin of the other divinities is beyond us, and we must accept the traditions of the men of old time who affirm themselves to be the offspring of the Gods—that is what they say—and they must surely have known their own ancestors. How can we doubt the word of the children of the Gods? Although they give no probable or certain proofs, still, as they declare that they are speaking of what took place in their own family, we must conform to custom and believe them.' 76E: 'Our creators well knew that women and other animals would some day be framed out of men, and they further knew that many animals would require the use of nails for many purposes; wherefore they fashioned in men at their first creation the rudiments of nails.' Or once more, let us reflect on two serious passages in which the order of the world is supposed to find a place in the human soul and to infuse harmony into it. 37A ff.: 'The soul, when touching anything that has essence, whether dispersed in parts or undivided, is stirred through all her powers to declare the sameness or difference of that thing and some other; and to what individuals are related, and by what affected, and in what way and how and when, both in the world of generation and in the world of immutable being. And when reason, which works with equal truth, whether she be in the circle of the diverse or of the same,—in voiceless silence holding her onward course in the sphere of the self-moved,—when reason, I say, is hovering around the sensible world, and when the circle of the diverse also moving truly imparts the intimations of sense to the whole soul, then arise opinions and beliefs sure and certain. But when reason is concerned with the rational, and the circle of the same moving smoothly declares it, then intelligence and knowledge are necessarily perfected'; where, proceeding in a similar path of contemplation, he supposes the inward and the outer world mutually to imply each other. And 47B: 'God invented and gave us sight to the end that we might behold the courses of intelligence in the heaven, and apply them to the courses of our own intelligence which are akin to them, the unperturbed to the perturbed; and that we, learning them and partaking of the natural truth of reason, might imitate the absolutely unerring courses of God and regulate our own vagaries.' Or let us weigh carefully some other profound thoughts, such as the following. 44C: 'He who neglects education walks lame to the end of his life, and returns imperfect and good for nothing to the world below.' 28C: 'The father and maker of all this universe is past finding out; and even if we found him, to tell of him to all men would be impossible.' 29D: 'Let me tell you then why the Creator made this world of generation. He was good, and the good can never have jealousy of anything. And being free from jealousy, he desired that all things should be as like himself as they could be. This is in the truest sense the origin of creation and of the world, as we shall do well in believing on the testimony of wise men: God desired that all things should be good and nothing bad, so far as this was attainable.' This is the leading thought in the *Timaeus*, just as the *idea* of Good is the leading thought of the *Republic*, the one expression describing the personal, the other the impersonal Good or God, differing in form rather than in substance, and both equally implying to the mind of Plato a divine reality. The slight touch, perhaps ironical, contained in the words, 'as we shall do well in believing on the testimony of wise men,' is very characteristic of Plato.

TIMAEUS

Persons of the Dialogue:
SOCRATES, CRITIAS, TIMAEUS, HERMOCRATES.

SOCRATES: One, two, three; but where, my dear Timaeus, is the fourth of those who were yesterday my guests and are to be my entertainers to-day?

TIMAEUS: He has been taken ill, Socrates; for he would not willingly have been absent from this gathering.

SOCRATES: Then, if he is not coming, you and the two others must supply his place.

TIMAEUS: Certainly, and we will do all that we can; having been handsomely entertained by you yesterday, those of us who remain should be only too glad to return your hospitality.

SOCRATES: Do you remember what were the points of which I required you to speak?

TIMAEUS: We remember some of them, and you will be here to remind us of anything which we have forgotten: or rather, if we are not troubling you, will you briefly recapitulate the whole, and then the particulars will be more firmly fixed in our memories?

SOCRATES: To be sure I will: the chief theme of my yesterday's discourse was the State—how constituted and of what citizens composed it would seem likely to be most perfect.

TIMAEUS: Yes, Socrates; and what you said of it was very much to our mind.

SOCRATES: Did we not begin by separating the husbandmen and the artisans from the class of defenders of the State?

TIMAEUS: Yes.

SOCRATES: And when we had given to each one that single employment and particular art which was suited to his nature, we spoke of those who were intended to be our warriors, and said that they were to be guardians of the city against attacks from within as well as from without, and to have no other employment; they were to be merciful in judging their subjects, of whom they were by nature friends, but fierce to their enemies, when they came across them in battle.

TIMAEUS: Exactly.

SOCRATES: We said, if I am not mistaken, that the guardians should be gifted with a temperament in a high degree both passionate and philosophical; and that then they would be as they ought to be, gentle to their friends and fierce with their enemies.

TIMAEUS: Certainly.

SOCRATES: And what did we say of their education? Were they not to be trained in gymnastic, and music, and all other sorts of knowledge which were proper for them?[1]

TIMAEUS: Very true.

SOCRATES: And being thus trained they were not to consider gold or silver or anything else to be their own private property; they were to be like hired troops, receiving pay for keeping guard from those who were protected by them—the pay was to be no more than would suffice for men of simple life; and they were to spend in common, and to live together in the continual practice of virtue, which was to be their sole pursuit.

TIMAEUS: That was also said.

SOCRATES: Neither did we forget the women; of whom we declared, that their natures should be assimilated and brought into harmony with those of the men, and that common pursuits should be assigned to them both in time of war and in their ordinary life.

TIMAEUS: That, again, was as you say.

SOCRATES: And what about the procreation of children? Or rather was not the proposal too singular to be forgotten? for all wives and children were to be in common, to the intent that no one should ever know his own child, but they were to imagine that they were all one family; those who were within a suitable limit of age were to be brothers and sisters, those who were of an elder generation parents and grandparents, and those of a younger, children and grandchildren.

TIMAEUS: Yes, and the proposal is easy to remember, as you say.

SOCRATES: And do you also remember how, with a view of securing as far as we could the best breed, we said that the chief magistrates, male and female, should contrive secretly, by the use of certain lots, so to arrange the nuptial meeting, that the bad of either sex and the good of either sex might pair with their like; and there was to be no quarrelling on this account, for they would imagine that the union was a mere accident, and was to be attributed to the lot?

TIMAEUS: I remember.

SOCRATES: And you remember how we said that the children of the good parents were to be educated, and the children of the bad secretly

---

[1] Or 'which are akin to these'; or τούτοις may be taken with ἐν ἅπασι.

dispersed among the inferior citizens; and while they were all growing up the rulers were to be on the look-out, and to bring up from below in their turn those who were worthy, and those among themselves who were unworthy were to take the places of those who came up?

TIMAEUS: True.

SOCRATES: Then have I now given you all the heads of our yesterday's discussion? Or is there anything more, my dear Timaeus, which has been omitted?

TIMAEUS: Nothing, Socrates; it was just as you have said.

SOCRATES: I should like, before proceeding further, to tell you how I feel about the State which we have described. I might compare myself to a person who, on beholding beautiful animals either created by the painter's art, or, better still, alive but at rest, is seized with a desire of seeing them in motion or engaged in some struggle or conflict to which their forms appear suited; this is my feeling about the State which we have been describing. There are conflicts which all cities undergo, and I should like to hear some one tell of our own city carrying on a struggle against her neighbours, and how she went out to war in a becoming manner, and when at war showed by the greatness of her actions and the magnanimity of her words in dealing with other cities a result worthy of her training and education. Now I, Critias and Hermocrates, am conscious that I myself should never be able to celebrate the city and her citizens in a befitting manner, and I am not surprised at my own incapacity; to me the wonder is rather that the poets present as well as past are no better—not that I mean to depreciate them; but every one can see that they are a tribe of imitators, and will imitate best and most easily the life in which they have been brought up; while that which is beyond the range of a man's education he finds hard to carry out in action, and still harder adequately to represent in language. I am aware that the Sophists have plenty of brave words and fair conceits, but I am afraid that being only wanderers from one city to another, and having never had habitations of their own, they may fail in their conception of philosophers and statesmen, and may not know what they do and say in time of war, when they are fighting or holding parley with their enemies. And thus people of your class are the only ones remaining who are fitted by nature and education to take part at once both in politics and philosophy. Here is Timaeus, of Locris in Italy, a city which has admirable laws, and who is himself in wealth and rank the equal of any of his fellow-citizens; he has held the most important and honourable offices in his own state, and, as I believe, has scaled the heights of all philosophy; and here is Critias, whom every Athenian knows to be no novice in the matters of which we are speaking; and as to Hermocrates, I am assured by many witnesses that his genius and ed-

ucation qualify him to take part in any speculation of the kind. And
therefore yesterday when I saw that you wanted me to describe the formation of the State, I readily assented, being very well aware, that, if
you only would, none were better qualified to carry the discussion further, and that when you had engaged our city in a suitable war, you of
all men living could best exhibit her playing a fitting part. When I had
completed my task, I in return imposed this other task upon you. You
conferred together and agreed to entertain me to-day, as I had entertained you, with a feast of discourse. Here am I in festive array, and no
man can be more ready for the promised banquet.

HERMOCRATES: And we too, Socrates, as Timaeus says, will not be
wanting in enthusiasm; and there is no excuse for not complying with
your request. As soon as we arrived yesterday at the guest-chamber of
Critias, with whom we are staying, or rather on our way thither, we
talked the matter over, and he told us an ancient tradition, which I
wish, Critias, that you would repeat to Socrates, so that he may help us
to judge whether it will satisfy his requirements or not.

CRITIAS: I will, if Timaeus, who is our other partner, approves.

TIMAEUS: I quite approve.

CRITIAS: Then listen, Socrates, to a tale which, though strange, is
certainly true, having been attested by Solon, who was the wisest of the
seven sages. He was a relative and a dear friend of my great-grandfather,
Dropides, as he himself says in many passages of his poems; and he told
the story to Critias, my grandfather, who remembered and repeated it
to us. There were of old, he said, great and marvellous actions of the
Athenian city, which have passed into oblivion through lapse of time
and the destruction of mankind, and one in particular, greater than all
the rest. This we will now rehearse. It will be a fitting monument of our
gratitude to you, and a hymn of praise true and worthy of the goddess,
on this her day of festival.

SOCRATES: Very good. And what is this ancient famous action of the
Athenians, which Critias declared, on the authority of Solon, to be not
a mere legend, but an actual fact?[2]

CRITIAS: I will tell an old-world story which I heard from an aged
man; for Critias, at the time of telling it, was, as he said, nearly ninety
years of age, and I was about ten. Now the day was that day of the
Apaturia which is called the Registration of Youth, at which, according
to custom, our parents gave prizes for recitations, and the poems of several poets were recited by us boys, and many of us sang the poems of
Solon, which at that time had not gone out of fashion. One of our tribe,

---

[2]Or 'which, though unrecorded in history, Critias declared, on the authority of Solon,
to be an actual fact?'

either because he thought so or to please Critias, said that in his judgment Solon was not only the wisest of men, but also the noblest of poets. The old man, as I very well remember, brightened up at hearing this and said, smiling: Yes, Amynander, if Solon had only, like other poets, made poetry the business of his life, and had completed the tale which he brought with him from Egypt, and had not been compelled, by reason of the factions and troubles which he found stirring in his own country when he came home, to attend to other matters, in my opinion he would have been as famous as Homer or Hesiod, or any poet.

And what was the tale about, Critias? said Amynander.

About the greatest action which the Athenians ever did, and which ought to have been the most famous, but, through the lapse of time and the destruction of the actors, it has not come down to us.

Tell us, said the other, the whole story, and how and from whom Solon heard this veritable tradition.

He replied:—In the Egyptian Delta, at the head of which the river Nile divides, there is a certain district which is called the district of Sais, and the great city of the district is also called Sais, and is the city from which King Amasis came. The citizens have a deity for their foundress; she is called in the Egyptian tongue Neith, and is asserted by them to be the same whom the Hellenes call Athene; they are great lovers of the Athenians, and say that they are in some way related to them. To this city came Solon, and was received there with great honour; he asked the priests who were most skilful in such matters, about antiquity, and made the discovery that neither he nor any other Hellene knew anything worth mentioning about the times of old. On one occasion, wishing to draw them on to speak of antiquity, he began to tell about the most ancient things in our part of the world—about Phoroneus, who is called 'the first man,' and about Niobe; and after the Deluge, of the survival of Deucalion and Pyrrha; and he traced the genealogy of their descendants, and reckoning up the dates, tried to compute how many years ago the events of which he was speaking happened. Thereupon one of the priests, who was of a very great age, said: O Solon, Solon, you Hellenes are never anything but children, and there is not an old man among you. Solon in return asked him what he meant. I mean to say, he replied, that in mind you are all young; there is no old opinion handed down among you by ancient tradition, nor any science which is hoary with age. And I will tell you why. There have been, and will be again, many destructions of mankind arising out of many causes; the greatest have been brought about by the agencies of fire and water, and other lesser ones by innumerable other causes. There is a story, which even you have preserved, that once upon a time Phaëthon, the son of

Helios, having yoked the steeds in his father's chariot, because he was not able to drive them in the path of his father, burnt up all that was upon the earth, and was himself destroyed by a thunderbolt. Now this has the form of a myth, but really signifies a declination of the bodies moving in the heavens around the earth, and a great conflagration of things upon the earth, which recurs after long intervals; at such times those who live upon the mountains and in dry and lofty places are more liable to destruction than those who dwell by rivers or on the seashore. And from this calamity the Nile, who is our never-failing saviour, delivers and preserves us. When, on the other hand, the gods purge the earth with a deluge of water, the survivors in your country are herdsmen and shepherds who dwell on the mountains, but those who, like you, live in cities are carried by the rivers into the sea. Whereas in this land, neither then nor at any other time, does the water come down from above on the fields, having always a tendency to come up from below; for which reason the traditions preserved here are the most ancient. The fact is, that wherever the extremity of winter frost or of summer sun does not prevent, mankind exist, sometimes in greater, sometimes in lesser numbers. And whatever happened either in your country or in ours, or in any other region of which we are informed — if there were any actions noble or great or in any other way remarkable, they have all been written down by us of old, and are preserved in our temples. Whereas just when you and other nations are beginning to be provided with letters and the other requisites of civilized life, after the usual interval, the stream from heaven, like a pestilence, comes pouring down, and leaves only those of you who are destitute of letters and education; and so you have to begin all over again like children, and know nothing of what happened in ancient times, either among us or among yourselves. As for those genealogies of yours which you just now recounted to us, Solon, they are no better than the tales of children. In the first place you remember a single deluge only, but there were many previous ones; in the next place, you do not know that there formerly dwelt in your land the fairest and noblest race of men which ever lived, and that you and your whole city are descended from a small seed or remnant of them which survived. And this was unknown to you, because, for many generations, the survivors of that destruction died, leaving no written word. For there was a time, Solon, before the great deluge of all, when the city which now is Athens was first in war and in every way the best governed of all cities, is said to have performed the noblest deeds and to have had the fairest constitution of any of which tradition tells, under the face of heaven. Solon marvelled at his words, and earnestly requested the priests to inform him exactly and in order about these former citizens. You are welcome to hear about them,

Solon, said the priest, both for your own sake and for that of your city, and above all, for the sake of the goddess who is the common patron and parent and educator of both our cities. She founded your city a thousand years before ours (Observe that Plato gives the same date (9000 years ago) for the foundation of Athens and for the repulse of the invasion from Atlantis (Crit.).), receiving from the Earth and Hephaestus the seed of your race, and afterwards she founded ours, of which the constitution is recorded in our sacred registers to be 8000 years old. As touching your citizens of 9000 years ago, I will briefly inform you of their laws and of their most famous action; the exact particulars of the whole we will hereafter go through at our leisure in the sacred registers themselves. If you compare these very laws with ours you will find that many of ours are the counterpart of yours as they were in the olden time. In the first place, there is the caste of priests, which is separated from all the others; next, there are the artificers, who ply their several crafts by themselves and do not intermix; and also there is the class of shepherds and of hunters,[3] as well as that of husbandmen; and you will observe, too, that the warriors in Egypt are distinct from all the other classes, and are commanded by the law to devote themselves solely to military pursuits; moreover, the weapons which they carry are shields and spears, a style of equipment which the goddess taught of Asiatics first to us, as in your part of the world first to you. Then as to wisdom, do you observe how our law from the very first made a study of the whole order of things, extending even to prophecy and medicine which gives health, out of these divine elements deriving what was needful for human life, and adding every sort of knowledge which was akin to them. All this order and arrangement the goddess first imparted to you when establishing your city; and she chose the spot of earth in which you were born, because she saw that the happy temperament of the seasons in that land would produce the wisest of men. Wherefore the goddess, who was a lover both of war and of wisdom, selected and first of all settled that spot which was the most likely to produce men likest herself. And there you dwelt, having such laws as these and still better ones, and excelled all mankind in all virtue, as became the children and disciples of the gods.

Many great and wonderful deeds are recorded of your state in our histories. But one of them exceeds all the rest in greatness and valour. For these histories tell of a mighty power which unprovoked made an expedition against the whole of Europe and Asia, and to which your city put an end. This power came forth out of the Atlantic Ocean, for in those days the Atlantic was navigable; and there was an island situ-

---

[3]Reading τὸ τῶν θηρευτῶν.

ated in front of the straits which are by you called the Pillars of
Heracles; the island was larger than Libya and Asia put together, and
was the way to other islands, and from these you might pass to the
whole of the opposite continent which surrounded the true ocean; for
this sea which is within the Straits of Heracles is only a harbour, having a narrow entrance, but that other is a real sea, and the surrounding
land may be most truly called a boundless continent. Now in this
island of Atlantis there was a great and wonderful empire which had
rule over the whole island and several others, and over parts of the continent, and, furthermore, the men of Atlantis had subjected the parts of
Libya within the columns of Heracles as far as Egypt, and of Europe as
far as Tyrrhenia. This vast power, gathered into one, endeavoured to
subdue at a blow our country and yours and the whole of the region
within the straits; and then, Solon, your country shone forth, in the excellence of her virtue and strength, among all mankind. She was pre-
eminent in courage and military skill, and was the leader of the
Hellenes. And when the rest fell off from her, being compelled to stand
alone, after having undergone the very extremity of danger, she de-
feated and triumphed over the invaders, and preserved from slavery
those who were not yet subjugated, and generously liberated all the rest
of us who dwell within the pillars. But afterwards there occurred violent earthquakes and floods; and in a single day and night of misfortune
all your warlike men in a body sank into the earth, and the island of
Atlantis in like manner disappeared in the depths of the sea. For which
reason the sea in those parts is impassable and impenetrable, because
there is a shoal of mud in the way; and this was caused by the subsi-
dence of the island.

I have told you briefly, Socrates, what the aged Critias heard from
Solon and related to us. And when you were speaking yesterday about
your city and citizens, the tale which I have just been repeating to you
came into my mind, and I remarked with astonishment how, by some
mysterious coincidence, you agreed in almost every particular with the
narrative of Solon; but I did not like to speak at the moment. For a long
time had elapsed, and I had forgotten too much; I thought that I must
first of all run over the narrative in my own mind, and then I would
speak. And so I readily assented to your request yesterday, considering
that in all such cases the chief difficulty is to find a tale suitable to our
purpose, and that with such a tale we should be fairly well provided.

And therefore, as Hermocrates has told you, on my way home yesterday I at once communicated the tale to my companions as I remembered it; and after I left them, during the night by thinking I recovered nearly the whole of it. Truly, as is often said, the lessons of our
childhood make a wonderful impression on our memories; for I am not

sure that I could remember all the discourse of yesterday, but I should be much surprised if I forgot any of these things which I have heard very long ago. I listened at the time with childlike interest to the old man's narrative; he was very ready to teach me, and I asked him again and again to repeat his words, so that like an indelible picture they were branded into my mind. As soon as the day broke, I rehearsed them as he spoke them to my companions, that they, as well as myself, might have something to say. And now, Socrates, to make an end of my preface, I am ready to tell you the whole tale. I will give you not only the general heads, but the particulars, as they were told to me. The city and citizens, which you yesterday described to us in fiction, we will now transfer to the world of reality. It shall be the ancient city of Athens, and we will suppose that the citizens whom you imagined, were our veritable ancestors, of whom the priest spoke; they will perfectly harmonize, and there will be no inconsistency in saying that the citizens of your republic are these ancient Athenians. Let us divide the subject among us, and all endeavour according to our ability gracefully to execute the task which you have imposed upon us. Consider then, Socrates, if this narrative is suited to the purpose, or whether we should seek for some other instead.

SOCRATES: And what other, Critias, can we find that will be better than this, which is natural and suitable to the festival of the goddess, and has the very great advantage of being a fact and not a fiction? How or where shall we find another if we abandon this? We cannot, and therefore you must tell the tale, and good luck to you; and I in return for my yesterday's discourse will now rest and be a listener.

CRITIAS: Let me proceed to explain to you, Socrates, the order in which we have arranged our entertainment. Our intention is, that Timaeus, who is the most of an astronomer amongst us, and has made the nature of the universe his special study, should speak first, beginning with the generation of the world and going down to the creation of man; next, I am to receive the men whom he has created, and of whom some will have profited by the excellent education which you have given them; and then, in accordance with the tale of Solon, and equally with his law, we will bring them into court and make them citizens, as if they were those very Athenians whom the sacred Egyptian record has recovered from oblivion, and thenceforward we will speak of them as Athenians and fellow-citizens.

SOCRATES: I see that I shall receive in my turn a perfect and splendid feast of reason. And now, Timaeus, you, I suppose, should speak next, after duly calling upon the Gods.

TIMAEUS: All men, Socrates, who have any degree of right feeling, at the beginning of every enterprise, whether small or great, always call upon God. And we, too, who are going to discourse of the nature of the universe, how created or how existing without creation, if we be not altogether out of our wits, must invoke the aid of Gods and Goddesses and pray that our words may be acceptable to them and consistent with themselves. Let this, then, be our invocation of the Gods, to which I add an exhortation of myself to speak in such manner as will be most intelligible to you, and will most accord with my own intent.

First then, in my judgment, we must make a distinction and ask, What is that which always is and has no becoming; and what is that which is always becoming and never is? That which is apprehended by intelligence and reason is always in the same state; but that which is conceived by opinion with the help of sensation and without reason, is always in a process of becoming and perishing and never really is. Now everything that becomes or is created must of necessity be created by some cause, for without a cause nothing can be created. The work of the creator, whenever he looks to the unchangeable and fashions the form and nature of his work after an unchangeable pattern, must necessarily be made fair and perfect; but when he looks to the created only, and uses a created pattern, it is not fair or perfect. Was the heaven then or the world, whether called by this or by any other more appropriate name—assuming the name, I am asking a question which has to be asked at the beginning of an enquiry about anything—was the world, I say, always in existence and without beginning? or created, and had it a beginning? Created, I reply, being visible and tangible and having a body, and therefore sensible; and all sensible things are apprehended by opinion and sense and are in a process of creation and created. Now that which is created must, as we affirm, of necessity be created by a cause. But the father and maker of all this universe is past finding out; and even if we found him, to tell of him to all men would be impossible. And there is still a question to be asked about him: Which of the patterns had the artificer in view when he made the world—the pattern of the unchangeable, or of that which is created? If the world be indeed fair and the artificer good, it is manifest that he must have looked to that which is eternal; but if what cannot be said without blasphemy is true, then to the created pattern. Every one will see that he must have looked to the eternal; for the world is the fairest of creations and he is the best of causes. And having been created in this way, the world has been framed in the likeness of that which is apprehended by reason and mind and is unchangeable, and must therefore of necessity, if this is admitted, be a copy of something. Now it is all-important that the beginning of everything should be according to nature. And in speaking of the copy and the original we may assume that words are akin to the matter which they describe; when they relate to the lasting and permanent and intelligible, they ought to be lasting and unalterable, and, as far as their nature allows, irrefutable and immovable—nothing less. But when they express only the copy or likeness and not the eternal things themselves, they need only be likely and analogous to the real words. As being is to becoming, so is truth to belief. If then, Socrates, amid the many opinions about the gods and the generation of the universe, we are not able to give notions which are altogether and in every respect exact and consistent with one another, do not be surprised. Enough, if we adduce probabilities as likely as any others; for we must remember that I who am the speaker, and you who are the judges, are only mortal men, and we ought to accept the tale which is probable and enquire no further.

SOCRATES: Excellent, Timaeus; and we will do precisely as you bid us. The prelude is charming, and is already accepted by us—may we beg of you to proceed to the strain?

TIMAEUS: Let me tell you then why the creator made this world of generation. He was good, and the good can never have any jealousy of anything. And being free from jealousy, he desired that all things should be as like himself as they could be. This is in the truest sense the origin of creation and of the world, as we shall do well in believing on the testimony of wise men: God desired that all things should be good and nothing bad, so far as this was attainable. Wherefore also finding the whole visible sphere not at rest, but moving in an irregular and disorderly fashion, out of disorder he brought order, considering that this was in every way better than the other. Now the deeds of the best could never be or have been other than the fairest; and the creator, reflecting on the things which are by nature visible, found that no unintelligent creature taken as a whole was fairer than the intelligent taken as a whole; and that intelligence could not be present in anything which was devoid of soul. For which reason, when he was framing the universe, he put intelligence in soul, and soul in body, that he might be the creator of a work which was by nature fairest and best. Wherefore, using the language of probability, we may say that the world became a living creature truly endowed with soul and intelligence by the providence of God.

This being supposed, let us proceed to the next stage: In the likeness of what animal did the Creator make the world? It would be an unworthy thing to liken it to any nature which exists as a part only; for nothing can be beautiful which is like any imperfect thing; but let us suppose the world to be the very image of that whole of which all other animals both individually and in their tribes are portions. For the original of the universe contains in itself all intelligible beings, just as this world comprehends us and all other visible creatures. For the Deity,

intending to make this world like the fairest and most perfect of intelligible beings, framed one visible animal comprehending within itself all
other animals of a kindred nature. Are we right in saying that there is
one world, or that they are many and infinite? There must be one only,
if the created copy is to accord with the original. For that which includes all other intelligible creatures cannot have a second or companion; in that case there would be need of another living being which
would include both, and of which they would be parts, and the likeness
would be more truly said to resemble not them, but that other which
included them. In order then that the world might be solitary, like the
perfect animal, the creator made not two worlds or an infinite number
of them; but there is and ever will be one only-begotten and created
heaven.

Now that which is created is of necessity corporeal, and also visible
and tangible. And nothing is visible where there is no fire, or tangible
which has no solidity, and nothing is solid without earth. Wherefore
also God in the beginning of creation made the body of the universe to
consist of fire and earth. But two things cannot be rightly put together
without a third; there must be some bond of union between them. And
the fairest bond is that which makes the most complete fusion of itself
and the things which it combines; and proportion is best adapted to effect such a union. For whenever in any three numbers, whether cube
or square, there is a mean, which is to the last term what the first term
is to it; and again, when the mean is to the first term as the last term is
to the mean,—then the mean becoming first and last, and the first and
last both becoming means, they will all of them of necessity come to be
the same, and having become the same with one another will be all
one. If the universal frame had been created a surface only and having
no depth, a single mean would have sufficed to bind together itself and
the other terms; but now, as the world must be solid, and solid bodies
are always compacted not by one mean but by two, God placed water
and air in the mean between fire and earth, and made them to have the
same proportion so far as was possible (as fire is to air so is air to water,
and as air is to water so is water to earth); and thus he bound and put
together a visible and tangible heaven. And for these reasons, and out
of such elements which are in number four, the body of the world was
created, and it was harmonized by proportion, and therefore has the
spirit of friendship; and having been reconciled to itself, it was indissoluble by the hand of any other than the framer.

Now the creation took up the whole of each of the four elements; for
the Creator compounded the world out of all the fire and all the water
and all the air and all the earth, leaving no part of any of them nor any
power of them outside. His intention was, in the first place, that the an-

imal should be as far as possible a perfect whole and of perfect parts: secondly, that it should be one, leaving no remnants out of which another such world might be created: and also that it should be free from old age and unaffected by disease. Considering that if heat and cold and other powerful forces which unite bodies surround and attack them from without when they are unprepared, they decompose them, and by bringing diseases and old age upon them, make them waste away—for this cause and on these grounds he made the world one whole, having every part entire, and being therefore perfect and not liable to old age and disease. And he gave to the world the figure which was suitable and also natural. Now to the animal which was to comprehend all animals, that figure was suitable which comprehends within itself all other figures. Wherefore he made the world in the form of a globe, round as from a lathe, having its extremes in every direction equidistant from the centre, the most perfect and the most like itself of all figures; for he considered that the like is infinitely fairer than the unlike. This he finished off, making the surface smooth all round for many reasons; in the first place, because the living being had no need of eyes when there was nothing remaining outside him to be seen; nor of ears when there was nothing to be heard; and there was no surrounding atmosphere to be breathed; nor would there have been any use of organs by the help of which he might receive his food or get rid of what he had already digested, since there was nothing which went from him or came into him: for there was nothing beside him. Of design he was created thus, his own waste providing his own food, and all that he did or suffered taking place in and by himself. For the Creator conceived that a being which was self-sufficient would be far more excellent than one which lacked anything; and, as he had no need to take anything or defend himself against any one, the Creator did not think it necessary to bestow upon him hands: nor had he any need of feet, nor of the whole apparatus of walking; but the movement suited to his spherical form was assigned to him, being of all the seven that which is most appropriate to mind and intelligence; and he was made to move in the same manner and on the same spot, within his own limits revolving in a circle. All the other six motions were taken away from him, and he was made not to partake of their deviations. And as this circular movement required no feet, the universe was created without legs and without feet.

Such was the whole plan of the eternal God about the god that was to be, to whom for this reason he gave a body, smooth and even, having a surface in every direction equidistant from the centre, a body entire and perfect, and formed out of perfect bodies. And in the centre he put the soul, which he diffused throughout the body, making it also to be the exterior environment of it; and he made the universe a circle moving in a circle, one and solitary, yet by reason of its excellence able to converse with itself, and needing no other friendship or acquaintance. Having these purposes in view he created the world a blessed god.

Now God did not make the soul after the body, although we are speaking of them in this order; for having brought them together he would never have allowed that the elder should be ruled by the younger; but this is a random manner of speaking which we have, because somehow we ourselves too are very much under the dominion of chance. Whereas he made the soul in origin and excellence prior to and older than the body, to be the ruler and mistress, of whom the body was to be the subject. And he made her out of the following elements and on this wise: Out of the indivisible and unchangeable, and also out of that which is divisible and has to do with material bodies, he compounded a third and intermediate kind of essence, partaking of the nature of the same[4] and of the other, and this compound he placed accordingly in a mean between the indivisible, and the divisible and material. He took the three elements of the same, the other, and the essence, and mingled them into one form, compressing by force the reluctant and unsociable nature of the other into the same. When he had mingled them with the essence and out of three made one, he again divided this whole into as many portions as was fitting, each portion being a compound of the same, the other, and the essence. And he proceeded to divide after this manner:—First of all, he took away one part of the whole [1], and then he separated a second part which was double the first [2], and then he took away a third part which was half as much again as the second and three times as much as the first [3], and then he took a fourth part which was twice as much as the second [4], and a fifth part which was three times the third [9], and a sixth part which was eight times the first [8], and a seventh part which was twenty-seven times the first [27]. After this he filled up the double intervals [i.e. between 1, 2, 4, 8] and the triple [i.e. between 1, 3, 9, 27] cutting off yet other portions from the mixture and placing them in the intervals, so that in each interval there were two kinds of means, the one exceeding and exceeded by equal parts of its extremes [as for example 1, $\frac{4}{3}$, 2, in which the mean $\frac{4}{3}$ is one-third of 1 more than 1, and one-third of 2 less than 2], the other being that kind of mean which exceeds and is exceeded by an equal number (e.g. $\bar{1}$, $\frac{4}{3}$, $\frac{3}{2}$, $\bar{2}$, $\frac{8}{3}$, 3, $\bar{4}$, $\frac{16}{3}$, 6, 8; and $\bar{1}$, $\frac{3}{2}$, 2, $\bar{3}$, $\frac{9}{2}$, 6, $\bar{9}$, $\frac{27}{2}$, 18, $\bar{27}$). Where there were intervals of $\frac{3}{2}$ and of $\frac{4}{3}$ and of $\frac{9}{8}$, made by the connecting terms in the former intervals, he

---

[4]Omitting ἂν πέρι.

filled up all the intervals of $\frac{4}{3}$ with the interval of $\frac{9}{8}$, leaving a fraction over; and the interval which this fraction expressed was in the ratio of 256 to 243 (e.g. $243:256::\frac{81}{64}.\frac{4}{3}..\frac{243}{128}.2..\frac{81}{32}.\frac{8}{3}..\frac{243}{64}.4..\frac{81}{16}.\frac{16}{3}..\frac{242}{32}.8.$). And thus the whole mixture out of which he cut these portions was all exhausted by him. This entire compound he divided lengthways into two parts, which he joined to one another at the centre like the letter X, and bent them into a circular form, connecting them with themselves and each other at the point opposite to their original meeting-point; and, comprehending them in a uniform revolution upon the same axis, he made the one the outer and the other the inner circle. Now the motion of the outer circle he called the motion of the same, and the motion of the inner circle the motion of the other or diverse. The motion of the same he carried round by the side (i.e. of the rectangular figure supposed to be inscribed in the circle of the Same) to the right, and the motion of the diverse diagonally (i.e. across the rectangular figure from corner to corner) to the left. And he gave dominion to the motion of the same and like, for that he left single and undivided; but the inner motion he divided in six places and made seven unequal circles having their intervals in ratios of two and three, three of each, and bade the orbits proceed in a direction opposite to one another; and three [Sun, Mercury, Venus] he made to move with equal swiftness, and the remaining four [Moon, Saturn, Mars, Jupiter] to move with unequal swiftness to the three and to one another, but in due proportion.

Now when the Creator had framed the soul according to his will, he formed within her the corporeal universe, and brought the two together, and united them centre to centre. The soul, interfused everywhere from the centre to the circumference of heaven, of which also she is the external envelopment, herself turning in herself, began a divine beginning of never-ceasing and rational life enduring throughout all time. The body of heaven is visible, but the soul is invisible, and partakes of reason and harmony, and being made by the best of intellectual and everlasting natures, is the best of things created. And because she is composed of the same and of the other and of the essence, these three, and is divided and united in due proportion, and in her revolutions returns upon herself, the soul, when touching anything which has essence, whether dispersed in parts or undivided, is stirred through all her powers, to declare the sameness or difference of that thing and some other; and to what individuals are related, and by what affected, and in what way and how and when, both in the world of generation and in the world of immutable being. And when reason, which works with equal truth, whether she be in the circle of the diverse or of the same—in voiceless silence holding her onward course in the sphere of the self-moved—when reason, I say, is hovering around the sensible world and when the circle of the diverse also moving truly imparts the intimations of sense to the whole soul, then arise opinions and beliefs sure and certain. But when reason is concerned with the rational, and the circle of the same moving smoothly declares it, then intelligence and knowledge are necessarily perfected. And if any one affirms that in which these two are found to be other than the soul, he will say the very opposite of the truth.

When the father and creator saw the creature which he had made moving and living, the created image of the eternal gods, he rejoiced, and in his joy determined to make the copy still more like the original; and as this was eternal, he sought to make the universe eternal, so far as might be. Now the nature of the ideal being was everlasting, but to bestow this attribute in its fulness upon a creature was impossible. Wherefore he resolved to have a moving image of eternity, and when he set in order the heaven, he made this image eternal but moving according to number, while eternity itself rests in unity; and this image we call time. For there were no days and nights and months and years before the heaven was created, but when he constructed the heaven he created them also. They are all parts of time, and the past and future are created species of time, which we unconsciously but wrongly transfer to the eternal essence; for we say that he 'was,' he 'is,' he 'will be,' but the truth is that 'is' alone is properly attributed to him, and that 'was' and 'will be' are only to be spoken of becoming in time, for they are motions, but that which is immovably the same cannot become older or younger by time, nor ever did or has become, or hereafter will be, older or younger, nor is subject at all to any of those states which affect moving and sensible things and of which generation is the cause. These are the forms of time, which imitates eternity and revolves according to a law of number. Moreover, when we say that what has become *is* become and what becomes *is* becoming, and that what will become *is* about to become and that the non-existent *is* non-existent,—all these are inaccurate modes of expression (compare *Parmen.*). But perhaps this whole subject will be more suitably discussed on some other occasion.

Time, then, and the heaven came into being at the same instant in order that, having been created together, if ever there was to be a dissolution of them, they might be dissolved together. It was framed after the pattern of the eternal nature, that it might resemble this as far as was possible; for the pattern exists from eternity, and the created heaven has been, and is, and will be, in all time. Such was the mind and thought of God in the creation of time. The sun and moon and five other stars, which are called the planets, were created by him in order to distinguish and preserve the numbers of time; and when he had made their several bodies, he placed them in the orbits in which the circle of the other was revolving,—in seven orbits seven stars. First, there was the moon in the orbit nearest the earth, and next the sun, in the second orbit above the earth; then came the morning star and the star sacred to Hermes, moving in orbits which have an equal swiftness with the sun, but in an opposite direction; and this is the reason why the sun and Hermes and Lucifer overtake and are overtaken by each other. To enumerate the places which he assigned to the other stars, and to give all the reasons why he assigned them, although a secondary matter, would give more trouble than the primary. These things at some future time, when we are at leisure, may have the consideration which they deserve, but not at present.

Now, when all the stars which were necessary to the creation of time had attained a motion suitable to them, and had become living creatures having bodies fastened by vital chains, and learnt their appointed task, moving in the motion of the diverse, which is diagonal, and passes through and is governed by the motion of the same, they revolved, some in a larger and some in a lesser orbit,—those which had the lesser orbit revolving faster, and those which had the larger more slowly. Now by reason of the motion of the same, those which revolved fastest appeared to be overtaken by those which moved slower although they really overtook them; for the motion of the same made them all turn in a spiral, and, because some went one way and some another, that which receded most slowly from the sphere of the same, which was the swiftest, appeared to follow it most nearly. That there might be some visible measure of their relative swiftness and slowness as they proceeded in their eight courses, God lighted a fire, which we now call the sun, in the second from the earth of these orbits, that it might give light to the whole of heaven, and that the animals, as many as nature intended, might participate in number, learning arithmetic from the revolution of the same and the like. Thus, then, and for this reason the night and the day were created, being the period of the one most intelligent revolution. And the month is accomplished when the moon has completed her orbit and overtaken the sun, and the year when the sun has completed his own orbit. Mankind, with hardly an exception, have not remarked the periods of the other stars, and they have no name for them, and do not measure them against one another by the help of number, and hence they can scarcely be said to know that their wanderings, being infinite in number and admirable for their variety, make up time. And yet there is no difficulty in seeing that the perfect number of time fulfils the perfect year when all the eight revolutions, having their relative degrees of swiftness, are accomplished together and attain their completion at the same time, measured by the rotation of the same and equally moving. After this manner, and for these reasons, came into being such of the stars as in their heavenly progress received reversals of motion, to the end that the created heaven might imitate the eternal nature, and be as like as possible to the perfect and intelligible animal.

Thus far and until the birth of time the created universe was made in the likeness of the original, but inasmuch as all animals were not yet comprehended therein, it was still unlike. What remained, the creator then proceeded to fashion after the nature of the pattern. Now as in the ideal animal the mind perceives ideas or species of a certain nature and number, he thought that this created animal ought to have species of a like nature and number. There are four such; one of them is the heavenly race of the gods; another, the race of birds whose way is in the air; the third, the watery species; and the fourth, the pedestrian and land creatures. Of the heavenly and divine, he created the greater part out of fire, that they might be the brightest of all things and fairest to behold, and he fashioned them after the likeness of the universe in the figure of a circle, and made them follow the intelligent motion of the supreme, distributing them over the whole circumference of heaven, which was to be a true cosmos or glorious world spangled with them all over. And he gave to each of them two movements: the first, a movement on the same spot after the same manner, whereby they ever continue to think consistently the same thoughts about the same things; the second, a forward movement, in which they are controlled by the revolution of the same and the like; but by the other five motions they were unaffected, in order that each of them might attain the highest perfection. And for this reason the fixed stars were created, to be divine and eternal animals, ever-abiding and revolving after the same manner and on the same spot; and the other stars which reverse their motion and are subject to deviations of this kind, were created in the manner already described. The earth, which is our nurse, clinging (or 'circling') around the pole which is extended through the universe, he framed to be the guardian and artificer of night and day, first and eldest of gods that are in the interior of heaven. Vain would be the attempt to tell all the figures of them circling as in dance, and their juxtapositions, and the return of them in their revolutions upon themselves, and their approximations, and to say which of these deities in their conjunctions meet, and which of them are in opposition, and in what order they get behind and before one another, and when they are severally eclipsed to our sight and again reappear, sending terrors and intimations of the future to those who cannot calculate their movements—to attempt to tell of all this without a visible representation of the heavenly system[5]

---

[5]Reading τοῖς οὐ δυν. and τούτων αὐτῶν.

would be labour in vain. Enough on this head; and now let what we have said about the nature of the created and visible gods have an end.

To know or tell the origin of the other divinities is beyond us, and we must accept the traditions of the men of old time who affirm themselves to be the offspring of the gods—that is what they say—and they must surely have known their own ancestors. How can we doubt the word of the children of the gods? Although they give no probable or certain proofs, still, as they declare that they are speaking of what took place in their own family, we must conform to custom and believe them. In this manner, then, according to them, the genealogy of these gods is to be received and set forth.

Oceanus and Tethys were the children of Earth and Heaven, and from these sprang Phorcys and Cronos and Rhea, and all that generation; and from Cronos and Rhea sprang Zeus and Herè, and all those who are said to be their brethren, and others who were the children of these.

Now, when all of them, both those who visibly appear in their revolutions as well as those other gods who are of a more retiring nature, had come into being, the creator of the universe addressed them in these words: 'Gods, children of gods, who are my works, and of whom I am the artificer and father, my creations are indissoluble, if so I will. All that is bound may be undone, but only an evil being would wish to undo that which is harmonious and happy. Wherefore, since ye are but creatures, ye are not altogether immortal and indissoluble, but ye shall certainly not be dissolved, nor be liable to the fate of death, having in my will a greater and mightier bond than those with which ye were bound at the time of your birth. And now listen to my instructions:— Three tribes of mortal beings remain to be created—without them the universe will be incomplete, for it will not contain every kind of animal which it ought to contain, if it is to be perfect. On the other hand, if they were created by me and received life at my hands, they would be on an equality with the gods. In order then that they may be mortal, and that this universe may be truly universal, do ye, according to your natures, betake yourselves to the formation of animals, imitating the power which was shown by me in creating you. The part of them worthy of the name immortal, which is called divine and is the guiding principle of those who are willing to follow justice and you—of that divine part I will myself sow the seed, and having made a beginning, I will hand the work over to you. And do ye then interweave the mortal with the immortal, and make and beget living creatures, and give them food, and make them to grow, and receive them again in death.'

Thus he spake, and once more into the cup in which he had previously mingled the soul of the universe he poured the remains of the ·

elements, and mingled them in much the same manner; they were not, however, pure as before, but diluted to the second and third degree. And having made it he divided the whole mixture into souls equal in number to the stars, and assigned each soul to a star; and having there placed them as in a chariot, he showed them the nature of the universe, and declared to them the laws of destiny, according to which their first birth would be one and the same for all,—no one should suffer a disadvantage at his hands; they were to be sown in the instruments of time severally adapted to them, and to come forth the most religious of animals; and as human nature was of two kinds, the superior race would hereafter be called man. Now, when they should be implanted in bodies by necessity, and be always gaining or losing some part of their bodily substance, then in the first place it would be necessary that they should all have in them one and the same faculty of sensation, arising out of irresistible impressions; in the second place, they must have love, in which pleasure and pain mingle; also fear and anger, and the feelings which are akin or opposite to them; if they conquered these they would live righteously, and if they were conquered by them, unrighteously. He who lived well during his appointed time was to return and dwell in his native star, and there he would have a blessed and congenial existence. But if he failed in attaining this, at the second birth he would pass into a woman, and if, when in that state of being, he did not desist from evil, he would continually be changed into some brute who resembled him in the evil nature which he had acquired, and would not cease from his toils and transformations until he followed the revolution of the same and the like within him, and overcame by the help of reason the turbulent and irrational mob of later accretions, made up of fire and air and water and earth, and returned to the form of his first and better state. Having given all these laws to his creatures, that he might be guiltless of future evil in any of them, the creator sowed some of them in the earth, and some in the moon, and some in the other instruments of time; and when he had sown them he committed to the younger gods the fashioning of their mortal bodies, and desired them to furnish what was still lacking to the human soul, and having made all the suitable additions, to rule over them, and to pilot the mortal animal in the best and wisest manner which they could, and avert from him all but self-inflicted evils.

When the creator had made all these ordinances he remained in his own accustomed nature, and his children heard and were obedient to their father's word, and receiving from him the immortal principle of a mortal creature, in imitation of their own creator they borrowed portions of fire, and earth, and water, and air from the world, which were hereafter to be restored—these they took and welded them together, not with the indissoluble chains by which they were themselves bound, but with little pegs too small to be visible, making up out of all the four elements each separate body, and fastening the courses of the immortal soul in a body which was in a state of perpetual influx and efflux. Now these courses, detained as in a vast river, neither overcame nor were overcome; but were hurrying and hurried to and fro, so that the whole animal was moved and progressed, irregularly however and irrationally and anyhow, in all the six directions of motion, wandering backwards and forwards, and right and left, and up and down, and in all the six directions. For great as was the advancing and retiring flood which provided nourishment, the affections produced by external contact caused still greater tumult—when the body of any one met and came into collision with some external fire, or with the solid earth or the gliding waters, or was caught in the tempest borne on the air, and the motions produced by any of these impulses were carried through the body to the soul. All such motions have consequently received the general name of 'sensations,' which they still retain. And they did in fact at that time create a very great and mighty movement; uniting with the ever-flowing stream in stirring up and violently shaking the courses of the soul, they completely stopped the revolution of the same by their opposing current, and hindered it from predominating and advancing; and they so disturbed the nature of the other or diverse, that the three double intervals [i.e. between 1, 2, 4, 8], and the three triple intervals [i.e. between 1, 3, 9, 27], together with the mean terms and connecting links which are expressed by the ratios of 3:2, and 4:3, and of 9:8 — these, although they cannot be wholly undone except by him who united them, were twisted by them in all sorts of ways, and the circles were broken and disordered in every possible manner, so that when they moved they were tumbling to pieces, and moved irrationally, at one time in a reverse direction, and then again obliquely, and then upside down, as you might imagine a person who is upside down and has his head leaning upon the ground and his feet up against something in the air; and when he is in such a position, both he and the spectator fancy that the right of either is his left, and the left right. If, when powerfully experiencing these and similar effects, the revolutions of the soul come in contact with some external thing, either of the class of the same or of the other, they speak of the same or of the other in a manner the very opposite of the truth; and they become false and foolish, and there is no course or revolution in them which has a guiding or directing power; and if again any sensations enter in violently from without and drag after them the whole vessel of the soul, then the courses of the soul, though they seem to conquer, are really conquered.

And by reason of all these affections, the soul, when encased in a mortal body, now, as in the beginning, is at first without intelligence; but when the flood of growth and nutriment abates, and the courses of the soul, calming down, go their own way and become steadier as time goes on, then the several circles return to their natural form, and their revolutions are corrected, and they call the same and the other by their right names, and make the possessor of them to become a rational being. And if these combine in him with any true nurture or education, he attains the fulness and health of the perfect man, and escapes the worst disease of all; but if he neglects education he walks lame to the end of his life, and returns imperfect and good for nothing to the world below. This, however, is a later stage; at present we must treat more exactly the subject before us, which involves a preliminary enquiry into the generation of the body and its members, and as to how the soul was created,—for what reason and by what providence of the gods, and holding fast to probability, we must pursue our way.

First, then, the gods, imitating the spherical shape of the universe, enclosed the two divine courses in a spherical body, that, namely, which we now term the head, being the most divine part of us and the lord of all that is in us: to this the gods, when they put together the body, gave all the other members to be servants, considering that it partook of every sort of motion. In order then that it might not tumble about among the high and deep places of the earth, but might be able to get over the one and out of the other, they provided the body to be its vehicle and means of locomotion; which consequently had length and was furnished with four limbs extended and flexible; these God contrived to be instruments of locomotion with which it might take hold and find support, and so be able to pass through all places, carrying on high the dwelling-place of the most sacred and divine part of us. Such was the origin of legs and hands, which for this reason were attached to every man; and the gods, deeming the front part of man to be more honourable and more fit to command than the hinder part, made us to move mostly in a forward direction. Wherefore man must needs have his front part unlike and distinguished from the rest of his body. And so in the vessel of the head, they first of all put a face in which they inserted organs to minister in all things to the providence of the soul, and they appointed this part, which has authority, to be by nature the part which is in front. And of the organs they first contrived the eyes to give light, and the principle according to which they were inserted was as follows: So much of fire as would not burn, but gave a gentle light, they formed into a substance akin to the light of every-day life; and the pure fire which is within us and related thereto they made to flow through the eyes in a stream smooth and dense, compressing the whole eye, and especially the centre part, so that it kept out everything of a coarser nature, and allowed to pass only this pure element. When the light of day surrounds the stream of vision, then like falls upon like, and they coalesce, and one body is formed by natural affinity in the line of vision, wherever the light that falls from within meets with an external object. And the whole stream of vision, being similarly affected in virtue of similarity, diffuses the motions of what it touches or what touches it over the whole body, until they reach the soul, causing that perception which we call sight. But when night comes on and the external and kindred fire departs, then the stream of vision is cut off; for going forth to an unlike element it is changed and extinguished, being no longer of one nature with the surrounding atmosphere which is now deprived of fire: and so the eye no longer sees, and we feel disposed to sleep. For when the eyelids, which the gods invented for the preservation of sight, are closed, they keep in the internal fire; and the power of the fire diffuses and equalizes the inward motions; when they are equalized, there is rest, and when the rest is profound, sleep comes over us scarce disturbed by dreams; but where the greater motions still remain, of whatever nature and in whatever locality, they engender corresponding visions in dreams, which are remembered by us when we are awake and in the external world. And now there is no longer any difficulty in understanding the creation of images in mirrors and all smooth and bright surfaces. For from the communion of the internal and external fires, and again from the union of them and their numerous transformations when they meet in the mirror, all these appearances of necessity arise, when the fire from the face coalesces with the fire from the eye on the bright and smooth surface. And right appears left and left right, because the visual rays come into contact with the rays emitted by the object in a manner contrary to the usual mode of meeting; but the right appears right, and the left left, when the position of one of the two concurring lights is reversed; and this happens when the mirror is concave and its smooth surface repels the right stream of vision to the left side, and the left to the right (He is speaking of two kinds of mirrors, first the plane, secondly the concave; and the latter is supposed to be placed, first horizontally, and then vertically.). Or if the mirror be turned vertically, then the concavity makes the countenance appear to be all upside down, and the lower rays are driven upwards and the upper downwards.

All these are to be reckoned among the second and co-operative causes which God, carrying into execution the idea of the best as far as possible, uses as his ministers. They are thought by most men not to be the second, but the prime causes of all things, because they freeze and heat, and contract and dilate, and the like. But they are not so, for they are incapable of reason or intellect; the only being which can properly have mind is the invisible soul, whereas fire and water, and earth and air, are all of them visible bodies. The lover of intellect and knowledge ought to explore causes of intelligent nature first of all, and, secondly, of those things which, being moved by others, are compelled to move others. And this is what we too must do. Both kinds of causes should be acknowledged by us, but a distinction should be made between those which are endowed with mind and are the workers of things fair and good, and those which are deprived of intelligence and always produce chance effects without order or design. Of the second or co-operative causes of sight, which help to give to the eyes the power which they now possess, enough has been said. I will therefore now proceed to speak of the higher use and purpose for which God has given them to us. The sight in my opinion is the source of the greatest benefit to us, for had we never seen the stars, and the sun, and the heaven, none of the words which we have spoken about the universe would ever have been uttered. But now the sight of day and night, and the months and the revolutions of the years, have created number, and have given us a conception of time, and the power of enquiring about the nature of the universe; and from this source we have derived philosophy, than which no greater good ever was or will be given by the gods to mortal man. This is the greatest boon of sight: and of the lesser benefits why should I speak? even the ordinary man if he were deprived of them would be-wail his loss, but in vain. Thus much let me say however: God invented and gave us sight to the end that we might behold the courses of intelligence in the heaven, and apply them to the courses of our own intelligence which are akin to them, the unperturbed to the perturbed; and that we, learning them and partaking of the natural truth of reason, might imitate the absolutely unerring courses of God and regulate our own vagaries. The same may be affirmed of speech and hearing: they have been given by the gods to the same end and for a like reason. For this is the principal end of speech, whereto it most contributes. Moreover, so much of music as is adapted to the sound of the voice[6] and to the sense of hearing is granted to us for the sake of harmony; and harmony, which has motions akin to the revolutions of our souls, is not regarded by the intelligent votary of the Muses as given by them with a view to irrational pleasure, which is deemed to be the purpose of it in our day, but as meant to correct any discord which may have arisen in the courses of the soul, and to be our ally in bringing her into harmony and agreement with herself; and rhythm too was given by them for the same reason, on account of the irregular and graceless ways which pre-vail among mankind generally, and to help us against them.

---

[6]Reading φωνῇ and placing the comma after ἀκοήν.

Thus far in what we have been saying, with small exceptions, the works of intelligence have been set forth; and now we must place by the side of them in our discourse the things which come into being through necessity—for the creation is mixed, being made up of necessity and mind. Mind, the ruling power, persuaded necessity to bring the greater part of created things to perfection, and thus and after this manner in the beginning, when the influence of reason got the better of necessity, the universe was created. But if a person will truly tell of the way in which the work was accomplished, he must include the other influence of the variable cause as well. Wherefore, we must return again and find another suitable beginning, as about the former matters, so also about these. To which end we must consider the nature of fire, and water, and air, and earth, such as they were prior to the creation of the heaven, and what was happening to them in this previous state; for no one has as yet explained the manner of their generation, but we speak of fire and the rest of them, whatever they mean, as though men knew their natures, and we maintain them to be the first principles and letters or elements of the whole, when they cannot reasonably be compared by a man of any sense even to syllables or first compounds. And let me say thus much: I will not now speak of the first principle or principles of all things, or by whatever name they are to be called, for this reason,—because it is difficult to set forth my opinion according to the method of discussion which we are at present employing. Do not imagine, any more than I can bring myself to imagine, that I should be right in undertaking so great and difficult a task. Remembering what I said at first about probability, I will do my best to give as probable an explanation as any other,—or rather, more probable; and I will first go back to the beginning and try to speak of each thing and of all.[7] Once more, then, at the commencement of my discourse, I call upon God, and beg him to be our saviour out of a strange and unwonted enquiry, and to bring us to the haven of probability. So now let us begin again.

This new beginning of our discussion of the universe requires a fuller division than the former; for then we made two classes, now a third must be revealed. The two sufficed for the former discussion: one, which we assumed, was a pattern intelligible and always the same; and the second was only the imitation of the pattern, generated and visible. There is also a third kind which we did not distinguish at the time, conceiving that the two would be enough. But now the argument seems to require that we should set forth in words another kind, which is difficult of explanation

---

[7]Putting the comma after μᾶλλον δὲ; or, following Stallbaum and omitting the comma, 'or rather, before entering on this probable discussion, we will begin again, and try to speak of each thing and of all.'

and dimly seen. What nature are we to attribute to this new kind of being? We reply, that it is the receptacle, and in a manner the nurse, of all generation. I have spoken the truth; but I must express myself in clearer language, and this will be an arduous task for many reasons, and in particular because I must first raise questions concerning fire and the other elements, and determine what each of them is; for to say, with any probability or certitude, which of them should be called water rather than fire, and which should be called any of them rather than all or some one of them, is a difficult matter. How, then, shall we settle this point, and what questions about the elements may be fairly raised?

In the first place, we see that what we just now called water, by con densation, I suppose, becomes stone and earth; and this same element, when melted and dispersed, passes into vapour and air. Air, again, when inflamed, becomes fire; and again fire, when condensed and extinguished, passes once more into the form of air; and once more, air, when collected and condensed, produces cloud and mist; and from these, when still more compressed, comes flowing water, and from water comes earth and stones once more; and thus generation appears to be transmitted from one to the other in a circle. Thus, then, as the several elements never present themselves in the same form, how can any one have the assurance to assert positively that any of them, whatever it may be, is one thing rather than another? No one can. But much the safest plan is to speak of them as follows:—Anything which we see to be continually changing, as, for example, fire, we must not call 'this' or 'that,' but rather say that it is 'of such a nature'; nor let us speak of water as 'this,' but always as 'such'; nor must we imply that there is any stability in any of those things which we indicate by the use of the words 'this' and 'that,' supposing ourselves to signify something thereby; for they are too volatile to be detained in any such expressions as 'this,' or 'that,' or 'relative to this,' or any other mode of speaking which represents them as permanent. We ought not to apply 'this' to any of them, but rather the word 'such'; which expresses the similar principle circulating in each and all of them; for example, that should be called 'fire' which is of such a nature always, and so of everything that has generation. That in which the elements severally grow up, and appear, and decay, is alone to be called by the name 'this' or 'that'; but that which is of a certain nature, hot or white, or anything which admits of opposite qualities, and all things that are compounded of them, ought not to be so denominated. Let me make another attempt to explain my meaning more clearly. Suppose a person to make all kinds of figures of gold and to be always transmuting one form into all the rest;—somebody points to one of them and asks what it is. By far the safest and truest answer is, That is gold; and not to call the triangle or any other figures which are formed in the gold 'these,' as though they had existence, since they are in process of change while he is making the assertion; but if the questioner be willing to take the safe and indefinite expression, 'such,' we should be satisfied. And the same argument applies to the universal nature which receives all bodies—that must be always called the same; for, while receiving all things, she never departs at all from her own nature, and never in any way, or at any time, assumes a form like that of any of the things which enter into her; she is the natural recipient of all impressions, and is stirred and informed by them, and appears different from time to time by reason of them. But the forms which enter into and go out of her are the likenesses of real existences modelled after their patterns in a wonderful and inexplicable manner, which we will hereafter investigate. For the present we have only to conceive of three natures: first, that which is in process of generation; secondly, that in which the generation takes place; and thirdly, that of which the thing generated is a resemblance. And we may liken the receiving principle to a mother, and the source or spring to a father, and the intermediate nature to a child; and may remark further, that if the model is to take every variety of form, then the matter in which the model is fashioned will not be duly prepared, unless it is formless, and free from the impress of any of those shapes which it is hereafter to receive from without. For if the matter were like any of the supervening forms, then whenever any opposite or entirely different nature was stamped upon its surface, it would take the impression badly, because it would intrude its own shape. Wherefore, that which is to receive all forms should have no form; as in making perfumes they first contrive that the liquid substance which is to receive the scent shall be as inodorous as possible; or as those who wish to impress figures on soft substances do not allow any previous impression to remain, but begin by making the surface as even and smooth as possible. In the same way that which is to receive perpetually and through its whole extent the resemblances of all eternal beings ought to be devoid of any particular form. Wherefore, the mother and receptacle of all created and visible and in any way sensible things, is not to be termed earth, or air, or fire, or water, or any of their compounds or any of the elements from which these are derived, but is an invisible and formless being which receives all things and in some mysterious way partakes of the intelligible, and is most incomprehensible. In saying this we shall not be far wrong; as far, however, as we can attain to a knowledge of her from the previous considerations, we may truly say that fire is that part of her nature which from time to time is inflamed, and water that which is moistened, and that the mother substance becomes earth and air, in so far as she receives the impressions of them.

Let us consider this question more precisely. Is there any self-existent fire? and do all those things which we call self-existent exist? or are only those things which we see, or in some way perceive through the bodily organs, truly existent, and nothing whatever besides them? And is all that which we call an intelligible essence nothing at all, and only a name? Here is a question which we must not leave unexamined or un-determined, nor must we affirm too confidently that there can be no decision; neither must we interpolate in our present long discourse a di-gression equally long, but if it is possible to set forth a great principle in a few words, that is just what we want.

Thus I state my view.—If mind and true opinion are two distinct classes, then I say that there certainly are these self-existent ideas un perceived by sense, and apprehended only by the mind; if, however, as some say, true opinion differs in no respect from mind, then everything that we perceive through the body is to be regarded as most real and certain. But we must affirm them to be distinct, for they have a distinct origin and are of a different nature; the one is implanted in us by in-struction, the other by persuasion; the one is always accompanied by true reason, the other is without reason; the one cannot be overcome by persuasion, but the other can: and lastly, every man may be said to share in true opinion, but mind is the attribute of the gods and of very few men. Wherefore also we must acknowledge that there is one kind of being which is always the same, uncreated and indestructible, never receiving anything into itself from without, nor itself going out to any other, but invisible and imperceptible by any sense, and of which the contemplation is granted to intelligence only. And there is another na-ture of the same name with it, and like to it, perceived by sense, created, always in motion, becoming in place and again vanishing out of place, which is apprehended by opinion and sense. And there is a third nature, which is space, and is eternal, and admits not of destruc-tion and provides a home for all created things, and is apprehended without the help of sense, by a kind of spurious reason, and is hardly real; which we beholding as in a dream, say of all existence that it must of necessity be in some place and occupy a space, but that what is nei-ther in heaven nor in earth has no existence. Of these and other things of the same kind, relating to the true and waking reality of nature, we have only this dreamlike sense, and we are unable to cast off sleep and determine the truth about them. For an image, since the reality, after which it is modelled, does not belong to it,[8] and it exists ever as the fleeting shadow of some other, must be inferred to be in another [i.e.

---

[8]Or, 'since in its very intention it is not self-existent'—which, though obscure, avoids any inaccuracy of construction.

in space], grasping existence in some way or other, or it could not be at all. But true and exact reason, vindicating the nature of true being, maintains that while two things [i.e. the image and space] are different they cannot exist one of them in the other and so be one and also two at the same time.

Thus have I concisely given the result of my thoughts; and my verdict is that being and space and generation, these three, existed in their three ways before the heaven; and that the nurse of generation, moistened by water and inflamed by fire, and receiving the forms of earth and air, and experiencing all the affections which accompany these, presented a strange variety of appearances; and being full of powers which were neither similar nor equally balanced, was never in any part in a state of equipoise, but swaying unevenly hither and thither, was shaken by them, and by its motion again shook them; and the elements when moved were separated and carried continually, some one way, some another; as, when grain is shaken and winnowed by fans and other instruments used in the threshing of corn, the close and heavy particles are borne away and settle in one direction, and the loose and light particles in another. In this manner, the four kinds or elements were then shaken by the receiving vessel, which, moving like a winnowing machine, scattered far away from one another the elements most unlike, and forced the most similar elements into close contact. Wherefore also the various elements had different places before they were arranged so as to form the universe. At first, they were all without reason and measure. But when the world began to get into order, fire and water and earth and air had only certain faint traces of themselves, and were altogether such as everything might be expected to be in the absence of God; this, I say, was their nature at that time, and God fashioned them by form and number. Let it be consistently maintained by us in all that we say that God made them as far as possible the fairest and best, out of things which were not fair and good. And now I will endeavour to show you the disposition and generation of them by an unaccustomed argument, which I am compelled to use; but I believe that you will be able to follow me, for your education has made you familiar with the methods of science.

In the first place, then, as is evident to all, fire and earth and water and air are bodies. And every sort of body possesses solidity, and every solid must necessarily be contained in planes; and every plane rectilinear figure is composed of triangles; and all triangles are originally of two kinds, both of which are made up of one right and two acute angles; one of them has at either end of the base the half of a divided right angle, having equal sides, while in the other the right angle is divided into unequal parts, having unequal sides. These, then, proceeding by a combination of probability with demonstration, we assume to be the original elements of fire and the other bodies; but the principles which are prior to these God only knows, and he of men who is the friend of God. And next we have to determine what are the four most beautiful bodies which are unlike one another, and of which some are capable of resolution into one another; for having discovered thus much, we shall know the true origin of earth and fire and of the proportionate and intermediate elements. And then we shall not be willing to allow that there are any distinct kinds of visible bodies fairer than these. Wherefore we must endeavour to construct the four forms of bodies which excel in beauty, and then we shall be able to say that we have sufficiently apprehended their nature. Now of the two triangles, the isosceles has one form only; the scalene or unequal-sided has an infinite number. Of the infinite forms we must select the most beautiful, if we are to proceed in due order, and any one who can point out a more beautiful form than ours for the construction of these bodies, shall carry off the palm, not as an enemy, but as a friend. Now, the one which we maintain to be the most beautiful of all the many triangles (and we need not speak of the others) is that of which the double forms a third triangle which is equilateral; the reason of this would be long to tell; he who disproves what we are saying, and shows that we are mistaken, may claim a friendly victory. Then let us choose two triangles, out of which fire and the other elements have been constructed, one isosceles, the other having the square of the longer side equal to three times the square of the lesser side.

Now is the time to explain what was before obscurely said: there was an error in imagining that all the four elements might be generated by and into one another; this, I say, was an erroneous supposition, for there are generated from the triangles which we have selected four kinds—three from the one which has the sides unequal; the fourth alone is framed out of the isosceles triangle. Hence they cannot all be resolved into one another, a great number of small bodies being combined into a few large ones, or the converse. But three of them can be thus resolved and compounded, for they all spring from one, and when the greater bodies are broken up, many small bodies will spring up out of them and take their own proper figures; or, again, when many small bodies are dissolved into their triangles, if they become one, they will form one large mass of another kind. So much for their passage into one another. I have now to speak of their several kinds, and show out of what combinations of numbers each of them was formed. The first will be the simplest and smallest construction, and its element is that triangle which has its hypotenuse twice the lesser side. When two such triangles are joined at the diagonal, and this is repeated three times, and the triangles rest their diagonals and shorter sides on the same point as a centre, a single equilateral triangle is formed out of six triangles; and four equilateral triangles, if put together, make out of every three plane angles one solid angle, being that which is nearest to the most obtuse of plane angles; and out of the combination of these four angles arises the first solid form which distributes into equal and similar parts the whole circle in which it is inscribed. The second species of solid is formed out of the same triangles, which unite as eight equilateral triangles and form one solid angle out of four plane angles, and out of six such angles the second body is completed. And the third body is made up of 120 triangular elements, forming twelve solid angles, each of them included in five plane equilateral triangles, having altogether twenty bases, each of which is an equilateral triangle. The one element [that is, the triangle which has its hypotenuse twice the lesser side] having generated these figures, generated no more; but the isosceles triangle produced the fourth elementary figure, which is compounded of four such triangles, joining their right angles in a centre, and forming one equilateral quadrangle. Six of these united form eight solid angles, each of which is made by the combination of three plane right angles; the figure of the body thus composed is a cube, having six plane quadrangular equilateral bases. There was yet a fifth combination which God used in the delineation of the universe.

Now, he who, duly reflecting on all this, enquires whether the worlds are to be regarded as indefinite or definite in number, will be of opinion that the notion of their indefiniteness is characteristic of a sadly indefinite and ignorant mind. He, however, who raises the question whether they are to be truly regarded as one or five, takes up a more reasonable position. Arguing from probabilities, I am of opinion that they are one; another, regarding the question from another point of view, will be of another mind. But, leaving this enquiry, let us proceed to distribute the elementary forms, which have now been created in idea, among the four elements.

To earth, then, let us assign the cubical form; for earth is the most immoveable of the four and the most plastic of all bodies, and that which has the most stable bases must of necessity be of such a nature. Now, of the triangles which we assumed at first, that which has two equal sides is by nature more firmly based than that which has unequal sides; and of the compound figures which are formed out of either, the plane equilateral quadrangle has necessarily a more stable basis than the equilateral triangle, both in the whole and in the parts. Wherefore, in assigning this figure to earth, we adhere to probability; and to water we assign that one of the remaining forms which is the least moveable; and the most moveable of them to fire; and to air that which is intermediate. Also we assign the smallest body to fire, and the greatest to water, and the intermediate in size to air; and, again, the acutest body to fire, and the next in acuteness to air, and the third to water. Of all these elements, that which has the fewest bases must necessarily be the most moveable, for it must be the acutest and most penetrating in every way, and also the lightest as being composed of the smallest number of similar particles: and the second body has similar properties in a second degree, and the third body in the third degree. Let it be agreed, then, both according to strict reason and according to probability, that the pyramid is the solid which is the original element and seed of fire; and let us assign the element which was next in the order of generation to air, and the third to water. We must imagine all these to be so small that no single particle of any of the four kinds is seen by us on account of their smallness: but when many of them are collected together their aggregates are seen. And the ratios of their numbers, motions, and other properties, everywhere God, as far as necessity allowed or gave consent, has exactly perfected, and harmonized in due proportion.

From all that we have just been saying about the elements or kinds, the most probable conclusion is as follows: — earth, when meeting with fire and dissolved by its sharpness, whether the dissolution take place in the fire itself or perhaps in some mass of air or water, is borne hither and thither, until its parts, meeting together and mutually harmonising, again become earth; for they can never take any other form. But water, when divided by fire or by air, on re-forming, may become one part fire and two parts air; and a single volume of air divided becomes two of fire. Again, when a small body of fire is contained in a larger body of air or water or earth, and both are moving, and the fire struggling is overcome and broken up, then two volumes of fire form one volume of air; and when air is overcome and cut up into small pieces, two and a half parts of air are condensed into one part of water. Let us consider the matter in another way. When one of the other elements is fastened upon by fire, and is cut by the sharpness of its angles and sides, it coalesces with the fire, and then ceases to be cut by them any longer. For no element which is one and the same with itself can be changed by or change another of the same kind and in the same state. But so long as in the process of transition the weaker is fighting against the stronger, the dissolution continues. Again, when a few small particles, enclosed in many larger ones, are in process of decomposition and extinction, they only cease from their tendency to extinction when they consent to pass into the conquering nature, and fire becomes air and air water. But if bodies of another kind go and attack them [i.e. the small particles], the latter continue to be dissolved until, being completely forced back and dispersed, they make their escape to their own kindred, or else, being overcome and assimilated to the conquering power, they remain where they are and dwell with their victors, and from being many become one. And owing to these affections, all things are changing their place, for by the motion of the receiving vessel the bulk of each class is distributed into its proper place; but those things which become unlike themselves and like other things, are hurried by the shaking into the place of the things to which they grow like.

Now all unmixed and primary bodies are produced by such causes as these. As to the subordinate species which are included in the greater kinds, they are to be attributed to the varieties in the structure of the two original triangles. For either structure did not originally produce the triangle of one size only, but some larger and some smaller, and there are as many sizes as there are species of the four elements. Hence when they are mingled with themselves and with one another there is an endless variety of them, which those who would arrive at the probable truth of nature ought duly to consider.

Unless a person comes to an understanding about the nature and conditions of rest and motion, he will meet with many difficulties in the discussion which follows. Something has been said of this matter already, and something more remains to be said, which is, that motion never exists in what is uniform. For to conceive that anything can be moved without a mover is hard or indeed impossible, and equally impossible to conceive that there can be a mover unless there be something which can be moved;—motion cannot exist where either of these are wanting, and for these to be uniform is impossible; wherefore we must assign rest to uniformity and motion to the want of uniformity. Now inequality is the cause of the nature which is wanting in uniformity; and of this we have already described the origin. But there still remains the further point—why things when divided after their kinds do not cease to pass through one another and to change their place—which we will now proceed to explain. In the revolution of the universe are comprehended all the four elements, and this being circular and having a tendency to come together, compresses everything and will not allow any place to be left void. Wherefore, also, fire above all things penetrates everywhere, and air next, as being next in rarity of the elements; and the two other elements in like manner penetrate according to their degrees of rarity. For those things which are composed of the largest particles have the largest void left in their compositions, and those which are composed of the smallest particles have the least. And the contraction caused by the compression thrusts the smaller particles into the interstices of the larger. And thus, when the small parts are placed side by side with the larger, and the lesser divide the greater and the greater unite the lesser, all the elements are borne up and down and hither and thither towards their own places; for the change in the size of each changes its position in space. And these causes generate an inequality which is always maintained, and is continually creating a perpetual motion of the elements in all time.

In the next place we have to consider that there are divers kinds of fire. There are, for example, first, flame; and secondly, those emanations of flame which do not burn but only give light to the eyes; thirdly, the remains of fire, which are seen in red-hot embers after the flame has been extinguished. There are similar differences in the air; of which the brightest part is called the aether, and the most turbid sort mist and darkness; and there are various other nameless kinds which arise from the inequality of the triangles. Water, again, admits in the first place of a division into two kinds; the one liquid and the other fusile. The liquid kind is composed of the small and unequal particles of water; and moves itself and is moved by other bodies owing to the want of uniformity and the shape of its particles; whereas the fusile kind, being formed of large and uniform particles, is more stable than the other, and is heavy and compact by reason of its uniformity. But when fire gets in and dissolves the particles and destroys the uniformity, it has greater mobility, and becoming fluid is thrust forth by the neighbouring air and spreads upon the earth; and this dissolution of the solid masses is called melting, and their spreading out upon the earth flowing. Again, when the fire goes out of the fusile substance, it does not pass into a vacuum, but into the neighbouring air; and the air which is displaced forces together the liquid and still moveable mass into the place which was occupied by the fire, and unites it with itself. Thus compressed the mass resumes its equability, and is again at unity with itself, because the fire which was the author of the inequality has retreated; and this departure of the fire is called cooling, and the coming together which follows upon it is termed congealment. Of all the kinds termed fusile, that which is the densest and is formed out of the finest and most uniform parts is that most precious possession called gold, which is hardened by filtration through rock; this is unique in kind, and has both a glittering and a yellow colour. A shoot of gold, which is so dense as to be very hard, and takes a black colour, is termed adamant. There is also another kind which has parts nearly like gold, and of which there are several species; it is denser than gold, and it contains a small and fine portion of earth, and is therefore harder, yet also lighter because of the great interstices which it has within itself; and this substance, which is one of the bright and denser kinds of water, when solidified is called copper. There is an alloy of earth mingled with it, which, when the two parts grow old and are disunited, shows itself separately and is called rust. The remaining phenomena of the same kind there will be no difficulty in reasoning out by the method of probabilities. A man may sometimes set aside meditations about eternal things, and for recreation turn to consider the truths of generation which are probable only; he will thus gain a pleasure not to be repented of, and secure for himself while he lives a wise and moderate pastime. Let us grant ourselves this indulgence, and go through the probabilities relating to the same subjects which follow next in order.

Water which is mingled with fire, so much as is fine and liquid (being so called by reason of its motion and the way in which it rolls along the ground), and soft, because its bases give way and are less stable than those of earth, when separated from fire and air and isolated, becomes more uniform, and by their retirement is compressed into itself; and if the condensation be very great, the water above the earth becomes hail, but on the earth, ice; and that which is congealed in a less degree and is only half solid, when above the earth is called snow, and when upon the earth, and condensed from dew, hoar-frost. Then, again, there are the numerous kinds of water which have been mingled with one another, and are distilled through plants which grow in the earth; and this whole class is called by the name of juices or saps. The unequal admixture of these fluids creates a variety of species; most of them are nameless, but four which are of a fiery nature are clearly distinguished and have names. First, there is wine, which warms the soul as well as the body: secondly, there is the oily nature, which is smooth and divides the visual ray, and for this reason is bright and shining and of a glistening appearance, including pitch, the juice of the castor berry, oil itself, and other things of a like kind: thirdly, there is the class of substances which expand the contracted parts of the mouth, until they return to their natural state, and by reason of this property create sweetness;—these are included under the general name of honey: and, lastly, there is a frothy nature, which differs from all juices, having a burning quality which dissolves the flesh; it is called *opos* (a vegetable acid).

As to the kinds of earth, that which is filtered through water passes into stone in the following manner:—The water which mixes with the earth and is broken up in the process changes into air, and taking this form mounts into its own place. But as there is no surrounding vacuum it thrusts away the neighbouring air, and this being rendered heavy, and, when it is displaced, having been poured around the mass of earth, forcibly compresses it and drives it into the vacant space whence the new air had come up; and the earth when compressed by the air into an indissoluble union with water becomes rock. The fairer sort is that which is made up of equal and similar parts and is transparent; that which has the opposite qualities is inferior. But when all the watery part is suddenly drawn out by fire, a more brittle substance is formed, to which we give the name of pottery. Sometimes also moisture may remain, and the earth which has been fused by fire becomes, when cool, a certain stone of a black colour. A like separation of the water which had been copiously mingled with them may occur in two substances composed of finer particles of earth and of a briny nature; out of either of them a half-solid body is then formed, soluble in water—the one, soda, which is used for purging away oil and earth, the other, salt, which harmonizes so well in combinations pleasing to the palate, and is, as the law testifies, a substance dear to the gods. The compounds of earth and water are not soluble by water, but by fire only, and for this reason:—Neither fire nor air melt masses of earth; for their particles, being smaller than the interstices in its structure, have plenty of room to move without forcing their way, and so they leave the earth unmelted and undissolved; but particles of water, which are larger, force a passage, and dissolve and melt the earth. Wherefore earth when not consolidated by force is dissolved by water only; when consolidated, by nothing but fire; for this is the only body which can find an entrance. The cohesion of water again, when very strong, is dissolved by fire only—when weaker, then either by air or fire—the former entering the interstices, and the latter penetrating even the triangles. But nothing can dissolve air, when strongly condensed, which does not reach the elements or triangles; or if not strongly condensed, then only fire can dissolve it. As to bodies composed of earth and water, while the water occupies the vacant interstices of the earth in them which are compressed by force, the particles of water which approach them from without, finding no entrance, flow around the entire mass and leave it undissolved; but the particles of fire, entering into the interstices of the water, do to the water what water does to earth and fire to air (The text seems to be corrupt.), and are the sole causes of the compound body of earth and water liquefying and becoming fluid. Now these bodies are of two kinds; some of them, such as glass and the fusible sort of stones, have less water than they have earth; on the other hand, substances of the nature of wax and incense have more of water entering into their composition.

I have thus shown the various classes of bodies as they are diversified by their forms and combinations and changes into one another, and now I must endeavour to set forth their affections and the causes of them. In the first place, the bodies which I have been describing are necessarily objects of sense. But we have not yet considered the origin of flesh, or what belongs to flesh, or of that part of the soul which is mortal. And these things cannot be adequately explained without also explaining the affections which are concerned with sensation, nor the latter without the former: and yet to explain them together is hardly possible; for which reason we must assume first one or the other and afterwards examine the nature of our hypothesis.[9] In order, then, that the affections may follow regularly after the elements, let us presuppose the existence of body and soul.

First, let us enquire what we mean by saying that fire is hot; and about this we may reason from the dividing or cutting power which it exercises on our bodies. We all of us feel that fire is sharp; and we may further consider the fineness of the sides, and the sharpness of the angles, and the smallness of the particles, and the swiftness of the motion;—all this makes the action of fire violent and sharp, so that it cuts whatever it meets. And we must not forget that the original figure of fire [i.e. the pyramid], more than any other form, has a dividing power which cuts our bodies into small pieces (κερματίζει), and thus naturally produces that affection which we call heat; and hence the origin of the name (θερμὸς, κέρμα). Now, the opposite of this is sufficiently manifest; nevertheless we will not fail to describe it. For the larger particles of moisture which surround the body, entering in and driving out the lesser, but not being able to take their places, compress the moist principle in us; and this from being unequal and disturbed, is forced by them into a state of rest, which is due to equability and compression. But things which are contracted contrary to nature are by nature at war, and force themselves apart; and to this war and convulsion the name of shivering and trembling is given; and the whole affection and the cause of the affection are both termed cold. That is called hard to which our flesh yields, and soft which yields to our flesh; and things are also termed hard and soft relatively to one another. That which yields has a small base; but that which rests on quadrangular bases is firmly posed and belongs to the class which offers the greatest resistance; so too does that which is the most compact and therefore most repellent. The nature of the light and the heavy will be best understood when examined in connexion with our notions of above and below; for it is quite a mistake to suppose that the universe is parted into two regions, separate from and opposite to each other, the one a lower to which all things tend which have any bulk, and an upper to which things only ascend against their will. For as the universe is in the form of a sphere, all the extremities, being equidistant from the centre, are equally extremities, and the centre, which is equidistant from them, is equally to be regarded as the opposite of them all. Such being the nature of the world, when a person says that any of these points is above or below, may he not be justly charged with using an improper expression? For the cen-

---

[9]Omitting ὕστερα.

tre of the world cannot be rightly called either above or below, but is
the centre and nothing else; and the circumference is not the centre,
and has in no one part of itself a different relation to the centre from
what it has in any of the opposite parts. Indeed, when it is in every direction similar, how can one rightly give to it names which imply opposition? For if there were any solid body in equipoise at the centre of
the universe, there would be nothing to draw it to this extreme rather
than to that, for they are all perfectly similar; and if a person were to go
round the world in a circle, he would often, when standing at the antipodes of his former position, speak of the same point as above and
below; for, as I was saying just now, to speak of the whole which is in
the form of a globe as having one part above and another below is not
like a sensible man. The reason why these names are used, and the circumstances under which they are ordinarily applied by us to the division of the heavens, may be elucidated by the following supposition: —
If a person were to stand in that part of the universe which is the appointed place of fire, and where there is the great mass of fire to which
fiery bodies gather — if, I say, he were to ascend thither, and, having the
power to do this, were to abstract particles of fire and put them in scales
and weigh them, and then, raising the balance, were to draw the fire by
force towards the uncongenial element of the air, it would be very evident that he could compel the smaller mass more readily than the
larger; for when two things are simultaneously raised by one and the
same power, the smaller body must necessarily yield to the superior
power with less reluctance than the larger; and the larger body is called
heavy and said to tend downwards, and the smaller body is called light
and said to tend upwards. And we may detect ourselves who are upon
the earth doing precisely the same thing. For we often separate earthy
natures, and sometimes earth itself, and draw them into the uncongenial element of air by force and contrary to nature, both clinging to
their kindred elements. But that which is smaller yields to the impulse
given by us towards the dissimilar element more easily than the larger;
and so we call the former light, and the place towards which it is im-
pelled we call above, and the contrary state and place we call heavy and
below respectively. Now the relations of these must necessarily vary, because the principal masses of the different elements hold opposite positions; for that which is light, heavy, below or above in one place will
be found to be and become contrary and transverse and every way diverse in relation to that which is light, heavy, below or above in an opposite place. And about all of them this has to be considered: — that the
tendency of each towards its kindred element makes the body which is
moved heavy, and the place towards which the motion tends below, but
things which have an opposite tendency we call by an opposite name.

Such are the causes which we assign to these phenomena. As to the smooth and the rough, any one who sees them can explain the reason of them to another. For roughness is hardness mingled with irregularity, and smoothness is produced by the joint effect of uniformity and density.

The most important of the affections which concern the whole body remains to be considered,—that is, the cause of pleasure and pain in the perceptions of which I have been speaking, and in all other things which are perceived by sense through the parts of the body, and have both pains and pleasures attendant on them. Let us imagine the causes of every affection, whether of sense or not, to be of the following nature, remembering that we have already distinguished between the nature which is easy and which is hard to move; for this is the direction in which we must hunt the prey which we mean to take. A body which is of a nature to be easily moved, on receiving an impression however slight, spreads abroad the motion in a circle, the parts communicating with each other, until at last, reaching the principle of mind, they announce the quality of the agent. But a body of the opposite kind, being immobile, and not extending to the surrounding region, merely receives the impression, and does not stir any of the neighbouring parts; and since the parts do not distribute the original impression to other parts, it has no effect of motion on the whole animal, and therefore produces no effect on the patient. This is true of the bones and hair and other more earthy parts of the human body; whereas what was said above relates mainly to sight and hearing, because they have in them the greatest amount of fire and air. Now we must conceive of pleasure and pain in this way. An impression produced in us contrary to nature and violent, if sudden, is painful; and, again, the sudden return to nature is pleasant; but a gentle and gradual return is imperceptible and *vice versa*. On the other hand the impression of sense which is most easily produced is most readily felt, but is not accompanied by pleasure or pain; such, for example, are the affections of the sight, which, as we said above, is a body naturally uniting with our body in the day-time; for cuttings and burnings and other affections which happen to the sight do not give pain, nor is there pleasure when the sight returns to its natural state; but the sensations are clearest and strongest according to the manner in which the eye is affected by the object, and itself strikes and touches it; there is no violence either in the contraction or dilation of the eye. But bodies formed of larger particles yield to the agent only with a struggle; and then they impart their motions to the whole and cause pleasure and pain—pain when alienated from their natural conditions, and pleasure when restored to them. Things which experience gradual withdrawings and emptyings of their nature, and great and sudden replenishments, fail to perceive the emptying, but are sensible of the replenishment; and so they occasion no pain, but the greatest pleasure, to the mortal part of the soul, as is manifest in the case of perfumes. But things which are changed all of a sudden, and only gradually and with difficulty return to their own nature, have effects in every way opposite to the former, as is evident in the case of burnings and cuttings of the body.

Thus have we discussed the general affections of the whole body, and the names of the agents which produce them. And now I will endeavour to speak of the affections of particular parts, and the causes and agents of them, as far as I am able. In the first place let us set forth what was omitted when we were speaking of juices, concerning the affections peculiar to the tongue. These too, like most of the other affections, appear to be caused by certain contractions and dilations, but they have besides more of roughness and smoothness than is found in other affections; for whenever earthy particles enter into the small veins which are the testing instruments of the tongue, reaching to the heart, and fall upon the moist, delicate portions of flesh—when, as they are dissolved, they contract and dry up the little veins, they are astringent if they are rougher, but if not so rough, then only harsh. Those of them which are of an abstergent nature, and purge the whole surface of the tongue, if they do it in excess, and so encroach as to consume some part of the flesh itself, like potash and soda, are all termed bitter. But the particles which are deficient in the alkaline quality, and which cleanse only moderately, are called salt, and having no bitterness or roughness, are regarded as rather agreeable than otherwise. Bodies which share in and are made smooth by the heat of the mouth, and which are inflamed, and again in turn inflame that which heats them, and which are so light that they are carried upwards to the sensations of the head, and cut all that comes in their way, by reason of these qualities in them, are all termed pungent. But when these same particles, refined by putrefaction, enter into the narrow veins, and are duly proportioned to the particles of earth and air which are there, they set them whirling about one another, and while they are in a whirl cause them to dash against and enter into one another, and so form hollows surrounding the particles that enter—which watery vessels of air (for a film of moisture, sometimes earthy, sometimes pure, is spread around the air) are hollow spheres of water; and those of them which are pure, are transparent, and are called bubbles, while those composed of the earthy liquid, which is in a state of general agitation and effervescence, are said to boil or ferment;—of all these affections the cause is termed acid. And there is the opposite affection arising from an opposite cause, when the mass of entering particles, immersed in the moisture of the mouth, is congenial to the tongue, and smooths and oils over the roughness, and relaxes the parts which are unnaturally contracted, and contracts the parts which are relaxed, and disposes them all according to their nature; — that sort of remedy of violent affections is pleasant and agreeable to every man, and has the name sweet. But enough of this.

The faculty of smell does not admit of differences of kind; for all smells are of a half-formed nature, and no element is so proportioned as to have any smell. The veins about the nose are too narrow to admit earth and water, and too wide to detain fire and air; and for this reason no one ever perceives the smell of any of them; but smells always proceed from bodies that are damp, or putrefying, or liquefying, or evaporating, and are perceptible only in the intermediate state, when water is changing into air and air into water; and all of them are either vapour or mist. That which is passing out of air into water is mist, and that which is passing from water into air is vapour; and hence all smells are thinner than water and thicker than air. The proof of this is, that when there is any obstruction to the respiration, and a man draws in his breath by force, then no smell filters through, but the air without the smell alone penetrates. Wherefore the varieties of smell have no name, and they have not many, or definite and simple kinds; but they are distinguished only as painful and pleasant, the one sort irritating and disturbing the whole cavity which is situated between the head and the navel, the other having a soothing influence, and restoring this same region to an agreeable and natural condition.

In considering the third kind of sense, hearing, we must speak of the causes in which it originates. We may in general assume sound to be a blow which passes through the ears, and is transmitted by means of the air, the brain, and the blood, to the soul, and that hearing is the vibration of this blow, which begins in the head and ends in the region of the liver. The sound which moves swiftly is acute, and the sound which moves slowly is grave, and that which is regular is equable and smooth, and the reverse is harsh. A great body of sound is loud, and a small body of sound the reverse. Respecting the harmonies of sound I must hereafter speak.

There is a fourth class of sensible things, having many intricate varieties, which must now be distinguished. They are called by the general name of colours, and are a flame which emanates from every sort of body, and has particles corresponding to the sense of sight. I have spoken already, in what has preceded, of the causes which generate sight, and in this place it will be natural and suitable to give a rational theory of colours.

Of the particles coming from other bodies which fall upon the sight, some are smaller and some are larger, and some are equal to the parts

of the sight itself. Those which are equal are imperceptible, and we call
them transparent. The larger produce contraction, the smaller dilation,
in the sight, exercising a power akin to that of hot and cold bodies on
the flesh, or of astringent bodies on the tongue, or of those heating bodies which we termed pungent. White and black are similar effects of
contraction and dilation in another sphere, and for this reason have a
different appearance. Wherefore, we ought to term white that which dilates the visual ray, and the opposite of this is black. There is also a
swifter motion of a different sort of fire which strikes and dilates the ray
of sight until it reaches the eyes, forcing a way through their passages
and melting them, and eliciting from them a union of fire and water
which we call tears, being itself an opposite fire which comes to them
from an opposite direction — the inner fire flashes forth like lightning,
and the outer finds a way in and is extinguished in the moisture, and
all sorts of colours are generated by the mixture. This affection is
termed dazzling, and the object which produces it is called bright and
flashing. There is another sort of fire which is intermediate, and which
reaches and mingles with the moisture of the eye without flashing; and
in this, the fire mingling with the ray of the moisture, produces a colour
like blood, to which we give the name of red. A bright hue mingled
with red and white gives the colour called auburn (ξανθόν). The law
of proportion, however, according to which the several colours are
formed, even if a man knew he would be foolish in telling, for he could
not give any necessary reason, nor indeed any tolerable or probable explanation of them. Again, red, when mingled with black and white, becomes purple, but it becomes umber (ὄρφνινον) when the colours are
burnt as well as mingled and the black is more thoroughly mixed with
them. Flame-colour (πυρρὸν) is produced by a union of auburn and
dun (φαιὸν), and dun by an admixture of black and white; pale yellow
(ὠχρὸν), by an admixture of white and auburn. White and bright meeting, and falling upon a full black, become dark blue (κυανοῦν), and
when dark blue mingles with white, a light blue (γλαυκὸν) colour is
formed, as flame-colour with black makes leek green (πράσιον). There
will be no difficulty in seeing how and by what mixtures the colours derived from these are made according to the rules of probability. He,
however, who should attempt to verify all this by experiment, would
forget the difference of the human and divine nature. For God only has
the knowledge and also the power which are able to combine many
things into one and again resolve the one into many. But no man either is or ever will be able to accomplish either the one or the other op-
eration.

These are the elements, thus of necessity then subsisting, which the
creator of the fairest and best of created things associated with himself,

when he made the self-sufficing and most perfect God, using the necessary causes as his ministers in the accomplishment of his work, but himself contriving the good in all his creations. Wherefore we may distinguish two sorts of causes, the one divine and the other necessary, and may seek for the divine in all things, as far as our nature admits, with a view to the blessed life; but the necessary kind only for the sake of the divine, considering that without them and when isolated from them, these higher things for which we look cannot be apprehended or received or in any way shared by us.

Seeing, then, that we have now prepared for our use the various classes of causes which are the material out of which the remainder of our discourse must be woven, just as wood is the material of the carpenter, let us revert in a few words to the point at which we began, and then endeavour to add on a suitable ending to the beginning of our tale.

As I said at first, when all things were in disorder God created in each thing in relation to itself, and in all things in relation to each other, all the measures and harmonies which they could possibly receive. For in those days nothing had any proportion except by accident; nor did any of the things which now have names deserve to be named at all—as, for example, fire, water, and the rest of the elements. All these the creator first set in order, and out of them he constructed the universe, which was a single animal comprehending in itself all other animals, mortal and immortal. Now of the divine, he himself was the creator, but the creation of the mortal he committed to his offspring. And they, imitating him, received from him the immortal principle of the soul; and around this they proceeded to fashion a mortal body, and made it to be the vehicle of the soul, and constructed within the body a soul of another nature which was mortal, subject to terrible and irresistible affections,—first of all, pleasure, the greatest incitement to evil; then, pain, which deters from good; also rashness and fear, two foolish counsellors, anger hard to be appeased, and hope easily led astray;—these they mingled with irrational sense and with all-daring love[10] according to necessary laws, and so framed man. Wherefore, fearing to pollute the divine any more than was absolutely unavoidable, they gave to the mortal nature a separate habitation in another part of the body, placing the neck between them to be the isthmus and boundary, which they constructed between the head and breast, to keep them apart. And in the breast, and in what is termed the thorax, they encased the mortal soul; and as the one part of this was superior and the other inferior they divided the cavity of the thorax into two parts, as the women's and men's

---

[10]Putting a colon after εὐπαράγωγον and reading αἰσθήσει δὲ ἀλόγω.

apartments are divided in houses, and placed the midriff to be a wall of partition between them. That part of the inferior soul which is endowed with courage and passion and loves contention they settled nearer the head, midway between the midriff and the neck, in order that it might be under the rule of reason and might join with it in controlling and restraining the desires when they are no longer willing of their own accord to obey the word of command issuing from the citadel.

The heart, the knot[11] of the veins and the fountain of the blood which races through all the limbs, was set in the place of guard, that when the might of passion was roused by reason making proclamation of any wrong assailing them from without or being perpetrated by the desires within, quickly the whole power of feeling in the body, perceiving these commands and threats, might obey and follow through every turn and alley, and thus allow the principle of the best to have the command in all of them. But the gods, foreknowing that the palpitation of the heart in the expectation of danger and the swelling and excitement of passion was caused by fire, formed and implanted as a supporter to the heart the lung, which was, in the first place, soft and bloodless, and also had within hollows like the pores of a sponge, in order that by receiving the breath and the drink, it might give coolness and the power of respiration and alleviate the heat. Wherefore they cut the air-channels leading to the lung, and placed the lung about the heart as a soft spring, that, when passion was rife within, the heart, beating against a yielding body, might be cooled and suffer less, and might thus become more ready to join with passion in the service of reason.

The part of the soul which desires meats and drinks and the other things of which it has need by reason of the bodily nature, they placed between the midriff and the boundary of the navel, contriving in all this region a sort of manger for the food of the body; and there they bound it down like a wild animal which was chained up with man, and must be nourished if man was to exist. They appointed this lower creation his place here in order that he might be always feeding at the manger, and have his dwelling as far as might be from the council-chamber, making as little noise and disturbance as possible, and permitting the best part to advise quietly for the good of the whole. And knowing that this lower principle in man would not comprehend reason, and even if attaining to some degree of perception would never naturally care for rational notions, but that it would be led away by phantoms and visions night and day,—to be a remedy for this, God combined with it the liver, and placed it in the house of the lower na-

---

[11]Reading ἄμμα.

ture, contriving that it should be solid and smooth, and bright and
sweet, and should also have a bitter quality, in order that the power of
thought, which proceeds from the mind, might be reflected as in a mirror which receives likenesses of objects and gives back images of them
to the sight; and so might strike terror into the desires, when, making
use of the bitter part of the liver, to which it is akin, it comes threaten-
ing and invading, and diffusing this bitter element swiftly through the
whole liver produces colours like bile, and contracting every part
makes it wrinkled and rough; and twisting out of its right place and
contorting the lobe and closing and shutting up the vessels and gates,
causes pain and loathing. And the converse happens when some gentle inspiration of the understanding pictures images of an opposite
character, and allays the bile and bitterness by refusing to stir or touch
the nature opposed to itself, but by making use of the natural sweetness
of the liver, corrects all things and makes them to be right and smooth
and free, and renders the portion of the soul which resides about the
liver happy and joyful, enabling it to pass the night in peace, and to
practise divination in sleep, inasmuch as it has no share in mind and
reason. For the authors of our being, remembering the command of
their father when he bade them create the human race as good as they
could, that they might correct our inferior parts and make them to attain a measure of truth, placed in the liver the seat of divination. And
herein is a proof that God has given the art of divination not to the wisdom, but to the foolishness of man. No man, when in his wits, attains
prophetic truth and inspiration; but when he receives the inspired
word, either his intelligence is enthralled in sleep, or he is demented
by some distemper or possession. And he who would understand what
he remembers to have been said, whether in a dream or when he was
awake, by the prophetic and inspired nature, or would determine by
reason the meaning of the apparitions which he has seen, and what indications they afford to this man or that, of past, present or future good
and evil, must first recover his wits. But, while he continues demented,
he cannot judge of the visions which he sees or the words which he ut-
ters; the ancient saying is very true, that 'only a man who has his wits
can act or judge about himself and his own affairs.' And for this reason
it is customary to appoint interpreters to be judges of the true inspiration. Some persons call them prophets; they are quite unaware that
they are only the expositors of dark sayings and visions, and are not to
be called prophets at all, but only interpreters of prophecy.

Such is the nature of the liver, which is placed as we have described
in order that it may give prophetic intimations. During the life of each
individual these intimations are plainer, but after his death the liver becomes blind, and delivers oracles too obscure to be intelligible. The

neighbouring organ [the spleen] is situated on the left-hand side, and is constructed with a view of keeping the liver bright and pure, — like a napkin, always ready prepared and at hand to clean the mirror. And hence, when any impurities arise in the region of the liver by reason of disorders of the body, the loose nature of the spleen, which is composed of a hollow and bloodless tissue, receives them all and clears them away, and when filled with the unclean matter, swells and festers, but, again, when the body is purged, settles down into the same place as before, and is humbled.

Concerning the soul, as to which part is mortal and which divine, and how and why they are separated, and where located, if God acknowledges that we have spoken the truth, then, and then only, can we be confident; still, we may venture to assert that what has been said by us is probable, and will be rendered more probable by investigation. Let us assume thus much.

The creation of the rest of the body follows next in order, and this we may investigate in a similar manner. And it appears to be very meet that the body should be framed on the following principles: —

The authors of our race were aware that we should be intemperate in eating and drinking, and take a good deal more than was necessary or proper, by reason of gluttony. In order then that disease might not quickly destroy us, and lest our mortal race should perish without fulfilling its end — intending to provide against this, the gods made what is called the lower belly, to be a receptacle for the superfluous meat and drink, and formed the convolution of the bowels, so that the food might be prevented from passing quickly through and compelling the body to require more food, thus producing insatiable gluttony, and making the whole race an enemy to philosophy and music, and rebellious against the divinest element within us.

The bones and flesh, and other similar parts of us, were made as follows. The first principle of all of them was the generation of the marrow. For the bonds of life which unite the soul with the body are made fast there, and they are the root and foundation of the human race. The marrow itself is created out of other materials: God took such of the primary triangles as were straight and smooth, and were adapted by their perfection to produce fire and water, and air and earth — these, I say, he separated from their kinds, and mingling them in due proportions with one another, made the marrow out of them to be a universal seed of the whole race of mankind; and in this seed he then planted and enclosed the souls, and in the original distribution gave to the marrow as many and various forms as the different kinds of souls were hereafter to receive. That which, like a field, was to receive the divine seed, he made round every way, and called that portion of the marrow, brain, intend-

ing that, when an animal was perfected, the vessel containing this substance should be the head; but that which was intended to contain the
remaining and mortal part of the soul he distributed into figures at
once round and elongated, and he called them all by the name 'marrow'; and to these, as to anchors, fastening the bonds of the whole soul,
he proceeded to fashion around them the entire framework of our
body, constructing for the marrow, first of all, a complete covering of
bone.

Bone was composed by him in the following manner. Having sifted
pure and smooth earth he kneaded it and wetted it with marrow, and
after that he put it into fire and then into water, and once more into fire
and again into water—in this way by frequent transfers from one to the
other he made it insoluble by either. Out of this he fashioned, as in a
lathe, a globe made of bone, which he placed around the brain, and in
this he left a narrow opening; and around the marrow of the neck and
back he formed vertebrae which he placed under one another like piv-
ots, beginning at the head and extending through the whole of the
trunk. Thus wishing to preserve the entire seed, he enclosed it in a
stone-like casing, inserting joints, and using in the formation of them
the power of the other or diverse as an intermediate nature, that they
might have motion and flexure. Then again, considering that the bone
would be too brittle and inflexible, and when heated and again cooled
would soon mortify and destroy the seed within—having this in view,
he contrived the sinews and the flesh, that so binding all the members
together by the sinews, which admitted of being stretched and relaxed
about the vertebrae, he might thus make the body capable of flexion
and extension, while the flesh would serve as a protection against the
summer heat and against the winter cold, and also against falls, softly
and easily yielding to external bodies, like articles made of felt; and
containing in itself a warm moisture which in summer exudes and
makes the surface damp, would impart a natural coolness to the whole
body; and again in winter by the help of this internal warmth would
form a very tolerable defence against the frost which surrounds it and
attacks it from without. He who modelled us, considering these things,
mixed earth with fire and water and blended them; and making a ferment of acid and salt, he mingled it with them and formed soft and suc-
culent flesh. As for the sinews, he made them of a mixture of bone and
unfermented flesh, attempered so as to be in a mean, and gave them a
yellow colour; wherefore the sinews have a firmer and more glutinous
nature than flesh, but a softer and moister nature than the bones. With
these God covered the bones and marrow, binding them together by
sinews, and then enshrouded them all in an upper covering of flesh.
The more living and sensitive of the bones he enclosed in the thinnest

film of flesh, and those which had the least life within them in the thickest and most solid flesh. So again on the joints of the bones, where reason indicated that no more was required, he placed only a thin covering of flesh, that it might not interfere with the flexion of our bodies and make them unwieldy because difficult to move; and also that it might not, by being crowded and pressed and matted together, destroy sensation by reason of its hardness, and impair the memory and dull the edge of intelligence. Wherefore also the thighs and the shanks and the hips, and the bones of the arms and the forearms, and other parts which have no joints, and the inner bones, which on account of the rarity of the soul in the marrow are destitute of reason—all these are abundantly provided with flesh; but such as have mind in them are in general less fleshy, except where the creator has made some part solely of flesh in order to give sensation,—as, for example, the tongue. But commonly this is not the case. For the nature which comes into being and grows up in us by a law of necessity, does not admit of the combination of solid bone and much flesh with acute perceptions. More than any other part the framework of the head would have had them, if they could have co-existed, and the human race, having a strong and fleshy and sinewy head, would have had a life twice or many times as long as it now has, and also more healthy and free from pain. But our creators, considering whether they should make a longer-lived race which was worse, or a shorter-lived race which was better, came to the conclusion that every one ought to prefer a shorter span of life, which was better, to a longer one, which was worse; and therefore they covered the head with thin bone, but not with flesh and sinews, since it had no joints; and thus the head was added, having more wisdom and sensation than the rest of the body, but also being in every man far weaker. For these reasons and after this manner God placed the sinews at the extremity of the head, in a circle round the neck, and glued them together by the principle of likeness and fastened the extremities of the jawbones to them below the face, and the other sinews he dispersed throughout the body, fastening limb to limb. The framers of us framed the mouth, as now arranged, having teeth and tongue and lips, with a view to the necessary and the good, contriving the way in for necessary purposes, the way out for the best purposes; for that is necessary which enters in and gives food to the body; but the river of speech, which flows out of a man and ministers to the intelligence, is the fairest and noblest of all streams. Still the head could neither be left a bare frame of bones, on account of the extremes of heat and cold in the different seasons, nor yet be allowed to be wholly covered, and so become dull and senseless by reason of an overgrowth of flesh. The fleshy nature was not therefore wholly dried up, but a large sort of peel was parted off and remained over, which is now called the skin. This met and grew by the help of the cerebral moisture, and became the circular envelopment of the head. And the moisture, rising up under the sutures, watered and closed in the skin upon the crown, forming a sort of knot. The diversity of the sutures was caused by the power of the courses of the soul and of the food, and the more these struggled against one another the more numerous they became, and fewer if the struggle were less violent. This skin the divine power pierced all round with fire, and out of the punctures which were thus made the moisture issued forth, and the liquid and heat which was pure came away, and a mixed part which was composed of the same material as the skin, and had a fineness equal to the punctures, was borne up by its own impulse and extended far outside the head, but being too slow to escape, was thrust back by the external air, and rolled up underneath the skin, where it took root. Thus the hair sprang up in the skin, being akin to it because it is like threads of leather, but rendered harder and closer through the pressure of the cold, by which each hair, while in process of separation from the skin, is compressed and cooled. Wherefore the creator formed the head hairy, making use of the causes which I have mentioned, and reflecting also that instead of flesh the brain needed the hair to be a light covering or guard, which would give shade in summer and shelter in winter, and at the same time would not impede our quickness of perception. From the combination of sinew, skin, and bone, in the structure of the finger, there arises a triple compound, which, when dried up, takes the form of one hard skin partaking of all three natures, and was fabricated by these second causes, but designed by mind which is the principal cause with an eye to the future. For our creators well knew that women and other animals would some day be framed out of men, and they further knew that many animals would require the use of nails for many purposes; wherefore they fashioned in men at their first creation the rudiments of nails. For this purpose and for these reasons they caused skin, hair, and nails to grow at the extremities of the limbs.

And now that all the parts and members of the mortal animal had come together, since its life of necessity consisted of fire and breath, and it therefore wasted away by dissolution and depletion, the gods contrived the following remedy: They mingled a nature akin to that of man with other forms and perceptions, and thus created another kind of animal. These are the trees and plants and seeds which have been improved by cultivation and are now domesticated among us; anciently there were only the wild kinds, which are older than the cultivated. For everything that partakes of life may be truly called a living being, and the animal of which we are now speaking partakes of the third kind of soul, which is said to be seated between the midriff and the navel, having no part in opinion or reason or mind, but only in feelings of pleasure and pain and the desires which accompany them. For this nature is always in a passive state, revolving in and about itself, repelling the motion from without and using its own, and accordingly is not endowed by nature with the power of observing or reflecting on its own concerns. Wherefore it lives and does not differ from a living being, but is fixed and rooted in the same spot, having no power of self-motion.

Now after the superior powers had created all these natures to be food for us who are of the inferior nature, they cut various channels through the body as through a garden, that it might be watered as from a running stream. In the first place, they cut two hidden channels or veins down the back where the skin and the flesh join, which answered severally to the right and left side of the body. These they let down along the backbone, so as to have the marrow of generation between them, where it was most likely to flourish, and in order that the stream coming down from above might flow freely to the other parts, and equalize the irrigation. In the next place, they divided the veins about the head, and interlacing them, they sent them in opposite directions; those coming from the right side they sent to the left of the body, and those from the left they diverted towards the right, so that they and the skin might together form a bond which should fasten the head to the body, since the crown of the head was not encircled by sinews; and also in order that the sensations from both sides might be distributed over the whole body. And next, they ordered the water-courses of the body in a manner which I will describe, and which will be more easily understood if we begin by admitting that all things which have lesser parts retain the greater, but the greater cannot retain the lesser. Now of all natures fire has the smallest parts, and therefore penetrates through earth and water and air and their compounds, nor can anything hold it. And a similar principle applies to the human belly; for when meats and drinks enter it, it holds them, but it cannot hold air and fire, because the particles of which they consist are smaller than its own structure.

These elements, therefore, God employed for the sake of distributing moisture from the belly into the veins, weaving together a network of fire and air like a weel, having at the entrance two lesser weels; further he constructed one of these with two openings, and from the lesser weels he extended cords reaching all round to the extremities of the network. All the interior of the net he made of fire, but the lesser weels and their cavity, of air. The network he took and spread over the newly-formed animal in the following manner:—He let the lesser weels pass into the mouth; there were two of them, and one he let down by the air-pipes into the lungs, the other by the side of the air-pipes into the belly. The former he divided into two branches, both of which he made to meet at the channels of the nose, so that when the way through the mouth did not act, the streams of the mouth as well were replenished through the nose. With the other cavity (i.e. of the greater weel) he enveloped the hollow parts of the body, and at one time he made all this to flow into the lesser weels, quite gently, for they are composed of air, and at another time he caused the lesser weels to flow back again; and the net he made to find a way in and out through the pores of the body, and the rays of fire which are bound fast within followed the passage of the air either way, never at any time ceasing so long as the mortal being holds together. This process, as we affirm, the name-giver named inspiration and expiration. And all this movement, active as well as passive, takes place in order that the body, being watered and cooled, may receive nourishment and life; for when the respiration is going in and out, and the fire, which is fast bound within, follows it, and ever and anon moving to and fro, enters through the belly and reaches the meat and drink, it dissolves them, and dividing them into small portions and guiding them through the passages where it goes, pumps them as from a fountain into the channels of the veins, and makes the stream of the veins flow through the body as through a conduit.

Let us once more consider the phenomena of respiration, and enquire into the causes which have made it what it is. They are as follows:— Seeing that there is no such thing as a vacuum into which any of those things which are moved can enter, and the breath is carried from us into the external air, the next point is, as will be clear to every one, that it does not go into a vacant space, but pushes its neighbour out of its place, and that which is thrust out in turn drives out its neighbour; and in this way everything of necessity at last comes round to that place from whence the breath came forth, and enters in there, and following the breath, fills up the vacant space; and this goes on like the rotation of a wheel, because there can be no such thing as a vacuum. Wherefore also the breast and the lungs, when they emit the breath, are replenished by the air which surrounds the body and which enters in through the pores of the flesh and is driven round in a circle; and again, the air which is sent away and passes out through the body forces the breath inwards through the passage of the mouth and the nostrils. Now the origin of this movement may be supposed to be as follows. In the interior of every animal the hottest part is that which is around the blood and veins; it is in a manner an internal fountain of fire, which we compare to the network of a creel, being woven all of fire and extended through the centre of the body, while the outer parts are composed of air. Now we must admit that heat naturally proceeds outward to its own place and to its kindred element; and as there are two exits for the heat, the one out through the body, and the other through the mouth and nostrils, when it moves towards the one, it drives round the air at the other, and that which is driven round falls into the fire and becomes warm, and that which goes forth is cooled. But when the heat changes its place, and the particles at the other exit grow warmer, the hotter air inclining in that direction and carried towards its native element, fire, pushes round the air at the other; and this being affected in the same way and communicating the same impulse, a circular motion swaying to and fro is produced by the double process, which we call inspiration and expiration.

The phenomena of medical cupping-glasses and of the swallowing of drink and of the projection of bodies, whether discharged in the air or bowled along the ground, are to be investigated on a similar principle; and swift and slow sounds, which appear to be high and low, and are sometimes discordant on account of their inequality, and then again harmonical on account of the equality of the motion which they excite in us. For when the motions of the antecedent swifter sounds begin to pause and the two are equalized, the slower sounds overtake the swifter and then propel them. When they overtake them they do not intrude a new and discordant motion, but introduce the beginnings of a slower, which answers to the swifter as it dies away, thus producing a single mixed expression out of high and low, whence arises a pleasure which even the unwise feel, and which to the wise becomes a higher sort of delight, being an imitation of divine harmony in mortal motions. Moreover, as to the flowing of water, the fall of the thunderbolt, and the marvels that are observed about the attraction of amber and the Heraclean stones, — in none of these cases is there any attraction; but he who investigates rightly, will find that such wonderful phenomena are attributable to the combination of certain conditions, — the non-existence of a vacuum, the fact that objects push one another round, and that they change places, passing severally into their proper positions as they are divided or combined.

Such as we have seen, is the nature and such are the causes of respiration, — the subject in which this discussion originated. For the fire cuts the food and following the breath surges up within, fire and breath rising together and filling the veins by drawing up out of the belly and pouring into them the cut portions of the food; and so the streams of food are kept flowing through the whole body in all animals. And fresh cuttings from kindred substances, whether the fruits of the earth or herb of the field, which God planted to be our daily food, acquire all sorts of colours by their inter-mixture; but red is the most pervading of them, being created by the cutting action of fire and by the impression which it makes on a moist substance; and hence the liquid which circulates in the body has a colour such as we have described. The liquid itself we call blood, which nourishes the flesh and the whole body, whence all parts are watered and empty places filled.

Now the process of repletion and evacuation is effected after the manner of the universal motion by which all kindred substances are drawn towards one another. For the external elements which surround us are always causing us to consume away, and distributing and sending off like to like; the particles of blood, too, which are divided and contained within the frame of the animal as in a sort of heaven, are compelled to imitate the motion of the universe. Each, therefore, of the divided parts within us, being carried to its kindred nature, replenishes the void. When more is taken away than flows in, then we decay, and when less, we grow and increase.

The frame of the entire creature when young has the triangles of each kind new, and may be compared to the keel of a vessel which is just off the stocks; they are locked firmly together and yet the whole mass is soft and delicate, being freshly formed of marrow and nurtured on milk. Now when the triangles out of which meats and drinks are composed come in from without, and are comprehended in the body, being older and weaker than the triangles already there, the frame of the body gets the better of them and its newer triangles cut them up, and so the animal grows great, being nourished by a multitude of similar particles. But when the roots of the triangles are loosened by having undergone many conflicts with many things in the course of time, they are no longer able to cut or assimilate the food which enters, but are themselves easily divided by the bodies which come in from without. In this way every animal is overcome and decays, and this affection is called old age. And at last, when the bonds by which the triangles of the marrow are united no longer hold, and are parted by the strain of existence, they in turn loosen the bonds of the soul, and she, obtaining a natural release, flies away with joy. For that which takes place according to nature is pleasant, but that which is contrary to nature is painful. And thus death, if caused by disease or produced by wounds, is painful and violent; but that sort of death which comes with old age and fulfils the debt of nature is the easiest of deaths, and is accompanied with pleasure rather than with pain.

Now every one can see whence diseases arise. There are four natures out of which the body is compacted, earth and fire and water and air, and the unnatural excess or defect of these, or the change of any of them from its own natural place into another, or—since there are more kinds than one of fire and of the other elements—the assumption by any of these of a wrong kind, or any similar irregularity, produces disorders and diseases; for when any of them is produced or changed in a manner contrary to nature, the parts which were previously cool grow warm, and those which were dry become moist, and the light become heavy, and the heavy light; all sorts of changes occur. For, as we affirm, a thing can only remain the same with itself, whole and sound, when the same is added to it, or subtracted from it, in the same respect and in the same manner and in due proportion; and whatever comes or goes away in violation of these laws causes all manner of changes and infinite diseases and corruptions. Now there is a second class of structures which are also natural, and this affords a second opportunity of observing diseases to him who would understand them. For whereas marrow and bone and flesh and sinews are composed of the four elements, and the blood, though after another manner, is likewise formed out of them, most diseases originate in the way which I have described; but the worst of all owe their severity to the fact that the generation of these substances proceeds in a wrong order; they are then destroyed. For the natural order is that the flesh and sinews should be made of blood, the sinews out of the fibres to which they are akin, and the flesh out of the clots which are formed when the fibres are separated. And the glutinous and rich matter which comes away from the sinews and the flesh, not only glues the flesh to the bones, but nourishes and imparts growth to the bone which surrounds the marrow; and by reason of the solidity of the bones, that which filters through consists of the purest and smoothest and oiliest sort of triangles, dropping like dew from the bones and watering the marrow. Now when each process takes place in this order, health commonly results; when in the opposite order, disease. For when the flesh becomes decomposed and sends back the wasting substance into the veins, then an over-supply of blood of diverse kinds, mingling with air in the veins, having variegated colours and bitter properties, as well as acid and saline qualities, contains all sorts of bile and serum and phlegm. For all things go the wrong way, and having become corrupted, first they taint the blood itself, and then ceasing to give nourishment to the body they are carried along the veins in all directions, no longer preserving the order of their natural courses, but at war with themselves, because they receive no good from one another, and are hostile to the abiding constitution of the body, which they corrupt and dissolve. The oldest part of the flesh which is corrupted, being hard to decompose, from long burning grows black, and from being everywhere corroded becomes bitter, and is injurious to every part of the body which is still uncorrupted. Sometimes, when the bitter element is refined away, the black part assumes an acidity which takes the place of the bitterness; at other times the bitterness being tinged with blood has a redder colour; and this, when mixed with black, takes the hue of grass;[12] and again, an auburn colour mingles

---

[12]Reading χλοῶδες.

with the bitter matter when new flesh is decomposed by the fire which surrounds the internal flame;—to all which symptoms some physician perhaps, or rather some philosopher, who had the power of seeing in many dissimilar things one nature deserving of a name, has assigned the common name of bile. But the other kinds of bile are variously distinguished by their colours. As for serum, that sort which is the watery part of blood is innocent, but that which is a secretion of black and acid bile is malignant when mingled by the power of heat with any salt substance, and is then called acid phlegm. Again, the substance which is formed by the liquefaction of new and tender flesh when air is present, if inflated and encased in liquid so as to form bubbles, which separately are invisible owing to their small size, but when collected are of a bulk which is visible, and have a white colour arising out of the generation of foam—all this decomposition of tender flesh when intermingled with air is termed by us white phlegm. And the whey or sediment of newly-formed phlegm is sweat and tears, and includes the various daily discharges by which the body is purified. Now all these become causes of disease when the blood is not replenished in a natural manner by food and drink but gains bulk from opposite sources in violation of the laws of nature. When the several parts of the flesh are separated by disease, if the foundation remains, the power of the disorder is only half as great, and there is still a prospect of an easy recovery; but when that which binds the flesh to the bones is diseased, and no longer being separated from the muscles and sinews,[13] ceases to give nourishment to the bone and to unite flesh and bone, and from being oily and smooth and glutinous becomes rough and salt and dry, owing to bad regimen, then all the substance thus corrupted crumbles away under the flesh and the sinews, and separates from the bone, and the fleshy parts fall away from their foundation and leave the sinews bare and full of brine, and the flesh again gets into the circulation of the blood and makes the previously-mentioned disorders still greater. And if these bodily affections be severe, still worse are the prior disorders; as when the bone itself, by reason of the density of the flesh, does not obtain sufficient air, but becomes mouldy and hot and gangrened and receives no nutriment, and the natural process is inverted, and the bone crumbling passes into the food, and the food into the flesh, and the flesh again falling into the blood makes all maladies that may occur more virulent than those already mentioned. But the worst case of all is when the marrow is diseased, either from excess or defect; and this is the cause of the very greatest and most fatal disorders, in which the whole course of the body is reversed.

---

[13]Reading αὐτό for αὖ τό and ἅμα for αἷμα.

There is a third class of diseases which may be conceived of as arising in three ways; for they are produced sometimes by wind, and sometimes by phlegm, and sometimes by bile. When the lung, which is the dispenser of the air to the body, is obstructed by rheums and its passages are not free, some of them not acting, while through others too much air enters, then the parts which are unrefreshed by air corrode, while in other parts the excess of air forcing its way through the veins distorts them and decomposing the body is enclosed in the midst of it and occupies the midriff; thus numberless painful diseases are produced, accompanied by copious sweats. And oftentimes when the flesh is dissolved in the body, wind, generated within and unable to escape, is the source of quite as much pain as the air coming in from without; but the greatest pain is felt when the wind gets about the sinews and the veins of the shoulders, and swells them up, and so twists back the great tendons and the sinews which are connected with them. These disorders are called tetanus and opisthotonus, by reason of the tension which accompanies them. The cure of them is difficult; relief is in most cases given by fever supervening. The white phlegm, though dangerous when detained within by reason of the air bubbles, yet if it can communicate with the outside air, is less severe, and only discolours the body, generating leprous eruptions and similar diseases. When it is mingled with black bile and dispersed about the courses of the head, which are the divinest part of us, the attack if coming on in sleep, is not so severe; but when assailing those who are awake it is hard to be got rid of, and being an affection of a sacred part, is most justly called sacred. An acid and salt phlegm, again, is the source of all those diseases which take the form of catarrh, but they have many names because the places into which they flow are manifold.

Inflammations of the body come from burnings and inflamings, and all of them originate in bile. When bile finds a means of discharge, it boils up and sends forth all sorts of tumours; but when imprisoned within, it generates many inflammatory diseases, above all when mingled with pure blood; since it then displaces the fibres which are scattered about in the blood and are designed to maintain the balance of rare and dense, in order that the blood may not be so liquefied by heat as to exude from the pores of the body, nor again become too dense and thus find a difficulty in circulating through the veins. The fibres are so constituted as to maintain this balance; and if any one brings them all together when the blood is dead and in process of cooling, then the blood which remains becomes fluid, but if they are left alone, they soon congeal by reason of the surrounding cold. The fibres having this power over the blood, bile, which is only stale blood, and which from being flesh is dissolved again into blood, at the first influx coming in lit-

tle by little, hot and liquid, is congealed by the power of the fibres; and
so congealing and made to cool, it produces internal cold and shuddering. When it enters with more of a flood and overcomes the fibres
by its heat, and boiling up throws them into disorder, if it have power
enough to maintain its supremacy, it penetrates the marrow and burns
up what may be termed the cables of the soul, and sets her free; but
when there is not so much of it, and the body though wasted still holds
out, the bile is itself mastered, and is either utterly banished, or is thrust
through the veins into the lower or upper belly, and is driven out of the
body like an exile from a state in which there has been civil war;
whence arise diarrhoeas and dysenteries, and all such disorders. When
the constitution is disordered by excess of fire, continuous heat and
fever are the result; when excess of air is the cause, then the fever is
quotidian; when of water, which is a more sluggish element than either
fire or air, then the fever is a tertian; when of earth, which is the most
sluggish of the four, and is only purged away in a four-fold period, the
result is a quartan fever, which can with difficulty be shaken off.

Such is the manner in which diseases of the body arise; the disorders
of the soul, which depend upon the body, originate as follows. We must
acknowledge disease of the mind to be a want of intelligence; and of
this there are two kinds; to wit, madness and ignorance. In whatever
state a man experiences either of them, that state may be called disease;
and excessive pains and pleasures are justly to be regarded as the greatest diseases to which the soul is liable. For a man who is in great joy or
in great pain, in his unreasonable eagerness to attain the one and to
avoid the other, is not able to see or to hear anything rightly; but he is
mad, and is at the time utterly incapable of any participation in reason.
He who has the seed about the spinal marrow too plentiful and over-
flowing, like a tree overladen with fruit, has many throes, and also ob-
tains many pleasures in his desires and their offspring, and is for the
most part of his life deranged, because his pleasures and pains are so
very great; his soul is rendered foolish and disordered by his body; yet
he is regarded not as one diseased, but as one who is voluntarily bad,
which is a mistake. The truth is that the intemperance of love is a disease of the soul due chiefly to the moisture and fluidity which is produced in one of the elements by the loose consistency of the bones.
And in general, all that which is termed the incontinence of pleasure
and is deemed a reproach under the idea that the wicked voluntarily
do wrong is not justly a matter for reproach. For no man is voluntarily
bad; but the bad become bad by reason of an ill disposition of the body
and bad education, things which are hateful to every man and happen
to him against his will. And in the case of pain too in like manner the
soul suffers much evil from the body. For where the acid and briny

phlegm and other bitter and bilious humours wander about in the body, and find no exit or escape, but are pent up within and mingle their own vapours with the motions of the soul, and are blended with them, they produce all sorts of diseases, more or fewer, and in every degree of intensity; and being carried to the three places of the soul, whichever they may severally assail, they create infinite varieties of ill-temper and melancholy, of rashness and cowardice, and also of forget-fulness and stupidity. Further, when to this evil constitution of body evil forms of government are added and evil discourses are uttered in private as well as in public, and no sort of instruction is given in youth to cure these evils, then all of us who are bad become bad from two causes which are entirely beyond our control. In such cases the planters are to blame rather than the plants, the educators rather than the educated. But however that may be, we should endeavour as far as we can by education, and studies, and learning, to avoid vice and attain virtue; this, however, is part of another subject.

There is a corresponding enquiry concerning the mode of treatment by which the mind and the body are to be preserved, about which it is meet and right that I should say a word in turn; for it is more our duty to speak of the good than of the evil. Everything that is good is fair, and the fair is not without proportion, and the animal which is to be fair must have due proportion. Now we perceive lesser symmetries or pro-portions and reason about them, but of the highest and greatest we take no heed; for there is no proportion or disproportion more productive of health and disease, and virtue and vice, than that between soul and body. This however we do not perceive, nor do we reflect that when a weak or small frame is the vehicle of a great and mighty soul, or con-versely, when a little soul is encased in a large body, then the whole an-imal is not fair, for it lacks the most important of all symmetries; but the due proportion of mind and body is the fairest and loveliest of all sights to him who has the seeing eye. Just as a body which has a leg too long, or which is unsymmetrical in some other respect, is an unpleas-ant sight, and also, when doing its share of work, is much distressed and makes convulsive efforts, and often stumbles through awkwardness, and is the cause of infinite evil to its own self—in like manner we should conceive of the double nature which we call the living being; and when in this compound there is an impassioned soul more power-ful than the body, that soul, I say, convulses and fills with disorders the whole inner nature of man; and when eager in the pursuit of some sort of learning or study, causes wasting; or again, when teaching or disput-ing in private or in public, and strifes and controversies arise, inflames and dissolves the composite frame of man and introduces rheums; and the nature of this phenomenon is not understood by most professors of medicine, who ascribe it to the opposite of the real cause. And once more, when a body large and too strong for the soul is united to a small and weak intelligence, then inasmuch as there are two desires natural to man,—one of food for the sake of the body, and one of wisdom for the sake of the diviner part of us—then, I say, the motions of the stronger, getting the better and increasing their own power, but making the soul dull, and stupid, and forgetful, engender ignorance, which is the greatest of diseases. There is one protection against both kinds of disproportion:—that we should not move the body without the soul or the soul without the body, and thus they will be on their guard against each other, and be healthy and well balanced. And therefore the mathematician or any one else whose thoughts are much absorbed in some intellectual pursuit, must allow his body also to have due exercise, and practise gymnastic; and he who is careful to fashion the body, should in turn impart to the soul its proper motions, and should cultivate music and all philosophy, if he would deserve to be called truly fair and truly good. And the separate parts should be treated in the same manner, in imitation of the pattern of the universe; for as the body is heated and also cooled within by the elements which enter into it, and is again dried up and moistened by external things, and experiences these and the like affections from both kinds of motions, the result is that the body if given up to motion when in a state of quiescence is overmastered and perishes; but if any one, in imitation of that which we call the foster-mother and nurse of the universe, will not allow the body ever to be inactive, but is always producing motions and agitations through its whole extent, which form the natural defence against other motions both internal and external, and by moderate exercise reduces to order according to their affinities the particles and affections which are wandering about the body, as we have already said when speaking of the universe, (See p. 198.) he will not allow enemy placed by the side of enemy to stir up wars and disorders in the body, but he will place friend by the side of friend, so as to create health. Now of all motions that is the best which is produced in a thing by itself, for it is most akin to the motion of thought and of the universe; but that motion which is caused by others is not so good, and worst of all is that which moves the body, when at rest, in parts only and by some external agency. Wherefore of all modes of purifying and re-uniting the body the best is gymnastic; the next best is a surging motion, as in sailing or any other mode of conveyance which is not fatiguing; the third sort of motion may be of use in a case of extreme necessity, but in any other will be adopted by no man of sense: I mean the purgative treatment of physicians; for diseases unless they are very dangerous should not be irritated by medicines, since every form of disease is in a manner akin to the living being, whose complex frame has an appointed term of life. For not the whole race only, but each individual—barring inevitable accidents—comes into the world having a fixed span, and the triangles in us are originally framed with power to last for a certain time, beyond which no man can prolong his life. And this holds also of the constitution of diseases; if any one regardless of the appointed time tries to subdue them by medicine, he only aggravates and multiplies them. Wherefore we ought always to manage them by regimen, as far as a man can spare the time, and not provoke a disagreeable enemy by medicines.

Enough of the composite animal, and of the body which is a part of him, and of the manner in which a man may train and be trained by himself so as to live most according to reason: and we must above and before all provide that the element which is to train him shall be the fairest and best adapted to that purpose. A minute discussion of this subject would be a serious task; but if, as before, I am to give only an outline, the subject may not unfitly be summed up as follows.

I have often remarked that there are three kinds of soul located within us, having each of them motions, and I must now repeat in the fewest words possible, that one part, if remaining inactive and ceasing from its natural motion, must necessarily become very weak, but that which is trained and exercised, very strong. Wherefore we should take care that the movements of the different parts of the soul should be in due proportion.

And we should consider that God gave the sovereign part of the human soul to be the divinity of each one, being that part which, as we say, dwells at the top of the body, and inasmuch as we are a plant not of an earthly but of a heavenly growth, raises us from earth to our kindred who are in heaven. And in this we say truly; for the divine power suspended the head and root of us from that place where the generation of the soul first began, and thus made the whole body upright. When a man is always occupied with the cravings of desire and ambition, and is eagerly striving to satisfy them, all his thoughts must be mortal, and, as far as it is possible altogether to become such, he must be mortal every whit, because he has cherished his mortal part. But he who has been earnest in the love of knowledge and of true wisdom, and has exercised his intellect more than any other part of him, must have thoughts immortal and divine, if he attain truth, and in so far as human nature is capable of sharing in immortality, he must altogether be immortal; and since he is ever cherishing the divine power, and has the divinity within him in perfect order, he will be perfectly happy. Now there is only one way of taking care of things, and this is to give to each the food and motion which are natural to it. And the motions which are naturally akin to the divine principle within us are the thoughts and revolutions of the universe. These each man should follow, and correct the courses of the head which were corrupted at our birth, and by learning the harmonies and revolutions of the universe, should assimilate the thinking being to the thought, renewing his original nature, and having assimilated them should attain to that perfect life which the gods have set before mankind, both for the present and the future.

Thus our original design of discoursing about the universe down to the creation of man is nearly completed. A brief mention may be made of the generation of other animals, so far as the subject admits of brevity; in this manner our argument will best attain a due proportion. On the subject of animals, then, the following remarks may be offered. Of the men who came into the world, those who were cowards or led unrighteous lives may with reason be supposed to have changed into the nature of women in the second generation. And this was the reason why at that time the gods created in us the desire of sexual intercourse, contriving in man one animated substance, and in woman another, which they formed respectively in the following manner. The outlet for drink by which liquids pass through the lung under the kidneys and into the bladder, which receives and then by the pressure of the air emits them, was so fashioned by them as to penetrate also into the body of the marrow, which passes from the head along the neck and through the back, and which in the preceding discourse we have named the seed. And the seed having life, and becoming endowed with respiration, produces in that part in which it respires a lively desire of emission, and thus creates in us the love of procreation. Wherefore also in men the organ of generation becoming rebellious and masterful, like an animal disobedient to reason, and maddened with the sting of lust, seeks to gain absolute sway; and the same is the case with the so-called womb or matrix of women; the animal within them is desirous of procreating children, and when remaining unfruitful long beyond its proper time, gets discontented and angry, and wandering in every direction through the body, closes up the passages of the breath, and, by obstructing respiration, drives them to extremity, causing all varieties of disease, until at length the desire and love of the man and the woman, bringing them together[14] and as it were plucking the fruit from the tree, sow in the womb, as in a field, animals unseen by reason of their smallness and without form; these again are separated and matured within; they are then finally brought out into the light, and thus the generation of animals is completed.

Thus were created women and the female sex in general. But the race of birds was created out of innocent light-minded men, who, al-

---

[14]Reading ξυνδυάζοντες (conj. Hermann).

though their minds were directed toward heaven, imagined, in their simplicity, that the clearest demonstration of the things above was to be obtained by sight; these were remodelled and transformed into birds, and they grew feathers instead of hair. The race of wild pedestrian animals, again, came from those who had no philosophy in any of their thoughts, and never considered at all about the nature of the heavens, because they had ceased to use the courses of the head, but followed the guidance of those parts of the soul which are in the breast. In consequence of these habits of theirs they had their front-legs and their heads resting upon the earth to which they were drawn by natural affinity; and the crowns of their heads were elongated and of all sorts of shapes, into which the courses of the soul were crushed by reason of disuse. And this was the reason why they were created quadrupeds and polypods: God gave the more senseless of them the more support that they might be more attracted to the earth. And the most foolish of them, who trail their bodies entirely upon the ground and have no longer any need of feet, he made without feet to crawl upon the earth. The fourth class were the inhabitants of the water: these were made out of the most entirely senseless and ignorant of all, whom the transformers did not think any longer worthy of pure respiration, because they possessed a soul which was made impure by all sorts of transgression; and instead of the subtle and pure medium of air, they gave them the deep and muddy sea to be their element of respiration; and hence arose the race of fishes and oysters, and other aquatic animals, which have received the most remote habitations as a punishment of their outlandish ignorance. These are the laws by which animals pass into one another, now, as ever, changing as they lose or gain wisdom and folly.

We may now say that our discourse about the nature of the universe has an end. The world has received animals, mortal and immortal, and is fulfilled with them, and has become a visible animal containing the visible—the sensible God who is the image of the intellectual,[15] the greatest, best, fairest, most perfect—the one only-begotten heaven.

---

[15]Or reading ποιητοῦ—'of his maker.'

DOVER·THRIFT·EDITIONS

NONFICTION

NARRATIVE OF THE LIFE OF FREDERICK DOUGLASS, Frederick Douglass. 96pp. 28499-9

SELF-RELIANCE AND OTHER ESSAYS, Ralph Waldo Emerson. 128pp. 27790-9

THE LIFE OF OLAUDAH EQUIANO, OR GUSTAVUS VASSA, THE AFRICAN, Olaudah Equiano. 192pp. 40661-X

THE AUTOBIOGRAPHY OF BENJAMIN FRANKLIN, Benjamin Franklin. 144pp. 29073-5

TOTEM AND TABOO, Sigmund Freud. 176pp. (Not available in Europe or United Kingdom.) 40434-X

LOVE: A Book of Quotations, Herb Galewitz (ed.). 64pp. 40004-2

PRAGMATISM, William James. 128pp. 28270-8

THE STORY OF MY LIFE, Helen Keller. 80pp. 29249-5

TAO TE CHING, Lao Tze. 112pp. 29792-6

GREAT SPEECHES, Abraham Lincoln. 112pp. 26872-1

THE PRINCE, Niccolò Machiavelli. 80pp. 27274-5

THE SUBJECTION OF WOMEN, John Stuart Mill. 112pp. 29601-6

SELECTED ESSAYS, Michel de Montaigne. 96pp. 29109-X

UTOPIA, Sir Thomas More. 96pp. 29583-4

BEYOND GOOD AND EVIL: Prelude to a Philosophy of the Future, Friedrich Nietzsche. 176pp. 29868-X

THE BIRTH OF TRAGEDY, Friedrich Nietzsche. 96pp. 28515-4

COMMON SENSE, Thomas Paine. 64pp. 29602-4

SYMPOSIUM AND PHAEDRUS, Plato. 96pp. 27798-4

THE TRIAL AND DEATH OF SOCRATES: Four Dialogues, Plato. 128pp. 27066-1

A MODEST PROPOSAL AND OTHER SATIRICAL WORKS, Jonathan Swift. 64pp. 28759-9

CIVIL DISOBEDIENCE AND OTHER ESSAYS, Henry David Thoreau. 96pp. 27563-9

SELECTIONS FROM THE JOURNALS (Edited by Walter Harding), Henry David Thoreau. 96pp. 28760-2

WALDEN; OR, LIFE IN THE WOODS, Henry David Thoreau. 224pp. 28495-6

NARRATIVE OF SOJOURNER TRUTH, Sojourner Truth. 80pp. 29899-X

THE THEORY OF THE LEISURE CLASS, Thorstein Veblen. 256pp. 28062-4

DE PROFUNDIS, Oscar Wilde. 64pp. 29308-4

OSCAR WILDE'S WIT AND WISDOM: A Book of Quotations, Oscar Wilde. 64pp. 40146-4

UP FROM SLAVERY, Booker T. Washington. 160pp. 28738-6

A VINDICATION OF THE RIGHTS OF WOMAN, Mary Wollstonecraft. 224pp. 29036-0

All books complete and unabridged. All 5³⁄₁₆" x 8¹⁄₄," paperbound. Available at your book dealer, online at **www.doverpublications.com**, or by writing to Dept. GI, Dover Publications, Inc., 31 East 2nd Street, Mineola, NY 11501. For current price information or for free catalogs (please indicate field of interest), write to Dover Publications or log on to **www.doverpublications.com** and see every Dover book in print. Dover publishes more than 500 books each year on science, elementary and advanced mathematics, biology, music, art, literary history, social sciences, and other areas.